"This timely book challenges investors to move away from the recently-popular 'Q Culture' of speculation to the 'V Culture' of value investing, based on business analysis that focuses on the basics of finance, accounting, and governance. The author reminds us that, 'earnings and cash flows are what give a business value'—the eternal message of long-run success in equity investing. It is the critical link in the investment chain, and Larry Cunningham's book forges it with heat, power, and persuasiveness."

John C. ("Jack") Bogle, Founder and Former Chairman,
The Vanguard Group

"Larry Cunningham masterfully tackles critical subjects at the heart of today's markets. A much-needed work on a unique style of investing, this book puts the ABCs of common sense valuation back into the business of investing. This is the place to look for insight and guidance in the age of volatile markets and colliding ideas."

Alan C. ("Ace") Greenberg, Chairman, Bear Stearns

"Anyone desiring to be a successful investor should read this excellent book presenting the important investing principles of Graham, Buffett, Fisher, and others in a most insightful and understandable manner."

David J. ("Sandy") Gottesman, Chairman, First Manhattan

"Remarkably timely. For stock players who realize they played the greatest fool in the Internet stock game, Cunningham offers a tool for rehabilitation: a guide to thoughtful investing. For earnest investors, he shows how to live profitably with the moodiness of Mr. Market."

David Henry, Associate Editor, Finance, *Business Week*

"While the stock market does not always behave rationally, Larry Cunningham's well-articulated and insightful views as to value investing are a refreshing reminder that, just as night follows day, a return to the principles at the core of Cunningham's commonsense approach to investing is inevitable."

Samuel J. Heyman, Chairman of the Board and CEO,
GAF Corporation

"Puzzled by acronyms, buzz words, the pop investing concepts? Cunningham explains then debunks them. He gets down to the fundamentals that investors must know about companies in order to choose reliable winners in the stock market."

Janet Lowe, Author, *Benjamin Graham on Value Investing* and *Warren Buffett Speaks*

HOW TO THINK LIKE BENJAMIN GRAHAM AND INVEST LIKE WARREN BUFFETT

HOW TO THINK LIKE BENJAMIN GRAHAM AND INVEST LIKE WARREN BUFFETT

Lawrence A. Cunningham

McGraw-Hill
New York   Chicago   San Francisco
Lisbon   London   Madrid   Mexico City
Milan   New Delhi   San Juan   Seoul
Singapore   Sydney   Toronto

Library of Congress Cataloging-in-Publication Data

Cunningham, Lawrence A., 1962–
    How to think like Benjamin Graham and invest like Warren Buffett / by
    Lawrence A. Cunningham.
       p. cm.
    Includes bibliographical references and index.
    ISBN 0-07-136992-9
       1. Investment analysis. 2. Securities—United States. 3. Graham, Benjamin,
1894–1976. Buffett, Warren. I. Title.

HG4529.C86 2001
332.6—dc21   00-060923

McGraw-Hill

A Division of The **McGraw·Hill** *Companies*

First McGraw-Hill paperback edition, 2002

1 2 3 4 5 6 7 8 9 0   DOC/DOC   0 9 8 7 6 5 4 3 2 1 0 (HC)
     4 5 6 7 8 9 0   DOC/DOC   0 9 8 7   (PBK)

ISBN 0-07-136992-9 (HC)
ISBN 0-07-140939-4 (PBK)

McGraw-Hill books are available at special quantity discounts to use as premiums and sales
promotions, or for use in corporate training programs. For more information, please write to
the Director of Special Sales, Professional Publishing, McGraw-Hill, Two Penn Plaza, New
York, NY 10121-2298. Or contact your local bookstore.

CONTENTS

PART II:
SHOW ME THE MONEY   89

PART III:
IN MANAGERS WE TRUST   169

ACKNOWLEDGMENTS

The main ideas in this book trace their intellectual lineage to Benjamin Graham, whom I never knew but must thank posthumously, and Warren Buffett, whom I have the great fortune to know and from whose writings, talks, and conversations I have gained knowledge and insight. Neither of these men, of course, has any responsibility for this book's content and no doubt would disagree with some of what it says, though it is written as a narrative interpretation of principles they developed, to which it tries to be faithful.

Mr. Buffett deserves my continuing thanks for permitting me to prepare a collection of his letters to the shareholders of Berkshire Hathaway, *The Essays of Warren Buffett: Lessons for Corporate America*, and for participating along with Berkshire Vice-Chairman Charles Munger in a symposium I organized to analyze it. Thanks also to the readers of that collection of wonderful writings for encouraging me to write the present book, especially the courageous college and business school professors who use that book in their courses and their many students who tell me how valuable it is.

Other fans of that book who encouraged me to write this one include my friends at Morgan Stanley Dean Witter, led by David Darst and John Snyder; Chris Davis and KimMarie Zamot at Davis Selected Advisers; the team at Edward D. Jones; and supporters too numerous to mention at other firms who appreciate the business analysis way of investing.

By training and professional habit I am a corporate lawyer, and as my students know, effectiveness as a corporate lawyer requires mastering not only (or mostly) law but also business, including finance, accounting, and governance. For tutelage in that philosophy, I thank my friends and former colleagues at Cravath, Swaine & Moore as well as that firm's clients.

Not all law faculties recognize the intersection of law and business. My colleagues at Cardozo Law School do and support my research and writing in the fields of finance, accounting, and governance that seem to others a step beyond law as such. Among these colleagues, special thanks to Monroe Price for introducing me to Warren Buffett through their mutual friend Bob Denham. For granting me a sabbatical to devote time to work on this book, I especially thank Dean Paul Verkuil and Dean Michael Herz.

My personal and institutional ability to span these and other subjects has been greatly aided by Samuel and Ronnie Heyman, both nonpracticing lawyers and astoundingly talented businesspeople, investors, and philanthropists. They generously endowed the Samuel and Ronnie Heyman Center on Corporate Governance at Cardozo, a multifaceted program I direct that explores this range of disciplines in teaching, research, and policy review.

My own teachers also deserve my thanks, particularly Elliott Weiss, now professor at the University of Arizona College of Law, who long ago drew my attention to Graham and Buffett's ideas and who generously shares his wealth of knowledge. For allowing me to use in modified form some materials from a textbook we worked on together, I also thank Professor Weiss, Professor Jeffrey D. Bauman of Georgetown University Law Center, and West Group, that book's publisher. Thanks also to West Group for allowing me to use in modified form some materials from another textbook I wrote, *Introductory Accounting and Finance for Lawyers*, which is not for lawyers only.

Many thanks to the whole team at McGraw-Hill for their confidence, enthusiasm, and guidance, particularly Kelli Christiansen, Jeffrey Krames and Scott Amerman.

Most of all, thanks to my wife, JoAnna Cunningham, who painstakingly edited the entire manuscript with precision and grace and encouraged me every step of the way.

INTRODUCTION: THE Q CULTURE

Common sense is the heart of investing and business management. Yet the paradox of common sense is that it is so uncommon. For example, people often refer to a stock or the market level as either "overvalued" or "undervalued." That is an empty statement. A share of stock or the aggregate of all shares in a market index have an intrinsic value. It is the sum of all future cash flows the share or the index will generate in the future, discounted to present value.

Estimating that amount of cash flow and its present value are difficult. But that defines value, and it is the same without regard to what people hope or guess it is. The result of the hoping and guessing game—sometimes the product of analysis, often not—is the share price or market level. Thus, it is more accurate to refer to a stock or a market index as over*priced* or under*priced* than as over*valued* or under*valued*.

The insight that prices vary differently from underlying values is common sense, but it defies prevalent sense. Think about the ticker symbol for the popular Nasdaq 100: QQQ. The marketing geniuses at the National Association of Securities Dealers may have chosen three Qs because Q is a cool and brandable letter (think Q-Tips). In choosing from the letters N, A, S, D, and Q, however, they selected the one (three times) that stands for Quotation and unwittingly reflect a quote-driven culture by this quintessentially New Economy index created in mid-1999.

Quotes of prices command constant attention in the mad, modern market where buyers and sellers of stocks have no idea of the businesses behind the paper they swap but precisely what the price is. Quote obsession trades analysis for attitude, minds for myopic momentum, intelligence for instinct. Quotations are the quotidian diet of the day trader, forging a casino culture where quickness of action fed by irrational impulses displaces both quality and quantity of thought. QQQ is an apt symbol for the most volatile index in stock market history.

In the Q culture, common sense is common nonsense, putting price on a pedestal and all but ignoring business value. The Q trader sees price as everything. The smart investor knows what value is. She focuses on value first, and then compares value to price to see if an investment holds the promise of a good return. That kind of focus requires the investor to operate as a business analyst, not as a market analyst or securities analyst and certainly not as a Q trader.

This book develops a mind-set for business analysis as the antidote to the Q culture. It discusses the tools of stock picking and highlights critical areas of thinking about markets and prices, and businesses and managers. It builds a latticework of common sense to fill the vast value void in today's markets.

The book first shows you why it is a mistake to operate as a market analyst or to look to the market to reveal value when all it can do is reveal prices. It then presents the tools to think about performance and value but also cautions about how financial information can be distorted in ways that can mislead you. Accordingly, it argues that an essential element of intelligent investing is a commonsense ability to assess the trustworthiness of corporate managers, principally the chief executive officer and board of directors.

The business analysis approach to investing shatters many myths of investment lore prevalent in the Q culture though not unique to it throughout history. For example, it rejects a distinction as pervasive as it is mistaken between growth investing and value investing (or between growth stocks and value stocks). To be sure, some companies show greater promise of earnings growth than others, but all rates of growth are a component of value so this distinction, crystalized in the early 1970s and a growing fixation ever since, is of no analytical value.

For another, the business analysis approach underscores a key distinction between investing on the one hand and speculation or gambling on the other. All investing involves risk and in that sense there is a speculative element in all of it. Intelligent investing, however, calls for a reasonably ascertainable valuation and comparison to the price.

Leading examples of speculating and gambling include people buying shares in IPOs or Internet start-ups they know little or nothing about and buying shares in any business without first reading its annual report or knowing what to look for in it. For every gambling success story you hear about, there are scores of failures you don't. As *The Wall Street Journal* recently quipped, no brother-in-law has ever been known to reveal how much money he lost in the stock market.

The focus on business analysis as opposed to market analysis is reinforced by the imaginary Mr. Market, created by the twentieth century's most astute investment thinker and business school teacher, Benjamin Graham. Price and value diverge in capital market trading because the market is best characterized as manic depressive, mostly either too euphoric or too gloomy. This is contrary to the popular but mistaken belief that markets are efficient and therefore accurately price securities.

Once you as a business analyst know *how* to look, the next question is *where* to look. The core idea is your circle of competence, created by the twentieth century's most successful investor and business educator, Warren Buffett. It is defined by your ability to understand a company's products and operating context. Circles of competence are as varied as the investors who must define them. All investors must grapple with the challenge of using current and past information to gauge future business performance.

For most people, it is easier to do this with businesses that have been around a long time, been through lots of business cycles, and faced economic recessions. Within that group of business are many whose long track records justify being called classics—well-established companies with powerful global products and market positions like Procter & Gamble, GE, Coca-Cola, and Disney. Some of these will endure as stalwarts, while others will be beaten down (as GE did to Westinghouse or as Wal-Mart did to Sears Roebuck). The ability to tell which is which will vary among people with different aptitudes in evaluating these companies, for different sets of skills are necessary to understand these various sorts of businesses.

So too will abilities vary with respect to assessing the future performance of newer companies that have been through fewer variations in their operating climate. These are "vintage businesses"—those that have been around for a while but which operate in newer and more dynamic industries that evolve at a rapid pace—companies like Cisco, Intel, or Microsoft, for example. They have less of a track record, and may be harder for lots of people to understand. But some people will have the ability to understand them quite well and be able to make informed judgments about their future prospects.

As with the classics, some vintage companies will turn out to be warriors and others wimps. For example, take the personal computer business. From 1990 to 1999 the erstwhile start-up Dell built a hugely profitable direct-sales PC business, growing its sales and profits at astonishing rates, with Compaq following respectably, Tandy and Apple lagging, and plenty of staggering wimps suffering erosion during the period, including AST, Digital, Atari, Tulip, Commodore, and Kaypro.*

A third group of companies are "rookies," brand-new companies, perhaps in brand-new industries, whose entire context has virtually no track record. These are frontier businesses, like steel in its day, automobiles in theirs, plastics a bit later, and the Internet at the turn of the twenty-first century. Apart from the first movers in such groups—say, Yahoo! and America Online (AOL) among the 1990s Internet companies—these have virtually no economic histories to speak of.

Even so, there will be investors who have the present-day tools to make intelligent estimates of where the rookies will be in the future. By mating with AOL in 2000, senior managers of Time-Warner expressed just such confidence in their ability to do so. Whether their judgment will be vindicated remains to be seen. But certainly although some of these companies will turn out to be fly-by-nights, others are true up-and-comers that will proceed up the ranks from vintage warriors to stalwart classics. After all, every company started out as a rookie.

The central feature of the circle of competence, then, is that it must be tailored to the individual. It is not the case that intelligent investors avoid businesses that are hard to understand or subject to rapid change. On the contrary, those investors equipped with the ability and fortitude to understand what is hard for others to understand and to gauge better than others how a business and its industry are evolving have a decided advantage. But it remains important for each investor to come to grips with what is and what is not within his circle of competence to make the informed judgments that intelligent investing requires.

---

* Kara Scannell, Anatomy of a Bull Run: "New Economy" Stocks Lead Charge: Blast From the Past—A Look at Yesterday's Tech Investments—A Few Thrive, Others Merely Survive, Some Fail, *The Wall Street Journal*, January 18, 2000.

The next inquiry is what to look for, within your circle of competence. The main question is the certainty with which you can evaluate the long-term economic characteristics of a business. A greater degree of confidence may be necessary for rookies, less for vintage companies, and least for classics; but in all cases, assessing the long-term characteristics of business performance is crucial.

Obtaining the necessary degree of confidence in valuation entails just a few quantitative inquiries. You'll see in the second part of the book that financial statements must enable you to answer three questions about a business:

- How likely is it the business will be able to pay its debts as they come due?
- How well is management running the business?
- What is it worth?

These questions can be gauged with a sufficient degree of confidence by a basic familiarity with key business ratios relating to working capital and debt, management of inventory and other short-term assets, returns on equity, and the future outlook for earnings.

Just as each investor's circle of competence will vary, so too will the assessment of these financial characteristics. Ultimately, the value of a business is the present value of all the cash it will generate for its owners over future time. Because no one can know the future with certitude, coming up with that number requires the right set of tools and good judgment.

Equipped with these tools and working within your circle of competence, you can determine how much and what sort of evidence is required to be comfortable with a valuation estimate. Yet there is no single reliable tool to pinpoint the value of a business, so intelligent investors must observe Benjamin Graham and Warren Buffett's cardinal rule of prudent investing: getting a margin of safety between the price you pay and the value you are paying for.

In your pursuit all these inquiries, reported figures must be treated with a healthy skepticism. Accounting conventions and judgments can distort business reality. For example, working capital figures can be distorted by accounting rules relating to inventory and receivables collection. Some fixed assets that are outmoded or noncompetitive may have an actual scrap value way less than the reported figure.

On the other hand, some assets may be understated on a balance sheet (such as reserves of a natural gas company as well as land values). Off–balance sheet liabilities relating to environmental problems, post-retirement health benefits for employees, and stock options for managers also must be included as adjustments to reported figures. You need not know every detail, but a working understanding is necessary and can be developed with a modicum of effort as part of a business analysis mind-set.

Tied to the question of certainty in evaluating the long-term characteristics of a business is the certainty with which you can rely upon management to channel rewards to shareholders. It remains true that mouth-watering economics is the most important variable in evaluating any business for investment. Poor economics can rarely, if ever, be cured, even by exceptional management, and inferior management can harm a good business (though it is harder for bad management to damage an outstanding business).

This management reality—coupled with the inadequacy of markets and the potential unreliability of numbers—demands that an investor also appreciate the qualitative dimensions of business analysis. The most important of these are those qualities that indicate that a company has an owner orientation.

Holding an owner orientation is not required of corporate managers as a matter of law or even by practice or custom. Nor will such an owner orientation be achieved merely by arranging the corporate rules in certain ways, such as having large numbers of outside directors or separating the functions of the CEO and the chairman of the board. Accordingly, the focus on managers is a focus on trustworthiness.

Assessing the trustworthiness of corporate managers is much like assessing the trustworthiness of a prospective son-in-law. It is a matter of common sense—again, a rare but acquirable mind-set. In the context of corporate managers, sources of insight into managerial trustworthiness include business records and qualities of communications to shareholders—the CEO letter in particular. Examples of this art finish off the book, the final chapter giving an account of the letters of Jack Welch (GE), Mike Eisner (Disney), and the late Roberto Goizueta (Coca-Cola).

The folk wisdom of "minding your Ps and Qs" does not refer to prices and quotes but to common sense. In investing, this means grasping the basics of finance, accounting, and governance to see that the following occurs:

- The efficient market story is at most four-fifths true and investors can take advantage of the remaining one-fifth
- Traditional tools of financial analysis remain an investor's best friends but that earnings management and accounting manipulation can be her worst enemies
- Intelligent investors pay special attention to who the managers are and whether they are trustworthy

Minding these Ps and Qs does not require enormous amounts of work, although it does require large doses of common sense as inoculation against Q fever.

This antidote takes you through the golden gates of the safer and more prosperous V culture world. The consummate teacher of V culture, Ben Graham, was also a successful practitioner. Warren Buffett, the consummate student and practitioner, is also a teacher. All good students take the lessons of their teachers and expand upon them in application. Buffett is no exception, nor are the many other Graham disciples who take the core lessons and extend them in a variety of successful ways.†

Yet the differences are subtle to say the least. Buffett keeps inviolate Graham's core ideas that call for a business analysis mindset, attention to the differences between price and value, and insisting on a margin of safety when making any investment. Only minor differences in application come up, including and pretty much limited to the following: Buffett places somewhat more significance on the role of managers in investing, is less beholden to bargain purchases of the type Graham favored, is a bit less committed to diversification of stock investment, and pays more attention to intangible asset values than did Graham. But these differences are not only overshadowed by what is common, they also reflect a broader unifying principle: the importance of independent judgment in investing.

Other Graham disciples choose different ways of applying the main ideas—some diversifying enormously, others concentrating enormously, and some paying far more or less attention to the underlying nature of businesses. With temerity and great humility, this book offers an account of Graham's ideas and Buffett's extension and application of them that reflect the example and tradition. It is

† Warren Buffett, The Superinvestors of Graham and Doddsville, *Hermes* (Columbia Business School), Fall 1984.

a broadened and extended narrative related specifically to the contemporary investing environment that Graham obviously can no longer address and that Buffett can do only in the relatively structured framework of annual shareholder letters.

At all times, the business analysis mind-set is anchored in the price-value distinction and the margin-of-safety principle, the deep moorings of the V culture, the deans of which will always be Graham and Buffett, though I am delighted to be on the faculty.

PART I

A TALE
OF TWO
MARKETS

CHAPTER 1

MR. MARKET'S BIPOLAR DISORDER

The patient exhibits classic manic depression—or bipolar disorder—combining episodes of euphoria with irritation. He goes on wild spending sprees for months on end, using money he does not have to buy things he does not need. In the buoyant periods he is talkative and full of ideas, but only in distracted, zigzaggy ways. He can charm you into buying the Brooklyn Bridge. Then, suddenly and swiftly, he shifts moods, falling into a months-long spell of dark depression, often provoked by the tiniest annoyances, such as minor bad news and modestly disappointing results.

Experts observe that the condition might be inherited, caused by innate chemistry affecting mood, appetite, and the perception of pain, which in turn could lead to dramatic weight gains followed by abrupt weight losses. There are safety nets to fall back on, such as government support, and government-approved treatments, such as mood stabilizers. But the patient lives in denial and can become angry and suspicious, sometimes not taking the medicine and precipitating more intense bouts of ups and downs.

The patient I am describing, of course, is the stock market. It mixes episodes of irrational fear with episodes of irrational greed. It rises with massive infusions of funds—often borrowed—then falls after the withdrawal of those funds. It bounces around like a circus clown on a pogo stick, weaving wild tales of untold riches to be made without effort. Then it pouts, plummets, and corrects, often on news that this or that company failed to meet earnings estimates by mere pennies per share.

Clear thinkers about market behavior rightly believe that this condition is incurable, with the market being prone to fat gains followed by fat losses without a nexus to business or economic reality. Nevertheless, government engines such as the Securities and Exchange Commission and private ones such as the New York Stock

Exchange monitor the extremes, imposing "circuit breakers" that shut the market down when it threatens to slip into a bout of depression (a sell-off) or raising the requirements for margin accounts, particularly those of day traders.

Yet no cure is in sight. Mr. Market, in Ben Graham's terms, denies its manic depression.[1] It does this in numerous studies extolling how "rational" it is. It does it in countless conversations and publications referring to its "efficiency." Reams of "beta books" are compiled in the belief that its gyrations simply and accurately reflect precisely the measurable risk that stocks pose for investors. Abstract advice to diversify portfolios is sold as the only way to minimize the rational risk that this efficient system manageably presents. Denial prevents cure.

Take Ben Graham's Mr. Market a diagnostic step deeper. Malicious microorganisms called rickettsia (named for Dr. Howard T. Ricketts, 1871–1910) cause diseases such as typhus. From the Greek word for "stupor," signifying a state of insensibility and mental confusion, typhus is characterized by bouts of depression and delirium. It is transmitted by bloodsucking parasites called ticks. These parasites transmit a similar disease called Q fever.

To avoid Q fever, those venturing into tick-infested forests prepare themselves. Hats, gloves, long sleeves, and pants are the dress code. If bitten, prudent forest denizens remove the parasite with tweezers, wash the bite, and apply rubbing alcohol, ice, and calamine lotion. They survive to enjoy the woods.

Fools in the tick-ridden forest go bare, leaving exposed their skin and, most daringly, their heads. After they find a tick, fear drives them to irrational action, such as burning the tick instead of tweezing it out. The kings and queens of fooldom then venture gleefully on their forest expedition, giddily unaware that they are infected with Q fever—until depression and delirium set in.

In the stock market forest, the ticks of price quotes infect the unprepared fools in the same way and with similar results. Trader obsession with price quotations spreads the Q fever epidemic, adding gas to the fire of Mr. Market's manic depression.

When venturing into the stock market, defend yourself just as you would when hiking in the forest: armed to fight the wealth-sucking parasite of the Q fever price tick. Ben Graham and Warren Buffett prescribe the same course for dealing with Mr. Market. They advise that just as it is foolish not to recognize his symptoms or diagnose his disease, it is equally foolish to play into them or expose oneself to the contagion. Instead, use Mr. Market to your advantage.

Neither Graham's Mr. Market nor this Q fever metaphor implies anything about the psychology of market participants. Rational people acting independently can produce irrational market results. Many investors simply defer to experts or majority opinion. Following the herd may seem rational and intelligent—until it stampedes straight off the cliff.

SWINGS, BUBBLES, AND CRASHES

Price ticks drive the wild volatility that plagues contemporary stock markets. Momentum traders and sector rotators are both victims and transmitters of Q fever. The disease reaches epidemic proportions when the crowd follows the "indelibly indicated trend," in the sarcastic words of Fred Schwed from his classic work *Where Are the Customers' Yachts?* referring to the illusion that patterns predictably persist.[2]

Average stock prices swing by 50% every year, while underlying business value is far more stable. Share turnover is enormous. The number of shares traded compared to the total shares outstanding spiked from 42% to 78% on the New York Stock Exchange between 1982 and 1999 and from 88% to 221% on the Nasdaq between 1990 and 1999.[3] Prices on particular stocks rise sharply and fall furiously within days and weeks without any link to underlying business values.

Speculation rages, and the speed of price fluctuation has multiplied dramatically compared to previous decades. Market volatility has increased roughly in proportion to the dramatic increase in information—both real and imagined—that is readily available. Getting in before the rise and out before the fall has become the day trader's mantra, one that reveals not only the presence of Mr. Market but the existence of his coconspirators by the thousands.

Roller coaster rides in stock levels have been known throughout the history of organized market exchanges, but these rides took major indexes either up or down together. A quite different trail was blazed in the late 1990s and early 2000s as the Dow Jones average of leading industrial companies went one way and the Nasdaq average of more technology-oriented or younger companies went another.

Frothy new economy devotees bid up the new stocks and tech stocks to wild heights compared to their pathetic or negative earnings while eschewing the stodgy old economy stocks that continued to generate steady earnings increases. The new giddiness subsided, and the Dow surged while the Nasdaq slumped. But then one recovered while the other dropped. Topsy-turvy is the only description for this wild world.

Anyone seeking to divine some deep logic in these flip-flopping patterns, however, could stop looking on April 14, 2000, when the indexes plunged together, the Dow by 6% and the Nasdaq by 10%. Then both rebounded the next trading day, with the Dow climbing back nearly 3% and the Nasdaq moving back up 6.6% (and the day after that experiencing up pumps of nearly 2% and over 7%, respectively).

No deep logic explains these swoons or this pricing divergence, and all you can really conclude is that Mr. Market was being his (un)usual self. Staggering as these data are, consider too that in the first quarter of 2000, the Nasdaq suffered four declines of 10% or more and then in each case rebounded. In April 2000 alone it recorded two jumps that were its largest in history and three drops that were its largest in history. In the late 1990s and early 2000s, Dow busts were equally commonplace, as other drops exceeding 3% show (see Table 1–1).

The Dow busts of August 1998 were particularly potent: They wiped out all the gains the Dow had made during that year. So was the March 2000 bust: It set the Dow back to where it had been about a year earlier.

If you prefer to focus on Mr. Market's euphoria, take the bursts

TABLE 1-1. Dow Busts

DATE	CLOSE	POINT CHANGE	PERCENT CHANGE
October 27, 1997	7,161.15	−554.26	−7.18
August 4, 1998	8,487.31	−299.43	−3.41
August 27, 1998	8,165.99	−357.36	−4.19
August 31, 1998	7,539.07	−512.61	−6.37
January 4, 2000	10,997.93	−359.58	−3.17
March 7, 2000	9,796.03	−374.47	−3.68

TABLE 1-2. Dow Bursts

Date	Close	Point Change	Percent Change
September 2, 1997	7,879.78	257.36	3.38
October 28, 1997	7,498.32	337.17	4.71
September 1, 1998	7,827.43	288.36	3.82
September 8, 1998	8,020.78	380.53	4.98
September 23, 1998	8,154.41	257.21	3.26
October 15, 1998	8,299.36	330.58	4.15
March 15, 2000	10,131.41	320.17	3.26
March 16, 2000	10,630.60	499.19	4.93

in the Dow exceeding 3% that occurred in the late 1990s and early 2000s (see Table 1–2).

Apart from their magnitude, consider the proximity of these Dow busts and bursts. The charts show two back-to-back reversals: The October 27, 1997, bust of −7.18% was followed the next day by a 4.71% burst, and the August 31, 1998, bust of −6.37% was followed the next day by a 3.82% burst. The three busts of August 1998 were promptly followed by three bursts of September 1998, much the way the bust of March 7, 2000, was followed by the bursts on March 15 and 16 of that year. It is hard to believe that these successive bursts and busts are based on changes in fundamental information investors were rationally and efficiently acting on.

Beyond busts and bursts on the Dow and the Nasdaq in the late 1990s and early 2000s, recall one of the most dramatic single episodes of Mr. Market's presence on Wall Street: the 1987 crash. The Dow vaporized by 22.6% on a single day and nearly 33% in the course of one month. The 1987 crash was not limited to the 30 common stocks on the Dow but was worldwide. The New York Stock Exchange, the London Stock Exchange, and the Tokyo Stock Exchange all crashed.

If stock market prices really obeyed the ever-popular efficient market theory (EMT) and accurately reflected information about business values, some major changes in the body of available information would be required to justify that crash. Many people tried to explain it as a rational response to a number of changes in and around mid-October 1987, including the following:

- On September 4, 1987, the Federal Reserve Board raised the discount rate.
- On October 13, 1987, the House Ways and Means Committee voted to approve income tax legislation that would disallow interest deductions on debt used to finance business acquisitions.
- On October 18, 1987, Treasury Secretary James Baker publicly announced an intention to reduce the value of the dollar.
- Market prices were already high by historical standards.[4]

Some experts attributed the 1987 crash to various institutional factors, including program trading and portfolio insurance that were set to sell off big chunks of the portfolios of large investors as prices fell. When prices fell, these program sales pushed them down even harder. Other experts pointed to derivative securities, often exotic instruments whose value fluctuates with changes in the value of benchmarks such as interest and exchange rates. These derivatives are usually intended to reduce risk and volatility in such benchmarks, though if poorly designed can exacerbate the volatility in stock market pricing.

But given the international nature of the crash and its depth, hardly anyone accepts these explanations. Most people also agree that it is impossible to explain rationally the radical price changes that have occurred at other times—whether the 1929 crash, the 1989 break, or the general 1990s and 2000s volatility. Market frenzy simply cannot be explained using EMT but is a product of a complex of forces in addition to actual changes in information about fundamental business values.

Market frenzies like these are not isolated and certainly not unique episodes in financial history. On the contrary, market bubbles—situations in which prices are way higher than values—happen all too often. There was a technology stock bubble from 1959 to 1961; a bubble in the so-called 'Nifty Fifty' stocks in the late 1960s and early 1970s; a gambling stock bubble in 1978; a bubble in oil and energy stocks in the late 1970s; a home shopping bubble in 1986 and 1987; and a biotechnology bubble in the early 1990s (with a resurgence in the early 2000s), and all of these resemble the Internet or dot-com bubble of the late 1990s and early 2000s.

The market capitalization (price times shares outstanding) of the Internet sector was about $1 trillion at the beginning of 2000, with sales of $30 billion and losses of $3 billion.[5] In 1999, scores of initial public offerings (IPOs) of Internet stocks were launched, many in the same industry where it is going to be impossible to have more than a handful of profitable companies. Deals included, for example, 17 health-care related companies, seven business-to-business e-commerce companies, six music distribution companies, five employee recruiters, and three travel agencies. It starts to sound like the "Twelve Days of Christmas."

Driving this funding is the fascination with technological innovation, a fascination that characterized previous market bubbles as well. The 1960s technology bubble arose from innovations such as color television and commercial jet aviation. It spawned an IPO boom in electronics and other businesses whose names ended with "tron" or "onics" not unlike that of 1999's dot-com boom.[6] Takeovers surged in both periods, fueled by high-priced stock that built many corporate empires. All the talk was of a new history-defying era— called a "new paradigm" in the 1960s and the "new economy" in the late 1990s and early 2000s. But as Warren Buffett quotes Herb Stein as saying, "If something can't go on forever, it will end."[7]

The Internet bubble may not end as abruptly as the 1960s electronics bubble did. It may instead follow the path of the stock market bubble in Japan in the 1980s, which ended in a gradual and total erosion of stock prices in the Nikkei average throughout the decade of the 1990s. One thing the two periods have in common—and one of the most striking common features of speculative bubbles generally—is the emergence of "new" ways to defend the high prices.

In 1980s Japan the fuel was stock prices based not on the earnings or cash that can be generated by a business, but on underlying asset values the businesses owned, which themselves had been rising to the stratosphere as a result of aggressive real estate speculation. We'll soon see that the same alchemy plagues the turn of the twenty-first-century United States.

These examples merely manifest in U.S. stock markets the emotional drives inherent in human market making, exemplified more generally not only by the 1980s Japanese experience but by classic episodes of bipolar disorder such as the Dutch tulip bulb mania of the 1630s and the British South Sea exuberance just prior to 1720. In each of those cases—as in most others—the initial reason to buy may have been sound. Rare tulip bulbs in Holland were valuable because the novelty of that flower in Holland turned it into a status symbol. Shares of Britain's South Sea Company were valuable when it began to exercise its royal grant of monopoly trade with Spain.

But the excitement of "getting in" on these deals got out of hand, more and more money was allocated to futures contracts on tulip bulbs and shares of the South Sea Company, and the more money that was led there, the more money seemed to follow—until the music stopped and panic set in. In Holland, the price got so high that speculators could not afford to pay for the bulbs they had bought the rights to. In Britain, the company simply did not generate the great gains from Spanish trade everyone had obviously been expecting.

If EMT were true, the U.S. stock markets would be unique among all markets throughout human history and across the contemporary globe.[8] Consider this selection from the writings of the market observer Joseph de la Vega from the late 1600s about the Amsterdam stock exchanges of his day, in the style of a tongue-in-cheek dialogue between a merchant and an investor:

MERCHANT: These stock-exchange people are quite silly, full of instability, insanity, pride and foolishness. They will sell without knowing the motive; they will buy without reason.

INVESTOR: They are very clever in inventing reasons for a rise in the price of the shares on occasions when there is a declining tendency, or for a fall in the midst of a boom. It is particularly worth remarking that in this gambling hell there are two classes of speculators. The first class consists of the bulls. The second faction consists of the bears. The bulls are like the giraffe which is scared by nothing. They love everything, they praise everything, they exaggerate everything. They are not impressed by a fire or disturbed by a debacle. The bears, on the contrary, are completely ruled by fear, trepidation, and nervousness. Rabbits become elephants, brawls in a tavern become rebellions, faint shadows appear to them as signs of chaos. The fall of prices need not have a limit, and there are also unlimited possibilities for the rise. Therefore the excessively high values need not alarm you.[9]

Sound familiar? Why, apart from hubris and chutzpah, should we believe the U.S. stock markets are so special in the history of the world?

BE AN ANOMALY

EMT also cannot explain many other things about how market prices operate apart from swings, bubbles, and crashes. Abundant evidence refuting EMT includes the extraordinary number of unexplained market phenomena, such as the following:

- The January effect (prices tend to rise in January).
- The insider effect (a stock's price tends to rise after insiders disclose purchases to the Securities and Exchange Commission and fall after insider sales are disclosed).
- The Value Line effect (stocks rated highly by the Value Line Investment Survey tend to outperform the market in terms of price).
- The analyst effect (stocks of companies followed by fewer analysts tend to become pricier compared to those followed by more analysts).
- The month effect (stock prices tend to rise at the end and the beginning of months).
- The weekend effect (stock prices tend to be lower on Mondays and higher on Fridays).

Weirder correlations also exist, including the hemline indicator (prices historically have risen and fallen in tandem with rises and falls in the average length of skirts in fashion) and the Super Bowl effect (prices tend to rise in the period after the Super Bowl if the winning team was a member of the original National Football League but fall otherwise).

Efficiency buffs call these and dozens of other well-known exhibits against market efficiency "anomalies." Some anomalies disappear over time. The January effect began to do so in the mid-1980s. When they do, EMT worshipers rejoice, citing the disappearance as evidence of market efficiency. This is strange evidence, however, when you note that the vanished anomalies persisted for decades (seven decades in the case of the January effect).

Even more bizarre, the anomaly label has been applied to the astonishing investing records of many prominent stock pickers, a list that is long and getting longer. It includes Ben Graham; Warren Buffett; Charlie Munger, vice chairman of Berkshire Hathaway; John Maynard Keynes; Bernard Baruch; Gerald Loeb; John Neff of the

Windsor Fund (Vanguard); Mario Gabelli; David Schafer; William Ruane and Richard Cuniff of the Sequoia Fund; Tom Knapp of Tweedy Browne; John Templeton; Mason Hawkins of Longleaf Partner Funds; and untold others.

BARREL OF MONKEYS?

Can it be, as EMT devotees resort to saying, that these are anomalies too—that these folks are all merely lucky? Is it plausible to believe that they are just like the imaginary monkey who would produce the entire script of *Hamlet* by randomly hitting the typewriter keys? Even if you agree that this is possible, to complete the argument the imaginary monkey would also have to be able to punch in the correct keys to generate the full scripts of *Romeo and Juliet, Macbeth, King Lear, Henry IV,* and pretty much the entire Shakespearean canon. Even if this is theoretically possible, such a prolific monkey (or a barrel of monkeys) seems incredible.

The monkey view acknowledges that luck plays a role in investing, as it does in other aspects of life. The leading populist apostle of this "lucky monkey" viewpoint is the Princeton professor Burton Malkiel, who explains it in his book *A Random Walk Down Wall Street* by using a coin-flipping contest.[10]

Start with a thousand people flipping a coin, with those flipping heads being the winners and going to the next round. By the laws of chance, on average 500 will flip heads and 500 will flip tails. The 500 flipping heads proceed to round two, where, again by the laws of chance, half will flip heads and half will flip tails. The 250 lucky heads flippers go to round three, where 125 of them win; 63 of those win round four; 31 win round five; 16 win round six; and 8 win the final round and are proclaimed "expert" coin flippers.

Yet resorting to luck as an explanation of investment success leaves the explanation incomplete. First, investing is simply not like coin flipping, though speculation and gambling may be. The great investors do some homework and develop a set of investment precepts to guide them in their selection of investments. They don't simply flip a coin in choosing which investments to make. They certainly do not decide between, say, IBM and Clorox by pasting their logos onto a coin, with the logo landing face up getting the capital.

Second, the lucky monkey would have to have been banging on

his keys every day for decades, much as a day trader would have to click his mouse every day for decades. But the great investors have not followed the daily trading strategy. On the contrary.

Buffett, for example, generated most of the billions of wealth Berkshire Hathaway has accumulated from about ten investments over about forty years. Many of those billions came from buying big stakes in large companies at times when their value was woefully underappreciated by the market.

Berkshire bought its stake in the Washington Post Company, for example, in mid-1973.[11] Not only had the Post's own stock price been battered by the Nixon White House's excoriation of its investigative reporting on Watergate, that was one of the few times in postwar American history that the U.S. stock market resembled its dismal stance during the Depression. Buffett's purchase price? About a fifth of intrinsic value, an 80% margin of safety. Luck plays a major role in a day trader's portfolio; discipline plays an obvious role in Berkshire's.

Luck is an inadequate though often partial explanation for any human endeavor that entails effort. Those who succeed in their endeavors catch butterflies not by luck alone but with the help of an expertly cast net. Ben Graham drew a fine link between luck and work by saying that "one lucky break, or one supremely shrewd decision—can we tell them apart?—may count for more than a lifetime of journeyman efforts. But behind the luck, or the crucial decision, there must usually exist a background of preparation and disciplined capacity."[12]

Whether they are characterized as value investors, growth investors, fundamental investors, opportunistic investors, or anything else, commonsense discipline is the unifying trait of all the superinvestors who make up this barrel of monkeys. It is true that Keynes and Loeb are associated with the "skittish" school of investing, an opportunistic strategy that rapidly exploits market gyrations fueled by alternating bouts of fear and greed. Their short-termism contrasts with the long-term views of the "value" school associated with Graham and Buffett, yet both schools recognize the price-value discrepancy that these alternating bouts of Mr. Market's bipolar disorder create.

All these stellar investors—and many others, such as Jack Bogle, Phil Carret, Phil Fisher, Peter Lynch, the Prices (Michael and T. Rowe), and George Soros—succeed by exercising common sense. The "systems" or "formulas" employed or the labels given to them are not important, but the quality of their analysis and the independence of their thought and judgment are.

The best investors employ a mind-set that takes account of just a few things, but those things are indispensable. Every extraordinary investor follows Ben Graham's first principle: The market does not perfectly price the business value of a stock. Warren Buffett takes that insight dead seriously by limiting his purchases to stocks that are way underpriced by the market. Both of these investment titans as well as Phil Carret emphasize the importance of avoiding bad deals, stocks that are way overpriced in the market.

These investors and other greats, such as Buffett's partner Charlie Munger, always remember that there are tens of thousands of investment options available to just about anyone. To opt for one requires a strong belief that the market is giving the best deal available compared to all the others. And opportunity does knock. One way to test opportunity is to take Loeb's approach: always ask whether you would be comfortable committing a large portion of your resources to a single stock you are considering.

Buffett and other outstanding investors, including Peter Lynch, know that an intelligent appraisal depends on your ability to understand a business. This gives you a basis for gauging points all these top investors consider crucial, such as a company's competitive strength, brand power, and ability to develop new products profitably.

The investment giants (not monkeys) don't worry much about whether their investments end up concentrated in certain companies. For example John Neff, the portfolio manager of the Windsor Fund from 1964 through 1995, generated returns exceeding the average by a steady 3% annually and did so while sometimes allocating as much as 40% of the fund into a single business sector. Buffett's Berkshire Hathaway is a wonderfully diverse collection of outstanding businesses, but that diversity was an accidental by-product of the tremendous growth in the capital it deployed rather than a conscious effort to participate in lots of different businesses or sectors.

This cast of illustrious investors extends the commonsense understanding of markets and businesses to the analysis of business fundamentals. Chief among these factors are economic characteristics such as strong financial condition, earnings stability and growth, strong sales and profit margins, and large amounts of internally generated cash to fund growth as opposed to a continuing reliance on external financing sources. These investors also pay attention to the quality and integrity of management, looking for companies which consistently maximize the full potential of a business, wisely allocate capital, and channel the rewards of this success to shareholders. They emphasize the importance of exceptionally competent managers who own substantial amounts of equity in their own companies and can rapidly adapt to dynamic business conditions. They also believe that managerial depth and integrity include assuring good relations with labor and promoting an entrepreneurial spirit.

The hedge fund master George Soros summed it up well by saying that "the prevailing wisdom is that markets are always right; I assume they are always wrong." The prevailing wisdom of market efficiency is one way to view markets. In this view, price changes are due almost exclusively to changes in fundamental values. Therefore, a diversified selection of stocks with different pricing behaviors compared to the overall market makes the most sense. The contrary view says that lots of price changes occur for nonfundamental reasons. The goal here is to identify those companies whose prices are below their business value. This perspective calls for thinking about individual businesses rather than the overall market.

The next two chapters offer the alternative foundations of these two competing ways to think about markets. Chapter 2 is a history of how the efficient market idea came into being. Chapter 3 is an account of evidence that contradicts EMT on its own terms. If you are already a skeptic of market efficiency, you can skip these two chapters as a practical matter (though they contain valuable insights on the merits of the competing views). If you are an efficiency devotee, you should read them and be prepared to change your mind.

Either way, Chapter 4 assesses the current environment for clues concerning whether the direction in which we are heading is better described by the efficient market idea or by what might be called the "chaotic" market idea. It finds that we are heading toward less rather than more efficient markets. The rest of the book adopts the view of the investment masters that stock markets are not perfectly efficient and provides the equipment you need to take advantage of the inefficiencies.

PROZAC MARKET

A long and interesting story lies behind the ever-popular efficient market theory, a story every investor should know. Knowing the EMT story will enable you to evaluate advice based on it, including advice about the value of diversification and ways of measuring risk. It will also help you decide for yourself whether to believe EMT. That is important because if you believe in market efficiency, you will adopt a style and philosophy of investing very different from the one you will be smart to adopt if you do not.

Investors who have already concluded that EMT is not the best account of how stock markets work could skip this chapter without being cheated, but even they may discover ways in which EMT has unwittingly affected their investing habits. All readers will also discover that the history of EMT is fascinating. It is a story about research designed to enlarge knowledge, to explain and understand the world, research whose results are intermittently neglected and then overblown. The story tells us that EMT is not the last word on how stock markets work, even though the power it has had over investors and teachers for several decades sometimes makes it seem that people think it is the last word.[1]

OBSCURITY

EMT traces its history to the random walk model of stock prices, the sensible idea that stock prices move in a way that cannot be predicted with any systematic accuracy. The model dates back to 1900, when it was elaborated in a doctoral dissertation by the French mathematician Louis Bachelier that though obscure in its time is now famous. That dissertation investigated linear correlation in the prices of options and futures traded on the French Bourse and concluded that such price changes behaved according to a random walk model.[2]

Bachelier's work was not widely noticed when it was published, perhaps because the mathematical parts of it preceded by five years Einstein's famous work on the random motion of colliding gas molecules. Einstein "discovered" the equation that describes the phenomenon of random molecular motion, known as Brownian motion (after the Scottish botanist Robert Brown, who first observed it), which was precisely the equation Bachelier developed to describe price behavior in financial markets.

Although the mathematical properties Bachelier employed were of direct and immediate interest to physicists and mathematicians (including Einstein and his intellectual progeny), economists paid little attention to the subject until the middle of the century. Indeed, virtually no studies before the early 1950s made any reference to Bachelier's work or to the theory of random processes in financial markets.

Maurice Kendall is frequently credited with bringing the random walk model to the attention of economists in the early 1950s. Bachelier's work itself, however, was not "discovered" by economists until they stumbled across it in the mid-1950s.

While rummaging through a library, Leonard Savage of the University of Chicago happened upon a small book by Bachelier published in 1914. He sent postcards to his economist friends asking if they had "ever heard of this guy." Paul Samuelson could not find the book in MIT's library but did locate and then read a copy of Bachelier's doctoral thesis. Just after Samuelson's discovery in 1959, the random walk model became a very popular area of research.

Bachelier's long obscurity was also due to a widely reported 1937 study by the renowned economist Alfred Cowles concluding that stock prices did move in a predictable way. This study shut down research on the random walk model for decades until in 1960 the Stanford professor Holbrook Working discovered a mistake in it. Cowles then corrected the mistake, and his revised study supported the random walk model.

SIMPLICITY

Once Samuelson and his colleagues rediscovered Bachelier, they also had the great fortune of being able to harness his insights on a large scale with the advent of the computer age and the widespread availability at universities and research foundations of high-speed computers. Using those new technologies in the early 1960s, stock market researchers went to work with a vengeance exploring random processes in these markets.

CORRELATION TESTS

One aspect of the investigation consisted of correlation tests that were used to determine whether specified data sequences move together to any degree. In the case of stock prices, price changes of a given stock are recorded over a specified time period—say, a number of days—and a subsequent period of the same length. These sequences (called time-series data) are then compared to determine whether they move together to any degree—whether they show any "correlation."

The comparison takes the form of a correlation coefficient, a number that reflects the degree to which the data are linearly related. In effect, the time series of data is tested for correlation by fitting a straight line to the data and then calculating that number. A correlation coefficient equal to zero provides evidence that the data in the series have the property of statistical independence; correlation coefficients that are close to zero (but not equal to zero) indicate that the data are uncorrelated. A time series of data is random if it is either independent or uncorrelated.

Consider televised lottery drawings in which winning lottery numbers are determined by selecting numbered balls from a bin containing numerous balls with different numbers painted on them. The auditor retrieves a ball, records its number, and replaces that ball. The auditor does this perhaps three times, each time retrieving, recording, and replacing. This process has the property of statistical independence because the number recorded after any retrieval indicates nothing about the numbers recorded either previously or subsequently.

Outside of a controlled context such as a lottery bin, particularly in the context of time-series data such as stock prices, it is extremely difficult to prove statistically that a series of data has the property of statistical independence. The less restrictive property—that data are uncorrelated—is susceptible to statistical proof and allows for conclusions substantially similar to those which follow from the independence property.

The correlation tests of the 1960s all resulted in correlation coefficients that did not differ significantly from zero. This meant that various series of actual stock market data were indistinguishable from various series of numbers generated by a random number table, roulette wheel, lottery drawing, or another device of chance.

These findings had an important practical implication: Traders could not systematically make above-normal gains from trading because a statistical lack of correlation implies that the best estimate of the future price of a stock is its present price. In other words, if prices follow a random walk, the price change from one time to the next will not affect the probability that a particular price change will follow that one. Past prices cannot predict future prices.

RUNS

A long known weakness of correlation tests is that the results can be skewed by a small number of extraordinary data in the time series. An alternative test that avoids this weakness is an analysis of runs in the data—an investigation of whether there is any persistence to the direction of successive changes.

A run is defined by an absence of directional change in a statistic in the series. Thus, a new run begins any time the direction changes (i.e., from negative to positive, from positive to negative, or from unchanged to either negative or positive).

Instead of testing the correlation of numerical changes in the data in the series, one investigates the relationship of the direction of those changes. If price changes follow the random walk model, the number of sequences and reversals in time-series data of stock prices will be roughly equal. If the same direction persists for a significantly longer period, the random walk model will be contradicted.

Among the numerous run studies conducted in the early 1960s, the University of Chicago economist Eugene Fama's is regarded as the most careful.[3] Fama found that the direction of price changes tended to persist but nevertheless concluded that no trading rule or strategy could be derived that outperformed the market consistently. Accordingly, almost everyone involved in the debate in the late 1960s agreed that the observed departures from randomness were negligible and believed that this constituted strong support for the random walk model.

TRADING RULES

Despite the widespread agreement, some participants in the debate remained skeptical. Indeed, prescient commentators of that era occasionally expressed the fear that the interrelationships of stock price changes are so complex that standard tools like these cannot reveal them. That fear led to efforts to dispute the model by designing trading rules that could achieve above-normal returns by uncovering and exploiting these greater complexities.

Among the most primitive though most illustrative trading rules was Sidney Alexander's "filter technique." This is a strategy designed to discern and exploit assumed trends in stock prices that, in Alexander's piquant phrase, may be "masked by the jiggling of the market."[4]

For instance, a "5% filter rule" for a stock would say to buy it when the price goes up 5% (and watch it rise to a higher peak); then sell it when the price goes down 5% from that peak (and watch it fall to a lower trough); then short the stock (i.e., borrow it and sell it at the prevailing price, promising to repay with the same stock, to be purchased for the price prevailing at the time of repayment); then, when the price rises 5% from that trough, cover the short position.

If this works, you get a gain on the initial sale plus a gain on the short position. More important, if it works, prices are following a peak-trough pattern. That means they are not random and the random walk model is contradicted.

Alexander's initial results indicated that such a technique could produce above-normal returns. Subsequent refinements of Alexander's work by himself and others, including Fama, however, demonstrated that relaxing or changing certain assumptions eliminated the abnormal returns, particularly the original filter technique's failure to note that dividends are a cost rather than a benefit when stocks are sold short.

Alexander's filter technique epitomizes the chartist or technical approach to stock analysis and trading, under which a study of past prices (or other data) is used as a basis for predicting future prices. Indeed, Alexander's filter technique is a conceptual cousin of limit orders and similar techniques prevalent in securities trading today. These techniques include conventional technical methods that rely on anomaly effects (the insider, month, weekend, and analyst effects) as well as the more unconventional methods (the hemline indicator, the Super Bowl indicator, and so on).

These and related philosophies such as "momentum investing" and "sector rotation" remain staples of Wall Street futurology. They are widely and increasingly used by traders and recommended by investment advisers and brokers. They are nonsense, as many students of the random walk model (and EMT) recognize based on the foregoing analysis.

They are nonsense not because of EMT but because they fly in the face of business analysis. As Ben Graham said of proponents of such technical methods in *The Intelligent Investor*: "We shall dismiss these with the observation that their work does not concern 'investors' as the term is used in this book."[5]

On their own terms, the trouble with all these tests of the random walk is that they are linear. They do not investigate the presence of nonlinear price dependence, something that in the early 1960s researchers simply lacked the computer horsepower to do.

The trading rule test, for example, is linear in that it operates in chronological time (or real time). Neither it nor the other old tests consider the possibility that market time may be better understood from a perspective that is nonlinear. We will get to that subject in the next chapter, but for now note that Einstein demonstrated that time is not absolute but works in dozens of different ways depending on the context, including forward (or linear), backward, circular, slow, and erratic (nonlinear), and can even stand still.

THE PERFECT DREAM

Many people suggest that EMT developed in a peculiar manner in scientific research. The proof of the hypothesis came first, beginning with Bachelier in 1900 and proceeding through the wealth of studies reporting randomness in the early 1960s.

Only then was a theory proposed to explain the randomness, beginning with the first explication of EMT in 1965 by Paul Samuelson, a recipient of the Nobel Prize in economics in 1970.[6] Economists welcomed this proof. The conditions necessary to produce it seemed tantalizingly close to those necessary to sustain every economist's dream: a perfect market.

The perfect market is a heuristic invented by making the following assumptions concerning a market: There are a large number of participants such that the actions of any individual participant cannot materially affect the market; participants are fully informed, have equal access to the market, and act rationally; the commodity is homogeneous; and there are no transaction costs.

A perfect market would give you exactly what the random walk model was implying: Prices of shares in stock markets should adjust instantaneously and accurately to new information concerning them. That prediction was embodied in EMT as it was first propounded. In its broadest terms, EMT said that the prices of shares traded in stock markets fully reflect all information concerning those shares.

Stock markets may or may not have the characteristics assumed by the perfect market model. As the 1976 Nobel laureate Milton Friedman reminds us, however, the cardinal rule of economic forecasting is that a model's predictive power is the only relevant test of its validity, not the assumptions underlying it.[7] Thus, the fact that investors are not rational or fully informed, for example, does not matter as long as these realities do not interfere with the predictive power of EMT. While many economists are reconsidering assumptions like these, for now this approach holds sway over accepted economic theory.

THREE FORMS OF EFFICIENCY

In its general form, EMT explains more than the random walk model. That model says simply that successive price changes are independent or uncorrelated, whereas EMT explains that by saying that stock prices fully reflect all the information (not just price histories) about a stock. As a result, virtually since the emergence of EMT as an explanation of the random walk model, EMT has been divided into three forms defined in terms of specified categories of information.

The three forms were first proposed to classify empirical tests of price behavior given specified kinds of information. The weak form tested the random walk model itself, using correlation and run tests like those just described to investigate whether past prices indicate anything about future prices. Semistrong-form testing investigated whether publicly available information other than prices was reflected in prevailing prices, and strong-form testing investigated whether private information was reflected in prevailing prices.

As the wealth of tests and discussion proceeded in the 1970s, the three forms of EMT came to be used to refer to the conclusions those tests suggested. Thus, the forms of EMT have since then been specified as follows: The weak form says that stock prices fully reflect all information consisting of past prices, the semistrong form says that stock prices fully reflect all information that is currently publicly available; and the strong form (hold your breath) says that stock prices fully reflect all existing information, whether publicly available or not.

There is thus a direct and logical link between the random walk model and weak-form efficiency but a more attenuated and contingent link between the random walk model and stronger forms of EMT. Recall that the random walk model holds that price changes are independent of or uncorrelated with prior price changes. That means that technical analysis of past price changes—sometimes called chartist analysis—cannot aid the prediction of future price changes in any systematic way.

Weak-form efficiency explains this independence and its implications for prediction by hypothesizing that the current price impounds all information contained in prior prices. Thus, any price change can only be the result of new information, the production of which is itself assumed to be random. This process of information absorption continues and thus explains the absence of substantial linear dependence in successive price changes discovered in the correlation and run tests of the 1960s. It also leads to the stronger forms of the hypothesis.

The semistrong form of EMT posits not only that current stock prices reflect all information consisting of prior stock prices but also that they reflect all publicly available information about the stock in question. Testing this more ambitious claim requires a focus not on correlation analysis of price changes but on the relative swiftness with which prices change given new information.

Despite this different testing methodology, semistrong efficiency depends on the validity of the random walk model, which depends in turn on empirical conclusions concerning the absence of statistical dependence in stock price data. In other words, if future price changes depend on prior price changes, any price change the semistrong form tests cannot be attributable solely to the new information the test is evaluating. Thus, both weak efficiency and semistrong efficiency depend on the proof provided by linear testing models.

The strong form of EMT extends much farther than the random walk model suggested. Indeed, the strong form is a theological proposition, holding that public capital markets are infinitely wise: even nonpublic information is reflected in public stock prices. Abundant evidence has decimated the strong form by showing that people who possess nonpublic information can use it to make abnormally high market returns, with the apotheosis being the insider trading scandals of the 1980s.

Since the strong form of EMT has been discredited, debate concerning EMT centers on the semistrong and weak forms. Debate over the weak form generally is defined by analysis of the random walk model itself, usually in terms of the linear empirical models used to test the relationship between successive price changes; this has cut into the random walk model.

A widely noted study by MIT's Andrew Lo and Wharton's A. Craig MacKinlay demonstrated strong positive serial correlation in stock prices for weekly and monthly holding period returns. Using 1,216 weekly stock return observations from 1962 to 1985, they found a weekly correlation coefficient of 30%, an extremely high level of correlation. These researchers point out in their book, *A Non-Random Walk Down Wall Street*, that this does not mean necessarily that the stock market is inefficient but that the random walk model cannot be the basis for any theory of efficiency.[8]

Though not conclusive, evidence like this led even Eugene Fama—a chief architect of EMT—to conclude that daily and weekly stock returns are predictable from past returns, thus rejecting the random walk model on a statistical basis.[9] Even so, Fama and the other fathers of EMT cling to the view that such discrepancies are merely anomalies that do not impair the basic model's validity, though others try to explain these results in a different way called noise.

NOISE

Consider John Maynard Keynes's well-known beauty contest metaphor for the stock market. In the contest, each judge picks the candidate he or she thinks others will pick rather than the candidate he or she thinks should win on merit. This replaces a fundamental or substantive sort of analysis (of the kind urged in this book) with a popular, speculative, and herd-pack mentality.

The 1981 Nobel laureate James Tobin of Yale took Keynes's beauty contest a step farther. He suggested that even if a public capital market is efficient in the sense of swiftly incorporating public information into stock prices (i.e., the semistrong form of EMT), that does not necessarily mean that stock prices in that market reflect fundamental values (i.e., the present value of expected future flows to stockholders).[10]

The quality of information digested by the market may be just as low as the quality of information that goes into the decisions of Keynes's beauty contest judges. Tobin has many followers who think he's right, including Nobel Prize winners William F. Sharpe and Kenneth Arrow of Stanford.[11] If it is true that many traders act as Keynes described, the semistrong form of EMT has to be further subdivided between strict informational efficiency and a more refined notion of fundamental efficiency.

Informational efficiency describes a market in which all public information about a stock is reflected in the price of that stock without regard to the quality of that information. Thus, information that concerns the fundamental value of a stock is reflected, but so is information wholly unrelated to that fundamental value, such as who won the Super Bowl. Fundamental efficiency is the more narrow but more ambitious idea that stock prices are accurate indicators of intrinsic value because they reflect only information concerning fundamental business values.[12]

The issue becomes whether the capital markets can distinguish among kinds of information so that only information about fundamental value is impounded and reflected in prices. That revives the basic question of whether humans behave rationally. EMT says it does not matter if individual actions are not rational because any individual irrationality will be corrected by others acting rationally. In effect, irrationally is "assumed out" of the EMT model.

The informational-fundamental distinction, however, is so intuitively and empirically potent that it had to be confronted. The result was the face-saving shelter of euphemism: The economist Fischer Black, borrowing a term from the field of statistics, renamed irrational behavior noise, thus enabling self-respecting economists to discuss the issue and try to model it.[13]

Noise theory is supported by substantial empirical evidence and a well-developed intellectual foundation. Noise theory models hold that stock markets are infected by a substantial volume of trading based on information unrelated to fundamental asset values (noise trading). These models attempt to explain both why noise trading occurs and why its effects persist.

The most common noise theory model says, for example, that noise trading is conducted by ill-informed investors who act on sentiment rather than rational analysis. Their actions move prices away from fundamental values. The price-value gap persists despite the presence of sophisticated arbitrageurs because they are risk-averse and cannot be sure that investor sentiment will not change adversely at any time.[14]

Evidence of the noisy investor approach to the stock market includes following tips or acting on rumors, rapidly turning over one's portfolio, selling good performers while retaining bad ones (thus triggering taxable gains rather than generating tax-deductible losses), paying huge mutual fund fees for poor managerial performance, and imitating others in running off market cliffs by using silly technical trading strategies.

The causes of this behavior remain poorly understood, but psychological research suggests a number of tendencies. These tendencies include attitudes toward risk that lead people to be more averse to loss than eager for gain; this explains the irrational tendency to hold losing stocks while selling winning stocks. Another is skewing the probabilities of uncertain future events by basing forecasts on past patterns, such as by forecasting that earnings growth over the next ten years will equal that of the last three.

In theory, smart money arbitrageurs could correct all these errors and profit from them, keeping EMT intact. But this is a risky business. If there is mispricing today, there may be mispricing tomorrow. If stocks are highly priced compared to value, an arbitrageur will sell short and await the correction. But the correction may not arrive before she has to cover. If stocks are lowly priced compared to value, an arb will buy and await the rise. But that correction could take a long time, during which those funds could be deployed at higher returns elsewhere.

Another possibility is that individual actions that are rational can produce aggregate results that are irrational. This happens all the time in business. After air-conditioning was invented, for example, retail stores spent substantial sums to install it, but once every store did this, none of them enjoyed any competitive advantage as a result. It is why you see a gas station at every corner of a suburban intersection. Buffett gives the example of what occurs when each person watching a parade decides he or she can see a little better by standing on tiptoe.

Despite these profound insights developed at the frontiers of thought about how markets work, they continue to be treated by many leading economists as variations on the theme. Maybe there is some deviation in EMT, its devotees admit, but the deviations are due to mere chance. Eugene Fama, for example, continues to argue that apparent overreaction to information is just as common as apparent underreaction to information, and the likelihood of abnormal returns continuing after an event are about as likely as those returns reversing after that event.

Thus, a whole group of leading economists thinks that the latest evidence against EMT does not add up to much. They cling to investment tools that are based on EMT and used to complete the theoretical picture with practical applications.

TIDYING UP THE TALE

EMT tells us that specified information sets are fully reflected in the price of public securities. EMT, however, does not provide any basis for determining what it means for any such information to be fully reflected in stock prices. Doing this requires a theory of asset pricing. It is composed of two popular ideas: modern portfolio theory, which provides the foundation, and the capital asset pricing model, which is the general paradigm.

MODERN PORTFOLIO THEORY

While the random walk model and EMT were being developed in the 1950s and 1960s, Harry Markowitz of the City University of New York and yet another Nobel Prize recipient (in 1990, along with Sharpe) was developing modern portfolio theory (MPT).[15] The basic idea here is that combining a group of noncorrelated stocks in a single portfolio results in a portfolio with less volatility than the average volatility of those individual stocks.

MPT proposes that all investments are reducible to two elements—risk and return—and assumes that investors are risk-averse in the sense that they will sacrifice returns to avoid risk and demand greater returns to assume risk. MPT says that such investors will best address their risk aversion by investing in a portfolio of investments in which they receive the greatest expected return for any given level of risk.

The expected return on an investment is simply the weighted average of all possible returns on it, and the risk of an investment is the dispersion of possible returns on that investment around the expected return. Under MPT, expected return on a portfolio of investments is simply the weighted sum of the expected returns on the individual investments; the risk, however, of a portfolio of investments is not necessarily the weighted sum of the risks (or dispersion in the returns) of the individual investments.

The central insight of MPT is thus that since variations in returns on individual investments may reduce the dispersion of returns on a portfolio of investments, portfolio risk is primarily a function of the degree of variance of individual investments compared to the portfolio as a whole. This means that portfolio risk is minimized through portfolio diversification.

MPT's understanding of risk has another important implication. With respect to any stock, two elements of risk can be distinguished: systematic risk and unsystematic risk. Systematic risk (also sometimes called market risk or undiversifiable risk) arises from the tendency of a stock to vary as the market in which it is traded varies. Unsystematic risk (also sometimes called unique risk, residual risk, specific risk, or diversifiable risk) arises from the peculiarities of the particular stock being investigated.

Because under MPT's diversification directive unsystematic risks can be diversified away to zero, market returns on a stock in a competitive market will not include any compensation for such risk. Thus, market returns will be a function solely of the systematic risk, or the extent to which a particular stock varies as the market of which it is a part varies. Measuring such risk and return is the main goal of capital asset pricing models.

THE CAPITAL ASSET PRICING MODEL

As MPT and EMT were maturing in the late 1960s, capital asset pricing theory was in its infancy. The capital asset pricing model (CAPM) that is most widely known today derives from MPT (and was pretty much invented by Markowitz's co-Nobelist, Sharpe).[16] Like MPT, CAPM assumes that investors are risk-averse in the sense just described. In addition, CAPM assumes that investors have rational expectations concerning expected returns. Under this assumption, CAPM says that the expected return on an investment is equal to the risk-free rate of return plus compensation for the systematic risk of the investment in the sense just described.

The systematic risk is measured by the degree of variability of the individual investment versus the market as a whole. It relates the risk premium associated with a particular stock (its return less the risk-free return) to that associated with the market as a whole.

That association for any stock is expressed by a number called the stock's β (beta). Under CAPM, stocks with higher β's are more risky than are stocks with lower β's because they tend to swing more widely than does the market—their returns exhibit greater dispersion versus market returns.

CRITIQUE AND COMMON SENSE

On their own terms, there are several weaknesses in MPT and CAPM. First, in evaluating EMT, the need for a pricing model creates a joint hypothesis problem: No one can ever be sure in testing a model whether its failure is due to market inefficiency or to an inadequately specified asset pricing model.

Indeed, many of the anomalies in EMT mentioned earlier are attributed to deficiencies in the asset pricing model rather than to the presence of market inefficiency. These deficiencies are most often associated with imprecision in defining risk or, equivalently, in specifying β.

The joint hypothesis problem has an important implication for EMT skeptics. To disprove EMT requires proof that does not use an asset pricing model. However, any linear or nonlinear dependence in stock price behavior is inconsistent with EMT itself. Thus, a discovery of linear or nonlinear dependence in successive stock prices (presented in the next chapter) means EMT is incomplete, period. It does not admit the alternative explanation of a "misspecified" asset pricing model.

In addition, CAPM says that expected returns from an investment are linearly related to expected returns on the portfolio of which that investment is a part. The linear relationship is given by β and is in turn dictated by CAPM's rational-expectations assumption.

If human behavior is itself inconsistent with the rational-expectations assumption, there is no reason to believe in such a linear relationship. This is another way of saying that the stock market is nonlinear rather than linear. In that case, β will not be an accurate measure of risk.

Finally, the rational-expectations assumption used in the CAPM requires that investors have homogeneous return expectations; this in turn requires that investors evaluate and understand information in identical ways. Heroic as that sounds, it would also require all investors to evaluate investment opportunities over identical time horizons. The patent dubiousness of these requirements recently has become an important aspect of the literature criticizing CAPM.

The literature demonstrates that demand for particular stocks is sensitive to price changes, just like demand for most other goods.[17] Investors have different appetites for particular stocks as their prices change. Thus, markets do not depict the right price of a stock because there is no such thing. Even rational people are not homogeneous automatons; they interpret information differently, and their judgment about the present value of a business's future cash flows will vary even if they are all rational.

As Francis Fukuyama has pointed out in another context, the neoclassical economic model of rational self-interested behavior with which EMT is ultimately linked is right only about 80% of the time.[18] Its devotees forget Adam Smith, the father of their thought, who emphasized that economic life is embedded in social life and that economic actors make decisions that vary from pure economic calculus as a result of social habits and contexts. That is why in Smith's day his field was called "political economy" rather than, as it is today, simply "economics."

If the rest of social science should be returned to economics, it is even possible to add some physics from the hard sciences. Recall that the random walk model got that name because public capital markets seemed to obey the principles of Brownian motion, which specify that molecules in motion behave randomly. Although molecules lack sentience, prices are strictly creatures of the ultimate sentience, human behavior.

Common sense thus suggests that the price-molecule parallel should not hold. More powerfully, current thought in physics concerning nonlinear dynamics and chaos theory extends well beyond Brownian motion and suggests further reasons to doubt and reconsider the validity of the analogy.

The next chapter shows how that analogy has been turned upside down and inside out. Before going on, though, pause to consider whether common sense supports β as a measure of risk. What β really measures is the price volatility of a stock. If you insist on associating the word "risk" with that measure, it at most means that β captures the risk of stock price gyrations. For a market analyst, that measurement may be of some interest.

But for a business analyst, price gyrations are useless analytic tools, and so therefore is β. What matters in business analysis might be called "business volatility," the gyrations in earnings or cash flows a business has experienced as grounds for gauging its future business performance. The earnings and cash flows are what give a business value and what are of interest; market prices do not, and β is therefore of no interest to a business analyst.

As the vogue of mathematical investing approaches raged in the late 1960s, Ben Graham declared that treating volatility in price changes as the meaning of risk is "more harmful than useful for sound investment decisions because it places too much emphasis on market fluctuations."[19] EMT sought to neutralize that objection by saying that market fluctuations were simply rational price changes reflecting information changes. Just so. Yet some things are not that simple. Charlie Munger is fond of quoting Einstein on this point: Everything should be made as simple as possible, but no more so.[20] Graham continues to be right.

CHAPTER 3

CHAOTIC MARKET

Today's investor can learn something from the elite group of Nobel Prize winners who brought us the "modern finance" summarized in the last chapter, but way less than is commonly believed. Although few informed students of EMT ever had great confidence in the strong form, the more modest forms—plus modern portfolio theory and beta (β)—have held sway over academic and popular investment thinking for nearly three decades.

Those hypotheses are based exclusively on simple linear analysis and thought, however, and so their descriptive power and normative implications are questionable. As in all fields of endeavor, knowledge continues to advance. Technology has enabled better ways to model market behavior than were available when EMT and the rest of modern finance were growing up. The new technology shows quite different results than did the old, results that confirm the common-sense intuitions behind Ben Graham's Mr. Market.[1]

NEW WAVE

The presence of noise in stock market trading shows the inadequacy of the linear testing models that led to the random walk model and EMT. Noise theory shows that the information-processing properties of public capital markets are so bluntly powerful that fundamental information about underlying business values is crowded out by extraneous information or noise. There is a feedback system in which individuals overreact to information or withhold action in the face of information.

Feedback processes are the hallmarks of a nonlinear system. They indicate a nonproportional relationship between a cause and its effect (e.g., between news and price changes). This insight of noise theory has not been recognized for its full power. The distinction between linear and nonlinear is fundamental to an understanding of stock market behavior and how investors and managers should think about markets and market prices.

Linearity means proportionality: A change in one variable produces a proportionate change in another specified variable. What makes the CAPM linear, for example, is its assertion that the expected risk premium of a stock varies in direct proportion to β.

EMT is linear in two ways. First, the statistical models underlying the weak form are simple linear regression analyses; correlation coefficients are statements about how variables are related on a straight-line basis over time. In other words, the time series of data is tested for correlation by fitting a straight line to the data and then calculating the correlation coefficient.

Second, the semistrong form of EMT is linear because it defines a proportional relationship between information changes and price changes. In particular, the semistrong form says that information is swiftly incorporated into prices without bias. In other words, there is a proportional relationship between information changes about business values and resulting price changes in the financial asset (stocks) representing those businesses.

In contrast and a bit simplistically, nonlinearity means the absence of proportionality: Changes in one variable will produce a change in another variable, but exponentially rather than proportionally. To take a prosaic example, the 1-gram straw that breaks the 1-ton camel's back is nonlinear because the cause is utterly disproportionate to the effect.

Volatile stock prices and roaring or crashing markets are often attributable to an incremental bit of information piled on top of cumulated bits of information. If one company announces that its earnings aren't going to be as strong as people had hoped, its stock price may take a haircut, but the market overall may not blush. But as the weeks go by and a few more companies in that sector say the same thing, Wall Street gets rattled. The shares of all the stocks in that sector can suddenly get punished, and the pounding can spread across the market as a whole. At some point, the creepy Wall Street saying that there is never only one cockroach starts to resonate.

The fact that the market may react slowly or may overreact to bits of new information is of course what noise theory teaches and explains. The distinction between nonlinear and linear systems goes well beyond noise theory, however, because noise theory itself is constrained by the efficiency paradigm. Nonlinear dynamics and chaos theory break from that context and imply a fundamentally different understanding of public capital market phenomena with a broader perspective on investor and market behavior.

There is no a priori reason to believe that public capital markets are linear systems rather than nonlinear systems. Therefore, one of the first questions that must be considered in understanding such markets is whether they follow linear or nonlinear processes. More sophisticated techniques than were available when the random walk model was first developed are now used to investigate precisely that question.

One reason such techniques were unavailable in the 1960s, 1970s, and even early 1980s was the need for powerful computer systems that not only could process data more swiftly but also could go beyond the simplified mathematical models of straight lines and investigate the curvatures of multidimensional data streams. Armed with such resources, researchers now start with the consensus view that empirical research shows that a random walk describes stock prices fairly well, subject to some anomalies. Then they dig deeper.

One tool for the digging actually dates to the early part of the twentieth century. It was developed by the hydrologist H. E. Hurst when he was working on the Nile River Dam project.[2] Hurst had to develop reservoir discharge policies to maintain reservoir water levels in the light of rainfall patterns.

To understand how the reservoir system worked, Hurst would record its water level each day at noon and calculate the range (essentially differences between the high and low levels and the average levels). If the range increased in proportion to the number of observations recorded, one could conclude that the reservoir system was a random one. Otherwise, it was nonrandom and exhibited some pattern, knowing either of which could enable the hydrologist to set the reservoir's discharge policies.

Hurst developed a simple tool called the H exponent to determine whether the range increased as would a random process or whether it exhibited a more patterned behavior. Skipping the mathematical details, if a system's H equals .50, then the system behaves according to a random walk. The probability that any particular move will follow any other move is 50-50 and thus completely up to chance.

If H is less than .50, the system is mean reverting. That means that if the system has moved up for a number of observations, it is more likely to move down over the next number of observations, and vice versa. Conversely, if H is greater than .50, the system is correlative or persistent: if the system has moved up for a number of observations, it is more likely to continue to move up over the next number of observations, and vice versa. If H is .60, for example, the probability that a positive move will follow a positive move is 60%.

H may change over time. For example, H may be in the .70s over some period and then drop to near .50 and subsequently increase again. The number of observations (or time periods) over which H is sustained at other than .50 (before returning to near .50) is a measure of the average cycle length of the system.

In the case where H exceeds .50 for a sustained period, the length of that period is a measure of the system's memory—the extent to which past events influence present and future events. In the context of investment analysis, it measures the period over which an investor can use information to his or her advantage.

During the 1990s, some market analysts figured out that the H exponent can also be applied to markets to determine whether they are random too. One of them even published his results. Edgar Peters, a money manager in Boston, applied it to the Standard and Poor's 500 Index (the S&P 500) for monthly data over a 38-year period from January 1950 through July 1988.[3]

Peters found that H was .78 for average periods of approximately four years, indicating a strong persistent element in the S&P 500 rather than a random process. Beyond average periods of four years, however, H was not significantly different from .50 (it was .52/-.02). So Peters concluded that the S&P 500 begins to lose memory of events after four years. The S&P 500 thus is not random, and events today continue to affect price changes for up to an average of four years.

NEXT WAVE

This dashing of the economist's dream of a perfect market has been amplified by studies of the chaotic behavior of markets. Just as Hurst's H suggests that markets are not linear as EMT assumes, EMT's assumption of market rationality is put into scientific doubt by principles first developed by physicists in the field of chaos theory.

Chaos theory was popularized by the publication of James Gleick's 1987 best-selling book *Chaos*, primarily an exposition of chaos in natural science. The potential role of chaos theory in economics and finance was made prominent by the Santa Fe Institute's publication of a volume in 1988. It has been carried into the realm of "phynance"—the merger of physics and finance—most spectacularly by Doyne Farmer and Norman Packard, whose phynance exploits are chronicled by Thomas Bass in his 1999 book *The Predictors*. As a result of these works, chaos theory became an important and growing field in the study of the nonlinear dynamic behavior of economic and financial systems.

Through chaos theory, physicists discovered that many phenomena in the universe previously thought to be random (unpredictable, exhibiting no pattern) are not random but exhibit a significant pattern. To oversimplify, chaos theory holds that there is a pattern to the seeming randomness of physical events occurring in the universe. Thus, systems that appear to be stochastic (to involve only random motion or behavior under conventional linear modeling) may be deterministic, or exhibit more complex internal dependence than simple linear modeling reveals.

Chaos theory has its roots in the nineteenth-century work of Henri Poincaré, a French mathematician and physicist who studied the famous three-body problem.[4] Newton, using his laws of motion and gravitation, proved that it was possible to calculate accurately the future positions and velocities of two mutually attractive material bodies. Neither Newton nor anyone since, however, has been able to do so for three or more bodies.

This three-body problem reveals itself repeatedly to scientists sending space probes to Mars and other planets: They chart a course directed to where the planet will be in its orbit when the probe arrives (not where the planet is upon sending the probe), but midcourse corrections are nevertheless necessary because Newtonian physics can predict accurately only the interaction of two bodies, not three. (This has led some probes to be lost in space.)

Poincaré attributed the three-body problem to nonlinearities inherent in multibody systems as the result of which "small differences in the initial conditions produce very great ones in the final phenomena. A small error in the former will produce an enormous error in the latter." This insight, now the unifying core of chaos theory, is known as "sensitive dependence upon initial conditions."

The classic example of sensitivity to initial conditions is the butterfly effect in meteorology. Its pioneer in the early 1960s was the MIT meteorologist Edward Lorenz, who said, "The dynamical equations governing the weather are so sensitive to the initial data that whether or not a butterfly flaps its wings in one part of the world may make the difference between a tornado occurring or not occurring in another part of the world."[5]

Picture an empty hockey rink. A person places a puck at midice and then rolls it toward the far end of the rink. He measures the angle of his hit, the angle of the puck's impact, and the angle of its rebound. He keeps measuring the puck's angles of impact and rebound as the puck bounces around the rink.

Assuming no friction, a rule of puck motion in the rink is that it will emerge from impacting a side of the rink at precisely its angle of approach (a similar thing will be familiar to anyone who has played billiards). That rule means we have defined a deterministic system under which the future position of the puck at any time can be forecast perfectly (assuming its actual or average speed is known).

But now assume that the initial position of the puck is varied by a few degrees, even an infinitesimally small variation, not observed by or known to the forecaster. The forecaster's predictions of the puck's location after it hits the first one or two sides may be imprecise—off by some small amount—but the imprecision will be negligible. The amount of error will grow exponentially, however, with each subsequent impact. In a short time the forecast will be wide of the mark.

Disturbing the measure of the puck's initial position causes its movement to appear random and unpredictable, whereas knowing that measure enables precise prediction. It is this sensitive dependence on initial conditions that is the signal characteristic of chaotic systems.[6] To detect its presence, Lorenz and his followers developed a couple of fascinating tools.

PICTURES AND ATTRACTORS

Time-series data are conventionally plotted using simple Cartesian geometry. For example, to plot a time series of a stock's price, price is plotted on the vertical axis and chronological time is plotted on the horizontal axis.

In physics, the usual Cartesian graphs can be turned into more powerful pictures called phase portraits plotted in phase space, a presentation that can depict the full range of possibilities for a system. The pendulum is the paradigm for illustrating the differences between Cartesian plots of time-series data and phase portraits of the same data as well as for introducing the notion of the attractor.

Consider a regularly swinging pendulum driven by mechanical

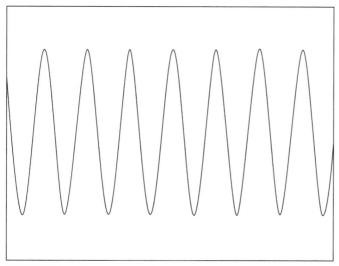

FIGURE 3-1 Driven pendulum time series.

force. It will swing back and forth at a steady speed and not come to rest (unless we withdraw its force). A Cartesian time-series plot would show such a pendulum's motion as a wavy up-and-down line whose height remains the same as time passes, as shown in Figure 3-1.[7]

The driven pendulum's portrait in phase space can be envisioned as a rectangle. At any moment in phase space, the pendulum's angle would dictate the location of a point horizontally and the pendulum's speed would dictate the location of a point vertically. As such, the pendulum's portrait in phase space would form a loop, illustrating the pendulum's continual motion through the same sequence of positions repeatedly, as shown in Figure 3-2. That continual repetition is described as a limit cycle or a limit cycle attractor because the pendulum (which can be called a system) is attracted to that one and only (limit) cycle.

Now consider a pendulum undriven by permanent mechanical force, having instead been started manually by lifting it to one end of its orbit and letting it go. Without the permanent mechanical force, the undriven pendulum will swing back and forth, gradually reducing speed and coming closer and closer to rest. A Cartesian time-series plot of this undriven pendulum would begin with the same wavy up-and-down line depicting the driven pendulum just

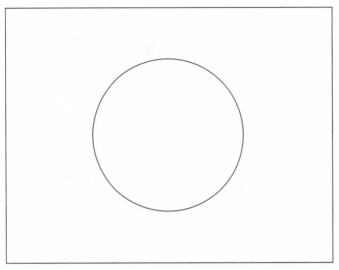

FIGURE 3-2   Driven pendulum phase space: "limit cycle attractor."

described, but this line's height would fall gradually and continuously as the pendulum's speed declined, as shown in Figure 3-3.

This pendulum's portrait in phase space also would begin as if it might form a loop, but owing to its declining speed, the plot would begin to spiral inward continuously as the pendulum slowed down. Correspondingly, the plot would converge to the origin, as shown in Figure 3-4. The origin in this case is described as a point attractor because the pendulum (or system) is attracted to that one and only point.

Another way to approach the pictures is to conceive of the phase space as a sideways view of the Cartesian time-series plot. It is in effect a collapsed side view of the gyrations of the simple time-series graph.

Keep that picture in mind as you consider a third type of attractor, which physicists call the strange attractor. The strange attractor describes a system whose phase portrait will be neither a loop nor a spiraling circle but instead will show some orbits that appear to be random: They do not repeat and are not periodic. They are, however, limited in range. In other words, the portrait will exist in a finite space but will admit of an infinite number of solutions in that finite space.

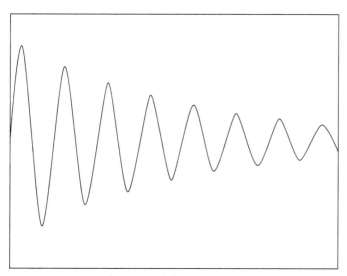

FIGURE 3-3 Undriven pendulum time series.

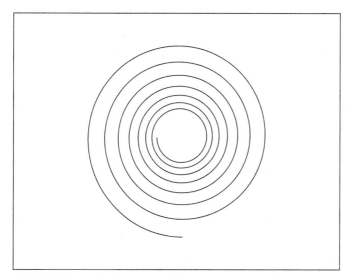

FIGURE 3-4 Undriven pendulum phase space: "point attractor."

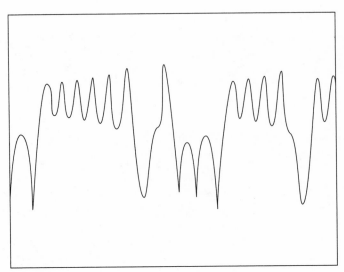

FIGURE 3-5 Simulated weather system time series.

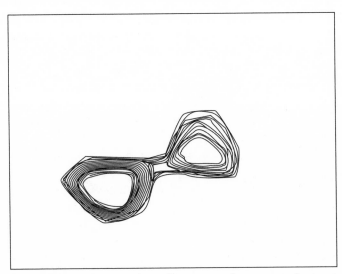

FIGURE 3-6 Simulated weather system phase space: "strange attractor."

Take a look at Figures 3-5 and 3-6. Figure 3-5 depicts the time series of a simulated weather system, suggesting behavior that is completely random and resembles typical graphs of stock market prices. Figure 3-6 depicts a phase portrait of the same system, revealing a strange attractor. Again, look at Figure 3-6 as a side shot of the time-series plot in Figure 3-5, condensing that Cartesian figure into a phase space portrait.

Limit cycle attractors and point cycle attractors do not exhibit any sensitive dependence on initial conditions: A pendulum without permanent mechanical force will always end up at the point of origin (its point attractor) no matter where it started, and a pendulum with permanent mechanical force will always orbit in its loop (its limit cycle attractor) no matter where it started.

Systems containing strange attractors do exhibit sensitive dependence on initial conditions: Where the system is at some future moment will be determined by where the system started (or by where it was at any time before).

STRETCHING

Phase portraits depict all possible states of a system by plotting a variable's value against the possible values of all other variables. The dimension of the phase space is equal to the number of variables that describe the system. Whether a system exhibits sensitive dependence on initial conditions can be determined by numbers called Lyapunov exponents (LEs), named for the Russian mathematician Aleksandr Lyapunov, who discovered them.[8]

LEs measure the speed of a variable's movements in phase space versus another variable. Positive LEs measure stretching in phase space—the speed of divergence of one variable with respect to another variable. Negative LEs measure contracting in phase space—the speed of system restoration after being perturbed. Thus, LEs for point attractors and limit cycles never are positive because such systems are always contracting.

In the case of a point attractor, the dimensions always converge to a fixed point, the origin; in the case of a limit cycle attractor, all the dimensions converge into one another except one, whose relative position creates the loop by not changing (and whose LE is therefore zero). For a strange attractor—involving a system that does exhibit sensitive dependence on initial conditions—at least one LE must be positive such that there is divergence in the nearby orbits.

LEs were created for use in connection with information theory, to specify the likelihood that information conveyed in binary computer language would be understood properly. LEs measured the increase in uncertainty of a communication as additional bits of information were added to the system.

The notion of bits of information has been reconceptualized for application to public capital markets as measures of our knowledge of current conditions. For example, in a time series of stock price data (e.g., daily returns), a positive LE would indicate the amount of information or predictive power lost each day.

An LE of .05 per day, for example, would mean that information becomes useless after 20 days (i.e., 1/.05). Thus, the LE is a measure of the reliability of information in making forecasts for specified periods.

Peters, the Boston money manager, also has calculated the LE for the S&P 500 (1950–1989), using monthly data. His calculations resulted in a stable LE equal to .0241 per month. An LE of .0241 per month means that information reliability decays at the rate of .0241 bit of accuracy each month; thus, the average cycle length of the system using this measure is approximately three and a half years (1/.0241 = approximately 42 months). Note that this result substantially matches the result that Peters got in his *H* analysis.

Peters also calculated the LE of 90-day trading data for the S&P 500 (1928–1990) and found an LE of .09883 per period. That result substantially matches both the monthly LE and the *H* analysis: The average cycle length of the system was approximately four years (1/.09883 = approximately ten 90-trading-day periods). Based on these calculations, the public capital markets do exhibit sensitive dependence on initial conditions and chaotic behavior rather than simple linear efficiency.

FRACTALS

Another way to test for chaos is to determine whether a system has a fractal dimension. Systems with fractal dimensions do not follow Euclidean laws. Euclidean geometry simplifies and organizes nature dimensionally: There are points, which lack dimension; lines, which have one dimension; planes, which have two dimensions; and solids, which have three dimensions. These simplifying images are heuristics: Natural objects do not conform to these images. Until fractal geometry was developed, however, these integral dimensions were all we had to go on.

Fractal geometry was developed initially by the mathematician and scientist Benoit Mandelbrot, who won the 1993 Wolf Prize in physics.[9] He observed that natural objects are not as simple as the descriptions offered by Euclidean geometry: "Clouds are not spheres [and] mountains are not cones." For example, how would we classify a piece of paper crumpled up an infinite number of times in terms of Euclidean geometry?

It is not three-dimensional because it is not a pure solid form (it has creases and crevices). (In mathematical terms, it is not completely differentiable across its entire surface.) It is also not two-dimensional because it has depth. In fact, its dimension is between two and three. That property makes the crumpled paper a fractal: Its dimension is a fraction (two point something).

With respect to time-series data, dimensionality depends on whether the system from which the data are taken is random or nonrandom. If a system is random, time-series data taken from it will reflect that randomness and have as large a dimension as can possibly be. In the case of data being presented on a sheet of paper, the highest possible dimension is two (the dimension of the paper itself). In any case, the data will fill a plane.

If a system is nonrandom, time series of data taken from it will reflect that nonrandomness and show a fractal dimension: The data will not fill the plane but will clump together. That clumping together reflects the correlations influencing the data (i.e., causing it to be nonrandom).

These properties distinguishing random from nonrandom time series may be conceptualized in a different way. For example, our conception of a crumpled piece of paper as a three-dimensional object can be regarded as embedding a fractal in a dimension greater than itself. That greater dimension is called the embedding dimension.

Fractals retain their fractal dimension when placed in an embedding dimension; random distributions do not. Thus, unlike nonrandom distributions, random distributions fill their space the way gas fills a volume: The gas spreads out because there is nothing to bind the molecules together. This is, of course, the defining characteristic of Brownian motion as discussed earlier.

Peters calculated the fractal dimension of the S&P 500 as 2.33 and did the same for other global stock markets, all of which also turned out to be fractals. Japan's was 3.05; Germany's, 2.41; and the United Kingdom's, 2.94. That is strong proof indeed that stock markets are not best described by EMT.

COMPLEXITY

Think about the 1987 crash (and other roller coaster market episodes) in terms of Einstein's point that time operates in different ways in different contexts. An intuitive case that market crashes exhibit chaotic behavior starts to emerge. The intuitive case begins by taking a nonlinear perspective of market time, under which market time expands (speeds up) when trading is heavy and compresses (slows down) when trading is thin. The speed of market time—called intrinsic time—evidences itself in pricing persistence and pricing discontinuity.

Pricing persistence is described in chaos theory as the Joseph effect, drawn from the familiar biblical story of Joseph interpreting the pharaoh's dream to mean seven years of feast followed by seven years of famine. The presence of this phenomenon in public capital markets is exhibited by bull markets and bear markets in that identifiable trends emerge and endure for significant time periods.

Pricing discontinuity is described in chaos theory as the Noah effect, taken from the biblical story of the Flood. Public capital markets exhibit the Noah effect in price changes. For example, suppose IBM opens at 50 and closes at 30. That does not necessarily mean that during some point in the trading day an investor could have traded IBM at 40 (or any other price between 50 and 30). Rather, the price of a stock moves discontinuously in the sense that at one moment it may be trading at 45 and at the next it cannot be sold for more than 35 (something that day traders see a lot of and that is discussed further in the next chapter).

The alternating presence of price persistence (the Joseph effect) and price discontinuity (the Noah effect) shows that chronological time—a linear concept—is not the most precise temporal measure of public capital market phenomena. When discontinuous pricing—the Noah effect—dominates a market, wide swings occur and market pricing is relatively unstable because intrinsic time and trading activity outpace chronological time and information gathering. When price persistence—the Joseph effect—dominates a market, pricing is relatively stable because intrinsic time is approximately equal to or slower than chronological time.

The speed of intrinsic time may differ from that of chronological time. Price changes would then move ahead of information changes. Investors and other market participants conform perfectly neither to the linear assumption of homogeneous expectations nor to the ubiquitous irrationality of noise theory.

Instead, investors have heterogeneous expectations that may or may not be rational and that may be defined according to a number of variables. Chief among them are investor time horizons that range from the very short term (for day traders and minute traders and market makers, say) to the very long term (for central banks, say).

The range of different time dimensions contributes to the Joseph and Noah effects, persistence, discontinuity, and premature and delayed adjustments to information. Short-term traders react more quickly to new information; long-term investors react more slowly. Therefore, information changes will not produce proportionate price changes. Indeed, volatility will increase when there are greater numbers of short-term traders (day traders) than long-term investors.

Changes that are produced constitute new information, producing another round of price changes again defined according to a range of discrete time dimensions. Adding further complexity to this mix of investor heterogeneity and time dimensions is the increasingly global nature of financial markets: News itself is dynamic, traveling around the world, usually in 24-hour cycles, and impacting Tokyo, then London/Frankfurt, then New York, and around again.

In this reality, it seems implausible to claim instantaneous, unbiased market adjustment to new information and it is not necessary to attribute all market preadjustment or readjustment to irrational noise trading. Incremental information changes in a perfect market would be expected to produce proportionate price changes.

But informational changes produce disproportionate changes. In terms of chaotic dynamics, these disproportionate changes may be seen as a result of initial measurement error that (as in the hockey puck example and the butterfly effect generally) leads to exponentially greater price changes over time.

BEHAVIORAL FINANCE

Not only do these systemic complexities and the stickiness of prices show new reasons to be skeptical of EMT, they also suggest partial explanations for the observed nonlinear dependence of stock prices and the possible presence of chaotic phenomena. They certainly show that market behavior is far more complex than EMT allows. While that is bad news for market efficiency, it is good news for investors who recognize reality.

EMT may remain valuable to economists in explaining portions of market processes—the public capital markets alternately may involve both random and nonrandom components. But this partial validity must not be misunderstood to suggest that markets are "relatively efficient," "reasonably efficient," "sufficiently efficient," or "more efficient than not" at any moment in time, as many devotees of EMT have been forced to argue since the market crash of 1987 shook confidence in that theory.

Since 1987, a new generation of economists has arisen in prominent universities to challenge EMT. Led by Robert Shiller of Yale, a school of thought called behavioral finance draws on a wide range of disciplines—including economics, psychology, biology, demography, sociology, and history—to challenge the essentially mathematical underpinnings of EMT.

The pioneers of behavioral finance have found substantial evidence supporting two of Buffett's long-held and most commonsense propositions. The first is that while stock prices over short horizons bounce around a lot, wedging price and value, over long horizons the price must correspond to value. As Andrei Shleifer of Harvard puts it, summarizing the studies: "Stocks with very high valuations relative to their assets or earnings (growth or glamour stocks), which tend to be stocks of companies with extremely high earnings growth over the previous several years, earn relatively low risk adjusted returns in the future, whereas stocks with low valuations (value stocks) earn relatively high returns."[10]

The second is evidence showing that investing in the latter group of stocks (mislabeled "value stocks," but the label is useful to simplify the discussion) offers superior returns over long horizons. However measured, the evidence Shleifer and his colleagues compiled shows that "value" stocks outperform "growth" stocks by spreads of about 8 to 10% annually over long horizons.

As early as 1981, Shiller showed that stock market prices are too volatile to accord with EMT. Shiller's peers at that time skewered him for this blasphemy, but his research has held up and attracted a still small but growing following, including former Harvard professor Lawrence Summers, who became secretary of the treasury. Shiller examined the relationship between price changes and subsequent cash paid to stockholders and found remarkable irregularity (bouncing around) in price changes in contrast to remarkable smoothness in the cash stream.

Shiller and his colleague John Campbell recognize that some of the price changes are due to changes in fundamental information and to uncertainty about the future trends of cash flows. But taking account of these factors, Shiller and Campbell estimated that only 27% of the annual return volatility in U.S. stock markets is justified in terms of fundamental information. Campbell followed up this research with John Ammer by using more recent data and reduced the estimate to only 15%.[11]

Markets may be relatively efficient only on some days but not on all days or may be relatively efficient for some stocks but not for others. Even if we are more generous than the 15 to 27% suggested by these studies and say EMT is 80% correct, it is a grave mistake to use market efficiency as the basis of a managerial or investor game plan. Buffett sums it up: "Observing correctly that the market was *frequently* efficient," EMT devotees "went on to conclude incorrectly that it was *always* efficient. The difference between these propositions is night and day."[12] That difference between night and day is all that Graham and Buffett need to recognize. Neither is enthused by mathematical accounts of markets, except to agree that EMT does not explain all of market behavior.

Buffett quotes one of Charlie Munger's favorite sayings to describe the modern economist's penchant for building EMT and related mathematical models of stock markets: "To a man with a hammer, every problem looks like a nail."[13] Graham quotes Aristotle: "It is the mark of an educated mind to expect that amount of exactness which the nature of the particular subject admits. It is equally unreasonable to accept merely probable conclusions from a mathematician and to demand strict demonstration from an orator."[14]

Graham concludes that "the work of a financial analyst falls somewhere in the middle between that of a mathematician and an orator."[15] The vanguard theorists of behavioral finance stand a better chance of finding that middle road than do the devotees of EMT, but they admit they still have a long way to go in understanding investors and markets, a task that is likely to get harder rather than easier, as the next chapter explains.

AMPLIFIED VOLATILITY

The efficient market story and the chaotic market story are neither exhaustive nor mutually exclusive accounts of market behavior. Rather, they depict end points on a continuum ranging from perfect pricing to substantial deviation between price and value. These polar points at the outer ranges of the continuum are a function of the amount of price volatility. Price volatility can move prices toward values (and is efficient) but can also push prices away from values (and is inefficient).

Measuring how much market behavior is captured by the efficiency story or the chaos story is hard. But if a generous estimate is that EMT has explained about 80% of stock market behavior in the past couple of decades, an important question is how much it is likely to explain in the future. To answer that question, we need to think about the sources of volatility in pricing and assess whether those sources are trending toward greater efficiency or greater price-value discrepancies.

The sources of volatility that lead prices to part from fundamental values are (1) the quality of information used by market participants in trading, (2) the complexity of the markets in which trades are effected, and (3) the discipline of market participants. A good prognosis is that with the rise of on-line and computer-based trading and the spread of fountains of noisy information all through the Internet, day and minute traders will drive market mania to an ever more acute state of bipolar disorder. Chaos rather than efficiency seems ascendant.

INFORMATION VOLATILITY

The first source of stock market volatility relates to information changes. Information volatility has both a positive (efficient) dimension and a negative (inefficient) dimension.

e efficient dimension of information volatility is simply the ket's facilitation of price changes in the light of fundamental formation about a company. That information alters the uncertainty associated with that company's future business prospects. When the U.S. Supreme Court announces that the U.S. Food and Drug Administration (FDA) lacks the authority to regulate tobacco products, for example, the prices of tobacco stocks change to reflect greater certainty about the regulatory environment.

This type of volatility is inherent in any market. It reflects the simple reality that stock market prices are gauges of the future value of cash flows to shareholders. The ineradicable uncertainty in that gauge means that prices in an efficient market will hover about the best estimates of value. But as information changes, the degree of uncertainty about that value changes and prices should change accordingly.

There is little reason to believe that positive information volatility is any worse or better now than it was a decade or longer ago. On the one hand, there may be greater uncertainty in business value as a result of globalization, the pervasiveness of new technology, and the seeming swiftness of its change. A portion of the substantial price volatility of the late 1990s and early 2000s may be a function of such greater business volatility. On the other hand, there are also superior ways to measure business and financial risk, manage it, and adapt to these changing landscapes. With these factors offsetting each other, there seems little basis for saying that positive information volatility will get better or worse in the future.

Negative information volatility is another story. This inefficient dimension of information volatility consists of trading on the basis of information either unrelated to fundamental values or inaccurate about them. The stuff of negative information volatility includes age-old accounting trickery (discussed in Chapter 9) and other tactics designed to prop up stock prices, such as share repurchases (discussed in Chapter 13). But none of these problems seem more (or less) severe than they ever did. Wacky trading strategies such as those based on hemline levels and Super Bowl winners also constitute negative information volatility, but these strategies are as fashionable (and foolish) as they ever were.

What's new is an increase in negative information volatility that arises from trading that is based on premature information dissemination, unfounded and untrue rumors, false speculative hunches, and hopes, dreams, and lies. Changes in the manner and speed of information flows produce fountains of high-quality information along with a deluge of low-quality junk masquerading as information. The result is increased negative information volatility that drives a wider wedge between price and value.

In the old economy, EMT seemed plausible in part because the information that markets digested had a superior quality compared to that in the new economy trading environment. Old economy news benefited from the major filtering role played by the mainstream press. You could count on the integrity of *The New York Times, USA Today, The Wall Street Journal*, and other great newspapers and magazines to deliver news and information that was professionally vetted under constraints imposed by long-nurtured and valuable reputations for journalistic quality and integrity.

While you still can count on such media for filtered and considered news reporting, the process of getting there has been littered with unfiltered information that gets out before its time. The days of getting vetted news from the morning paper and the evening news are numbered. Americans get a steady diet of news throughout the day, with the newspaper and the evening broadcasts sandwiching nonstop cable news programs, Internet reports, and e-mails forwarding rumor-based "news" that your friends or colleagues fear you might otherwise miss.

The deluge of "news by the second" disrupts the old fixture of the news cycle. Reporters who used to work on a 24-hour news cycle that entailed gathering, researching, writing, rewriting, and printing the news now announce their results as they go. Print journalists broadcast tomorrow's stories on today's market wraps, and the reports flash around every other news outlet—cable, Internet, and traditional wires.

By the time this new news cycle is finished, the news that actually gets reported in print is often either stale or discovered to be less important than first believed. Reporting quality is sacrificed for speed. In this world you get data earlier, but you get it the way journalists in the middle of the old news cycle used to get it: unfiltered—the draft of a story in progress.

These forces were behind the $2 billion price plunge of Emulex, manufacturer of fiber optic communications equipment, in August 2000. Major news organizations, including Bloomberg, Dow Jones, and CBS.Marketwatch.com, distributed what turned out to be a fake press release announcing that Emulex's CEO had resigned and that it planned to restate its earnings for the prior two years.

The hoax was engineered by a former employee of a press service who knew the ropes of getting releases onto the Internet and reported by organizations eager to be first to get news out. Apart from the devastation to the stock of Emulex, the hoax appeared responsible for dragging down the stock prices of numerous other fiber optic companies as well as the broader Nasdaq composite.[1]

Webcasting by brokerage firms can also be a source of negative information volatility. Supplanting the traditional news media, analysts of major brokerages increasingly post reports directly on their own Web sites by video streaming. They opine on market conditions and call attention to favored stocks. Most firms admit they are not reporting news but claim instead to be giving information. The difference is often lost on investors consuming the data, who trade on its basis without recognizing that it is furnished as a marketing device for the brokerage rather than as news vetted and constrained by traditional journalistic ethics of independence.

But the real villains of negative information volatility are the cobwebs of Web sites that pump out unfiltered information on the Internet with unbridled abandon, particularly on bulletin boards and chat rooms. The ease and often anonymous character of information dissemination over these Internet forums eliminates an important filter for vast channels of what only passes for news and information. If it has always been hard to believe that the market is as omniscient as EMT says it is, the increasing ability of anyone, anywhere—identified or anonymous—to spread lies, rumors, hunches, and other disinformation to millions at a time makes that concept downright fantastic.

On a typical day over thirty thousand messages flood the four largest boards: Yahoo!, Silicon Investor, Motley Fool, and Raging Bull. None of these board providers screen the messages for accuracy, and all leave them up after they are posted. All of them permit anonymous messages, and all posters can use as many different names as they want.

For less than it costs to buy a cappuccino, anybody can drop by a cyber café, log on, use one of many services that facilitate anonymous postings that are nearly impossible to trace (cutely called "anonymizers"), and say anything he or she wants to about any company (or anything else, for that matter). The SEC has some investigators who regularly review sites looking for possible fraud and some companies try to address the rumors they see flying around, but these efforts cannot assure you that what you are reading is worth anything.

The most innocuous form of the risk of negative information volatility is the rumor mill—Internet postings that stop way short of fraud—but these rumors can have equally significant effects on stock prices. Berkshire Hathaway's stock price was hurt when wholly unfounded and viscous rumors that Warren Buffett's health was failing spread all over the Internet in early 2000. Equally vicious were the rumors spread in 1996 that executives of Quigley Corporation, a company that had just introduced a cold remedy called Cold-Eaze, were really mobsters: Its stock price dropped from $37 to $10 on the lies. Worst of all was the day when Michael Hackworth, president and chief executive officer of Cirrus Logic, clicked on a Yahoo! site to a message pronouncing him "dead after a long illness."[2]

More pernicious than rumors in motive and in their effect on stock price accuracy are the deliberate defrauders, those who have adapted a host of age-old fraud techniques to the Internet at a very low cost and a very low risk of detection.[3] Spamming is one of the Internet defrauders cheapest mechanisms of deceit. For a few hundred dollars, a spammer can buy software that enables the harvesting of thousands of e-mail addresses from Internet files. A whole e-mailing list can be devised. For higher stakes—say, $10,000—spammers can buy e-mailing lists numbering tens of millions of addresses. They blitz them for bogus bucks.

These spammers sometimes get caught. One who did promoted stocks by spamming to several million e-mailees, touting the stocks of two companies in exchange for a fee. The spammer did not disclose his true identify or the fact that he was being paid to do the hawking. A California court in October 1998 slammed the spammer with a fine and an injunction against doing it again.[4] In a similar case, a convicted felon just out of jail and on probation for previous securities fraud spammed 30 million e-mailees with lies about his company that were intended to prop up its price precisely so that he could generate enough money to repay the victims of his earlier fraud![5] What a Ponzi scheme.

A more elaborate spamming technique seeks to disguise the source of the e-mail and the identity of its sender, making it look as if the message were misdirected to the recipient and making her feel she had "overheard" a hot tip being exchanged between friends. In one case, two men indicted in early 2000 on charges of securities fraud "made" more than $1 million by sending hundreds of thousands of e-mail messages about dozens of small companies to subscribers of America Online (AOL).[6] The subject stocks were just the kind lots of 2000s maniacs salivate for: no earnings and no revenue, though most of them also had no continuing operations. In a number of other cases, spammers disguised the sender of e-mails to make it look as if the recipient were reading an internal memo at a major investment banking house containing "inside" information about various stocks.[7]

It has always been true that "tips" are suspect—whether from your neighbor across the back fence, your hairdresser, or your dentist. The great investor Phil Carret advised avoiding them like the plague;[8] an astute chronicler of trading markets, Edwin LeFèvre, stingingly observed that "Wall Street professionals know that acting on 'inside' tips will break a man more quickly than famine, pestilence, crop failures, political readjustments, or what might be called normal accidents";[9] and Ben Graham was terser: "Much bad advice is given free."[10]

What is different about the new tips is that more people create them, more people hear them, and more people act on them than ever before. When adapted for the Internet, not only do classic fraud schemes dramatically enlarge the number of possible victims (and the dollar receipts of the perpetrator), when peddled on many finance bulletin boards and chat rooms they can carry special weight. This is the case because these boards and rooms often create a spirit of camaraderie among their users that generates trust in other participants and what they have to say.

The most classic scam being adapted to the Internet is the pump-and-dump, and it has been going on for many years. As early as October 1996, for example, a pumper bought shares of Omnigene Diagnostics for around $1 each and then posted a slew of pretty much identical lies on AOL boards saying that the company was hot and sales were growing rapidly. The stock sprinted to nearly $7 in about six weeks, whereupon the pumper dumped the stock for an illicit but huge gain. The lies were dispelled when an employee of Omnigene announced on the company's own Web site all sorts of operational and financial problems. The SEC ordered a halt in trading of the company's stock. When it later lifted that halt, the stock traded back below the $1 a share it had been resting at before the pump-and-dump.[11]

A more recent pump-and-dump example began one Friday afternoon in late November 1999, when three Beverly Hills twentysomethings bought fifty thousand shares of a bankrupt commercial printing company, NEI Webworld, for nickels and dimes a share.

They then spent the weekend on computers at UCLA bombarding three popular finance message boards—Yahoo!, Raging Bull, and Freerealtime—with some five hundred fabricated messages hyping a pending buyout of the worthless company. The lies jacked up NEI's stock price to open at $8 Monday morning and move to a high that day of $15, while the troika cashed in their shares for a net booty of about $364,000, plunging the price back to the nickels and dimes they had "invested."[12]

The SEC and the U.S. attorney's office in California jumped on this scam and in a matter of days identified the looters and charged them with violating federal securities laws against telling material lies in connection with the purchase or sale of securities. The SEC rightly denounced much of the nonsense that is spewed in Internet bulletin boards and chat rooms as having no more value than graffiti, and *The Wall Street Journal* rightly declared that some of them can be worse than trash.

Of all the known Internet trashers, Yun Soo Oh Park is the most notorious. Called Tokyo Joe, he was subjected to civil fraud charges in early 2000 by the SEC for putting misleading investment information on his Internet site. During 1998 and 1999, the SEC said, Tokyo Joe made hundreds of thousands of fraudulent dollars through a scalping strategy that involved buying stocks, saying wonderful things about them on his Web site, and then selling them after the buying of the masses pushed their price up.[13]

It may not even be those looking for fast money who sponsor this negative information volatility. Early in 1999 an employee of PairGain Technologies put a message on a Yahoo! site directing users to a fake Bloomberg News page containing a fabricated story that PairGain was going to be taken over. Its stock price soared on this "news," and while the fabricator apparently did not gain any money from the ploy, he is spending five years on probation for the crime.[14]

Hard as it is to identify Internet scammers, you cannot count on the authorities to punish and deter the new defrauders when they are traced. When the SEC discovered in early 2000 that four third-year Georgetown University law students (and the mother of one of them, who happened to be a councilwoman for Colorado Springs!) had generated nearly $350,000 in illegal profits from a pump-and-dump scam on their Web site, the SEC "settled" with the scoundrels. No jail time, no fine, not even disgorgement of the dirty money. The losers simply had to agree not to do it again.[15]

In a world where it is just as easy for anyone to buy a share of stock as to sell it short, the pump-and-dump scheme can be run just as easily as a bust-and-buy scam. The buster is a short seller who benefits if a stock price falls because he buys stock today but promises to pay for it at a price to be determined later. So he spreads false rumors that a company's sales are falling and that it is plagued with all kinds of problems. The price busts, and the scammer gets his shares at a low price—and then gets to watch the price rise as people figure out there was no reason for the bust in the first place.[16] That is precisely what the drafter of the fake press release about Emulex was trying to do.

Outdoing the brazen fraud of the perpetrators of these stories and the lax enforcement is the galactic stupidity of those who fall for the schemes. To take just one example, any eighth-grader could have looked up NEI on the SEC's Web site or any other reputable database and found that it had filed for bankruptcy a year earlier and that it no longer had a listed telephone number for its Dallas headquarters, let alone any assets or operations. Yet you would be surprised how many people buy stocks on the basis of such Internet gibberish and buy them without even knowing anything about their business climate, let alone management or other basic financial information.

Speaking of eighth-graders, an astonishing number of people who should have known better lost over a quarter of a million dollars to a junior high school kid who apparently took Internet securities fraud up as an after-school hobby. The child, 14 years old when he began his scam, posted hundreds of manufactured messages concerning nine different obscure stocks in chat rooms and bulletin boards and entered automatic orders to sell the stocks once they reached hype-inflated price levels. Without admitting or denying guilt, he agreed with the SEC to refrain from doing it again and to disgorge his profits (though without paying any additional fine or other penalty).[17]

These anecdotal accounts and hundreds more untold indicate a dramatic increase in negative information volatility. Certainly they do not evidence an efficient market or one that is getting more efficient. Rather, they help explain the market manias and greed-gloom gyrations cataloged in Chapter 1. Their limited detectability and policing, coupled with the public's evident gullibility, suggest they will continue to plague the market.

You can be sure not only that there are other crooks and swindlers looking for and sometimes finding fast and fraudulent dollars but that negative information volatility will result. That bad news for market efficiency is not entirely bad news for you as an investor, however, so long as you steer clear of the pump-and-dump set and take advantage of the widening spread between price and value that results from their dirty work.

TRANSACTION VOLATILITY

The second source of stock price volatility is transaction-related.[18] This arises from the way prices are formed by market trading. It is not possible for any party acting alone to set the price of a stock. Share pricing in stock markets arises solely as a result of traders' orders meeting in the market. How they meet in the market to determine prices is important to know but often overlooked.

Trades on traditional markets such as the New York Stock Exchange (NYSE) begin with a customer who instructs a broker to effect a trade, say, to buy 100 shares of Dell at $50. The broker takes that order to the trading floor, where a crowd of traders are at work. If there were another broker who had gotten a customer's order to sell 100 shares of Dell at $50, the two could just swap shares for their customers. No price change would result, and so there would be no transaction volatility. That perfect matching of buy and sell orders seldom happens on traditional exchanges (or on the Nasdaq, where the chief difference is only that matching is done more by computer routing of orders than through the physical presence of people on the floor).

Instead, buyers and sellers place orders with their brokers at different times, want to trade different amounts of shares, and want to buy or sell at different prices. In these more typical cases, the customers have to wait until someone else arrives looking for a trade on the same terms or have someone else in the market make the trade. That someone else is there, and she is called a market maker (on the NYSE) or specialist (on the Nasdaq) in that stock.

When a broker can't find another broker looking for a precise swap with his customer's order, these middlemen (market makers and specialists) do the trade so that the broker's customers don't have to wait until a counterpart comes along. The middlemen do the waiting for them, making markets in stocks by buying and selling shares when buyers and sellers arrive.

Middlemen make money for providing this service by buying

stocks at a lower price (called the bid) and selling them at a higher price (called the ask). The difference between the bid and the ask price is called the bid-ask spread. It is the price buyers and sellers pay so that they don't have to wait.

The bid-ask spread also compensates the market maker for the risks he is exposed to in taking positions in stocks so that others don't have to wait. Making a market in stocks exposes her to the risk of error in her own valuations and the valuations of others. Market makers can make a market at a price below or above a stock's fundamental value.

If they make a market at a price below value, more buyers should arrive. But the price goes up when buyers arrive (they pay the ask price). Therefore, a maker will sell more shares at the ask than it buys at the bid. It may then have to buy more shares to make a market, and the price will be pushed up, exposing it to losses if the bid-ask spread is too small.

Market makers respond to that risk by widening the bid-ask spread—raising the price at which they will sell to buyers and/or lowering the price at which they will buy from sellers. Transaction volatility in stock prices arises from such changes in the bid-ask spread. It is undesirable volatility because it is driven not by changes in fundamental values but by a market maker's exposure to loss from value errors amid orders arriving at different times seeking different things.

Market makers also create transaction volatility when they respond to changes in order flow. If more buy orders than sell orders are coming in, they raise the bid and ask quotes. They do this because they must assume that the order imbalance reflects changes in fundamental values. When they are right about that, their raise reflects positive information volatility (i.e., price moving closer to value). But when they are wrong about that, their prices deviate from value and the change creates transaction volatility.

The rise of electronic computer networks (ECNs) has put regulatory and economic pressure on the traditional exchanges to reduce transaction volatility resulting from market making. ECNs conduct trading solely on computer screens rather than through brokers, traders, and market makers. The swiftness and transparency of this computerized technique allows trades to be handled as in the first example above, where two brokers swap their respective customers' mirror trades, and with far less or no waiting time.

Each customer posts his desired trade on the ECN's screen, say, one seeking to buy 100 shares of Dell at $50 and one seeking to sell the same. When the price of an offer to buy matches the price of an offer to sell (as in this case), the trade occurs automatically. The middleman disappears, and the price is formed directly by two orders meeting in the market. ECNs can thus reduce transaction volatility caused by the bid-ask spread required by market makers.

If particular ECN offer prices do not match, however, they still get posted on the computer along with the bid and ask offers of specialists and market makers. When the orders don't match, there is an "order imbalance" and the screens cannot do anything about it. A middleman must step in to buy or sell to eliminate the imbalance and keep the market alive.

Even if it were theoretically possible for ECNs to eliminate transaction volatility caused by the bid-ask spread required by middlemen, that could not happen without effectively shutting down the market. Thus, any reduction in transaction volatility you see coming from ECNs is not going to eliminate it. And there is some reason to believe it won't even reduce it—depending on how markets shape up.

ECNs shook up market trading as they proliferated in the late 1990s and early 2000s. The leading players in this market are Island and Instinet, both of which do a huge business in this kind of computer trading. Any business they get, however, is business that the traditional exchanges—and the brokers, traders, and market makers who participate in them—do not get. At stake for traditional brokerage firms is the franchise value from their roles as specialists and market makers in stocks. At stake for the proprietors of the ECNs and the on-line and discount brokers who get more order flow through their use is a new franchise value the systems can create.

Not surprisingly, then, the explosion of ECNs as alternative trading places produced an excited debate among the traditional firms and the newer firms and at the SEC and in Congress. All factions recite a variation of the same mantra: The goal is to help investors get the best price available each time they trade.

Traditional firms say the goal of getting customers the best price would be best accomplished by having a single source of pricing information,[19] and so they call for a centralized order book where all orders would be posted and through which all participants could insure that their customers get the best price. The ECNs and on-line and discount firms say you will get better pricing if you have lots of competition between firms, and so they call for permitting a fragmented system with lots of different order books. The pressure on all sides is revealed by merger talks between the NYSE and Nasdaq on the one hand and between ECN leaders Instinet and Island on the other.[20]

Given this environment, elimination of transaction volatility is unlikely. Not only that, any reduction in it through enhanced use of electronic computer systems as opposed to market makers is likely to be offset by another development in market trading: quoting share prices down to the penny ("decimal pricing") rather than in fractional increments of 1/8 or 1/16.

In theory, decimal pricing would help produce prices that equal value. Suppose the value of a share is $50.03. In a decimal pricing system it is quoted at exactly $50.03, whereas in a fractional pricing system it is quoted either at $50 or at $50.06 (i.e., 50 1/16).

Decimal pricing also has the effect of narrowing the bid-ask spread for the same reason. But it means the spread is changed more frequently, itself a cause of transaction volatility. While the move to decimal pricing may not contribute as much to increasing transaction volatility as the rise of ECNs subtracts, on balance the reduction from ECNs makes only a modest case for improved market efficiency.

The case is cloudier yet when you add the move toward 24-hour trading. Market volatility tends to lighten when trading sessions are interrupted, as occurs on the Thursday following Ash Wednesday, for example. However, some of the greatest market plummets have occurred on Mondays, following two days off. Whether continuous trading will promote or retard efficiency is thus hard to predict, though one lesson from history suggests the latter. The Evening Exchange operated in New York in the 1860s as a place to continue trading stocks and gold after the NYSE's regular daytime hours. It lasted only a few years, apparently creating and suffering from a staggering speculative and volatile bubble that led to its demise.[21]

Whatever value ECNs add in terms of reduced transaction volatility is offset by what they create in a third kind of volatility. The rise of ECNs has meant a proliferation of places to trade and get prices. For investors and traders, this means faster and cheaper ways to trade stocks, at lower commissions, with swifter trade executions and more after-hours trading. This promotes the democratization of capital, which sounds nice. But is it?

As anyone who knows anything about Warren Buffett knows, the best investors see themselves as part owners of a business rather than of a piece of tradable paper or cyberspace. But this mind-set is hard to maintain when price quotes proliferate and distract attention to value by both existing owners and new shareholders who buy on spec.

All this action across a broad spectrum of people and places means more room for psychological influences. That remains true whether all these trades arise in thousands of different places or occur in a single place. The resulting prices bear less resemblance to business values. The irony is that volatility exists no matter what system emerges, though with the rise of ECNs a greater danger lurks: trader volatility.

TRADER VOLATILITY

Trader volatility arises when trades are made for purposes unrelated to the fundamental values of a business. These trades drive prices to points related more to the motives of the trader than to the business value of the company.

The wide range of trading decisions that cause price moves unrelated to business value includes: trading for identifiable economic reasons of the trader, such as portfolio "rebalancing"; selling shares to fund personal needs or desires, such as a child's education or the remodeling of a kitchen; and, most notoriously of all, day trading for purposes of speculation and gambling. Let's start with that one.

Day trading is usually not based on fundamental values but on momentum, sector rotation, and other technical tactics of the type ridiculed earlier. When trades are based on these things, they move prices. Those moves, having nothing to do with values, widen the gap between price and value. This exacerbates Mr. Market's peaks and valleys and feeds irrational exuberance and irrational despair. Day trading is thus among the worst developments capital markets have seen in their history for purposes of maintaining an orderly or sensible market, much less an efficient one.

Many day traders are probably perfectly rational people; many are not. Aberrations may get headlines, but some of the day trader stunts captured by the mainstream press warrant attention. The Atlanta day trader who gunned down nine people and then himself in the summer of 1999 after suffering staggering day trading losses is a glaring example. So too is the fun-loving 44-year-old family man who took early retirement with his wife and their $780,000 nest egg only to murder the money day trading and then attempt to murder his wife (he wound up in a South Carolina prison).[22]

Hardly tales of high rationality, and the woeful tales of these hapless folks are not isolated examples or aberrations. A Senate committee held hearings on day trading in early 2000 accompanied by a blistering report cataloging its numerous plagues. The report focused on the industry that supports day trading and emphasized the need for greater industry risk disclosure, licensing, and minimum financial requirements for traders. But it is also a brief against the sagacity of the pernicious practice.[23]

The most compelling conclusions of the report are that 75% of day traders lose money and that a typical day trader has to generate gains of $110,000 a year just to break even after costs! That figure is breathtaking, but the idea is not new. Classic studies have shown that someone who tries to time the market and move in and out of it quickly to exploit its gyrations has to be right 70% of the time to profit. Do you know anybody who can perform that well consistently? Even the best hitters in baseball—say, Rod Carew, George Brett, and even Ted Williams—bat at most .400 (the equivalent of "being right" only 40% of the time).

An equally important—if slightly more benign—source of trader volatility is the practice of "rebalancing." Ironically, this practice was promoted mainly by those who use modern portfolio theory and believe in market efficiency. Rebalancing goes something like this: If you start with ten stocks each bought for 10% of the total cost of your portfolio, some will rise in price and some will fall. The rebalancer says that after a year or another arbitrary interval, look at the new pricing. Suppose five went up and five went down, both in proportion. Now your portfolio has five stocks constituting 75% of the holdings and five stocks constituting 25%. The rebalancer says you should shed some of those in the 75% group to reduce their role in the overall holdings.

This must rank among the dumbest things people could do with investments, yet it is very prevalent. You end up selling the stocks that seem to be performing relatively well and keeping those which come up behind. Why would you do that?

It may be rational, but not because your portfolio is somehow out of balance. It makes sense to sell the good performers only if you examine the business fundamentals of the companies and decide that they no longer meet your requirements for holding them: the price exceeds the value by large amounts, there are clearly superior opportunities for wider price-value gaps, the economic characteristics have deteriorated, or management has changed hands for the worse.

The famed investor Gerald Loeb gave the opposite advice, which is not easy to follow in the best of circumstances, much less when contemporary advisers are telling you something else: "If you want to sell some of your stocks and not all, invariably go against your emotional inclinations and sell first the issues with losses, small profits, or none at all. Always get rid of the weakest and keep your best issues for last."[24]

Like Loeb, Peter Lynch regards the prevalent practice of rebalancing as backward, saying it is like gardening by watering the weeds and pulling the flowers. The beneficiaries of this backward gardening are not the investors or traders who do the rebalancing but their advisers—who generate fees from trading—and the U.S. federal and local treasuries—which get tax payments. Buffett put it best in asking whether it would have made sense for the Chicago Bulls to trade Michael Jordan on the grounds that he had become too important and valuable to the team.[25]

Apart from the stupidity of trading the best picks, the strategy's contribution to trader volatility is significant. When trades are made to rebalance a portfolio in this way, they are by definition trades unrelated to business value (other than fortuitously). The sale of stock that no longer "fits" a portfolio puts price change pressures on that stock. But that pressure, having nothing to do with actual or even perceived value in that stock, simply widens the price-value gulf.

Finally, plenty of people have turned to the stock market as a savings account. It is the place where they repose regular sums to build wealth for planned projects such as buying a home, paying for a child's education, and enjoying retirement. It is also the place where money is stored and drawn on for unplanned funding needs, such as paying to remodel a kitchen, buying a sports utility vehicle, and taking trips to exotic vacation spots.

It is hard to quarrel with those who use the stock market as a way to build wealth for planned future needs such as home ownership, education, and retirement. These tend to be long-term goals that enable long-term investing, and so the stock market is a rational place to store some of that wealth.

It is far easier to rebuke the use of the stock market for more short-term-oriented expenditures. For one thing, there is extraordinary risk in stock market investing, especially over short periods of time. It is simply not a rational place to put resources that may be needed to fund ordinary needs such as home repair and ordinary desires such as recreation.

As to either form of using the stock market, however, the net effect on market efficiency is the same. Trading decisions are based on needs (or desires) rather than on the fundamental values of the stock being sold. That has the effect, again, of separating the resulting prices from the actual values.

As more Americans use the stock market for these purposes— as traders rather than as investors—EMT explains less market activity. And as *The New York Times* said when day trader mania took hold, America has gone from a nation of savers, to a nation of investors, to a nation of traders.[26]

ECNs and discount on-line brokers facilitate trading, rebalancing, and savings via stocks. Although this positively reduces the costs of incremental trading, it has an offsetting negative effect of encouraging more trades. In the aggregate market, negative information volatility and a wilder Mr. Market ensue.

It is like Reaganomics for brokers, as people end up spending more in commissions under this lower pricing per trade because they trade more often. Charles Schwab, to give a representative example of this industry, reduced its average revenue per trade from $64.27 in 1997 to $45.55 two years later while increasing daily trading volume from 106,000 to 208,000 and growing.[27] Schwab's revenues soared; you know who paid.

Day trading funds on the horizon will make all these matters worse. Marrying low-cost trading, screen-based clearing, and the insatiable day trader appetite, a former commissioner of the SEC launched a company in mid-2000 called Folio(fn) to cater to the rebalancing and day trading set. It offers a fixed annual fee that is not only much lower than typical mutual fund fees but also lower than the average cost per trade Schwab and others charge. It uses a proprietary trading system to match customer trading orders in house, going to market twice a day with compiled customer orders to clear any imbalance. Touted as a way to help investors, this day trading fund will increase trader volatility.[28]

PROGNOSIS

The main effect of amplified volatility—from low-quality information, market fragmentation, and noise traders—is less efficient pricing of stocks. The spread has widened between Mr. Market's currency (prices, what you pay) and corporate management's currency (value, what you get).

The symptoms of that inefficiency and the consequences of that amplification consist of all the phenomena cataloged in Chapter 1, including bifurcation of markets (for example, between the Dow and the Nasdaq) and roller coaster rides of crashes and breaks. Episodes such as the crash of 1987 and the break of 1989 no longer look like isolated aberrations; rather, these and the spasmodic bursts and busts of the late 1990s and early 2000s evidence a disease that is not only epidemic but chronic.

EMT was never a perfect explanation of the stock market, but whatever purchase it once held is declining further and rapidly in today's market climate. It may have had some appeal in an era when trading enjoyed the benefits of a major filtering role for the financial press and investment professionals. While these institutions were never perfect in those roles, their training, knowledge, and professionalism (and, for advisers, interest in stable markets for underwriting and merger advisory businesses) took some of the edge off their human infirmities. It didn't make EMT right, but it did make it seem plausible.

The rise of the Web, ECNs, day traders, and the individual investor have produced unfiltered stock markets that retard rather than promote efficiency. SEC Chairman Arthur Levitt testified before Congress that market fragmentation created by the rise of ECNs could lead the same stock to trade at substantially different prices in different trading forums. Maybe that would create new and exciting arbitrage opportunities, but the chairman's insight makes the case against existing stock market efficiency airtight.

As the next chapter shows, these trends in market behavior imply that managers and investors should ignore how the market is behaving with respect to pricing securities and focus instead on their own knitting: running businesses with strong economic characteristics and looking for them, respectively.

CHAPTER 5

TAKE THE FIFTH

Knowing that the average cycle length of public capital markets is approximately four years does not give you any tricks to investing, for there are none. That, plus knowing that stock market efficiency is at most about 80% true and getting less so, corroborates the endurance of Ben Graham's intuition: Mr. Market is alive and still not well. The question is what to do with the 20% or more of market pricing EMT does not capture, and the answer is to take advantage of it.

Maybe Mr. Market's manic depression has been better diagnosed if still not widely understood. Maybe the detection of nonlinear dependence and the upsetting of EMT are like superior clinical diagnoses of bipolar disorder in medicine. Maybe increasing recognition of the disease has reduced the denial and given some hope of treatability. But these are just maybes.

What is certain is that the market is complex. Also certain, given the alternative accounts of market phenomena, is that trading rule tests and other pat formulas for investing remain nonsensical gibberish, though not because the market is efficient but because it is plagued by emotional disorder.

It remains to navigate the market's Scylla of gloom and its Charybdis of euphoria. It is possible to do so because there are bounds to the mania. The greater fool theory may be true: Buying stocks for profitable resale at some future time requires that there be someone out there who will buy what you want to sell. It may be true that the entire market operation rests upon confidence that in the long run the market gets things right without too much static or dislocation over the shorter run that it takes to get there.

Market traits of irrationality and chaos undermine efficiency claims, but that is as far as they go. They do not undermine confidence in the long-run stability of markets. To the contrary, they mean that opportunities exist for the wise and the cautious, those armed with the tools of business analysis that enable one to decide when the time is right to take advantage of Mr. Market's festering gloom and when the time is right to steer clear of his maniacal euphoria.

The debate over how much of market behavior EMT captures is an endless one. This is the case because its devotees tell us that as it starts to explain less, opportunities arise for informed people (such as those who act on the mind-set they develop from reading this book) to step in and correct things. Thus, EMT gets restored. The endlessly open empirical question is the degree to which one effect swamps the other.

On balance, the Internet's negligible business information quality and the frolicsome day traders acting on it suggest plenty of incentive for real investors to get informed and plenty of room left over after they do. In other words, if the current trading environment makes it seem that EMT's descriptive power is going to look more like 70% in the coming years, people acting on it may be able to return its power to about 80% after that. Those most able to participate in taking advantage of that process are investors equipped with a business analysis mind-set.

WHO'S IN CHARGE?

From a manager's perspective, an important consequence of market complexity is that directors and officers cannot control a company's stock price. Hence, shareholders should not expect or require them to maximize it. Managers can only be expected and required to manage their own business and its fundamental values, not how the market understands that performance. Investors and traders make those determinations, not managers.

It would be a mistake, however, to allow this reality to immunize managers from reproach for poor stock price performance over long periods of time. What this means is only that managers cannot be held responsible for fluctuations in the company's stock price that result from the passions of the marketplace. It does not mean that a long-term subpar stock price is not a reflection of actual managerial ineptitude.

Good managers will enjoy average stock prices of the company above the norm; bad ones will suffer average prices below it. Neither is responsible for, or can claim credit for, the intermittent ups and downs. As Ben Graham said, "Good managements produce a good average market price, and bad managements produce bad market prices."[1]

Managers also undoubtedly attempt to influence the company's stock price all the time in ways ranging from the mundane (casting unfavorable announcements in the rosiest light subject to antifraud constraints), to the unlawful (manipulating earnings, a subject considered in Part II), to something in between (say, extraordinary distributions to shareholders from the sale of debt or assets).

Those attempts, however, are not motivated primarily by a desire to produce stock prices equivalent to underlying business value. On the contrary, most managers want the company's stock to trade at the highest possible prices in the market, without regard to business value. This is a mistake, as Buffett emphasizes repeatedly, for such delinkage means that business results during one period will not necessarily benefit the people who owned the company during that period.[2]

While investors rather than managers are in the best position to evaluate and translate into market prices a company's performance as measured by its underlying business value, they cannot guarantee a perfect translation. Information, transaction, and trader volatility all interfere with the identity between business value and market price. Even subject to these distortions, however, it is worth an investor's time to understand business values and promote their identity with market prices. The larger investors have greater incentives to do this and to reap its rewards, which increase in proportion to shareholding size.

Together, therefore, these insights justify active, informed, large, and long-term investors focused on business analysis or, in Buffett's characterization of Berkshire Hathaway, "major, stable and interested shareholders" who are "supportive, analytical and objective."[3] Instead of asking whether such investors will make EMT more than about 70 to 80% correct, however, this perspective confirms the prospect that such investing can take advantage of what EMT has papered over for nearly three decades: the systemic separation of business value from market price.

STICKING TO YOUR KNITTING

The separation of business value from market price calls for inverting the usual thinking about investing. Too often tools and people use market prices as a metric in valuing a business. That gets the process backward. Market price is the *last* thing an investor should look at in a valuation exercise. All the market price tells you is what you can buy (or sell) a share of stock for.

The market does not at all tell you whether that is a good or bad deal. Answering that question requires conducting a valuation based on the fundamental business and economic characteristics of the issuing company. These are the tools considered in the rest of this book.

In using these tools, all investors—institutional and individual—also should appreciate a few other implications of market complexity that follow from the question suggested at the beginning of this chapter: What does a stock market's four-year cycle length mean? It certainly means that the most revolutionary investing ideas of the last 30 years—EMT, MPT, and CAPM—can be misleading.

These are the lessons to relearn:

- It is not a waste of time to study individual investment opportunities in stocks.
- You are likely to do better by thinking about whether individual investment opportunities make sense than by randomly selecting a group of stocks for a portfolio by throwing darts at the stock tables (as contests sponsored by publications such as *The Wall Street Journal* lead many to believe).
- Nor will you do better by using modern portfolio theory's strategy of putting your eggs in lots of different baskets based on what β tells you the risk of each basket is.

It should also be noted that one of the costliest lessons of modern finance theory was the proliferation of portfolio insurance—a computerized technique for readjusting a portfolio in declining markets. The widespread use of portfolio insurance helped precipitate the stock market crash of October 1987 as well as the market break of October 1989, for the models prescribed selling off blocks of stock as their prices fell.

That massive an error—on the scale of the entire market and its participants—suggests that similar errors occurred throughout the investing population, including missed opportunities for gain by small investors. Accordingly, you should ignore modern finance theory and other quasi-sophisticated views of the market and stick to investment knitting.

Strategies

You might ask whether it is worth your time to do hardheaded analysis of business or whether you would be better off letting other people do the work and then free riding on their effort. Economists illustrate this free rider strategy by positing a country that taxes its citizens in order to build a good military. Everyone agrees that this is desirable to defend against foreign enemies. A tax dodger free rides on the public good of a strong military while not contributing to it.

Is it possible for an investor to let others do the investment research (pay the taxes) yet participate as a free rider in the market anyway? Not quite. First, in the classic free rider example, there are two classes of people: those who pay their taxes and those who free ride. In stock investing, there are three: those who do their homework, those who speculate, and those who free ride. The addition of the speculators makes it possible for those who would otherwise be content with a free ride to exploit the folly of the speculators by doing their homework.

You might ask, If those doing the homework can gain so much from the speculators, why doesn't everyone shift from speculating to homework? Good question. People should. But they don't. Ben Graham and Warren Buffett—the consummate homework devotees—repeatedly marvel at the inertia of speculators and can only wonder why so many people choose lemming-like laziness over active analysis. Yet the speculator is here to stay, as the trends identified earlier suggest (and not everyone will read or heed this book). *Plus ça change, plus ça la même chose.*

Even the strategies that come closest to resembling the free rider gambit require some work. The most common version of a free rider strategy, which may be best for many people, is long-term investment in an index fund. An index fund is a mutual fund that buys the same securities that are in a given index, such as the S&P 500. They have grown to gigantic proportions of total invested capital.[4]

People are attracted to such funds for lots of reasons. For one thing, the S&P 500 and similar indexes consistently outperform the managers of active portfolio funds. Indexes also change relatively little, and so index funds have low stock turnover and therefore lower costs and better management of taxable gains.

The chief potential downside of indexing is that it pays no attention to fundamentals, emphasizing past returns rather than evaluating future prospects. The trade-off hinges on an investor's ability and inclination to conduct business analysis. While using an index fund gives a reasonable assurance of obtaining the average market return with very little effort, the investor should still have some reasonable basis for believing that the basket of stocks that constitutes the index—whether the S&P 500 or something else—is cheap relative to the value it contains. Making such a decision requires some sense of the business analysis discussed in this book even if it does not require precise or detailed application of it.

Monitoring of fundamentals is plain common sense. Buyers of a market index need to know what value they are getting, just as buyers of shares do. Both can fluctuate on the upside and the downside. There is no assurance that the overall stock market will go up any more than there is any assurance that attendance at major league baseball games will go up. Both can and do go down.

Patience while holding is not as valuable as research before buying, for many bear markets extend for long periods of time. Whether a market is heading up or down is impossible to predict, even over long periods, whereas there is at least some possibility of predicting, over long periods, which way a particular stock is likely to go.

Stock mutual funds are managed portfolios consisting of selected stocks from the broader market. An investment committee regularly buys and sells stocks for the fund. The fund's shareholders pay the costs of these trades, plus other fees, making mutual funds more expensive than index funds. They are also more expensive from a tax standpoint. Mutual fund portfolio changes often produce capital gains, and shareholders pay the taxes.

The tax consequence of mutual fund ownership shows an advantage to holding individual stocks. When you make a mistake in purchasing a stock—it declines in both price and value to the point where it no longer meets your requirements for holding it—selling it at least gives you the modest break of a tax deduction for the loss on the sale.

For individual stocks, regular and periodic investing in dividend reinvestment plans (DRIPs) using the concept of dollar-cost averaging is a sensible alternative for many people. All this concept means is that regular purchases of a particular stock in set dollar amounts each month (or another interval) lower the average cost of those shares compared to the average of the prices when the shares were bought. It insulates an investor from the effects of Mr. Market's euphoria by taking advantage of his episodic gloom.

Suppose you invested $200 per month in Procter & Gamble during three months when its stock price on the purchase dates was $80, $120, and $100, respectively. The average price during that period was $100 (80 + 120 + 100 divided by 3), but your average cost would have been $97 (you would have acquired 2.5 shares at $80, 1.66 shares at $120, and 2 shares at $100, and so you would have invested $600 and acquired 6.16 shares). This strategy can beat Mr. Market by substantial margins when used over long periods of time.

Staying the course is prudent only if there is a basis for deciding that price is less than value. Adopting the mind-set developed in this book is important in making that kind of judgment. Monitoring the relationship of the DRIP's price to its value using this mind-set is prudent. Beware, however, that dollar-cost averaging works to reduce your average purchase price only if you participate during Mr. Market's gloomy moods. It defeats the goal of defeating Mr. Market to try to time the market by periodically terminating and later resuming participation.

For all investors (those in index or mutual funds, DRIPs, or individual stocks) the key point is to develop a mind-set that attends to the price-value distinction. You can achieve this without necessarily doing all the detailed computations or extensive research discussed in this book, but it is imperative to embrace the mind-set these tools reflect as a way to understand business analysis and intelligent investing. There are no free rides any more than there are free lunches.

DIVERSIFICATION OF STOCK INVESTMENTS

Unlike modern finance theory, investment knitting does not prescribe a particular diversification of a stock portfolio. It may result in diversification, but not as a requirement. Ending up with a concentrated portfolio is sometimes perfectly fine. As Gerald Loeb noted, most of the really great fortunes were made by concentration.[5] If you think about Johnson & Johnson or Papa John's Pizza and find that the prices at which they can be bought are very low compared to your reasonable valuation, buying only those two stocks may be all you need or prudently should do.

You should certainly avoid starting a portfolio on day one with a dozen diversified stocks. It is almost certain that you will not be able to find that number of stocks on a single day that are offered at prices substantially lower than their values. Over long periods of time, some degree of diversification will probably occur, and it is not imprudent to maintain it as long as it does not impair your ability to concentrate on selecting new candidates or keeping up with what you already own.

An excessively diversified portfolio gives you a different version of the free rider problem. Just as a tax dodger benefits from a strong national defense without contributing to it, a bad stock enjoys the price you paid for it without contributing value to your portfolio. Free riders are less noticeable in larger settings; it is easier to catch a tax cheat in Canada than in the United States, for example. Likewise, the more stocks you have in your portfolio, the less likely it is that you will catch and punish (sell) those which are free riding on your wealth and devouring it.

These principles of limited diversification hold only for well-chosen common stocks that carry a margin of safety between the price paid and the reasonable value estimated. For those, Buffett believes finding between 5 and 10 stocks would be sensible; Graham says between 10 and 30. Graham and Buffett both emphasize that investors taking more aggressive stances, as professional money managers do, require the same kind of wide diversification casino houses adopt: The house needs, in Buffett's words, "lots of action because it is favored by probabilities, but will refuse to accept a single, huge bet."[6]

ASSET ALLOCATION

Excessive stock diversification (and portfolio rebalancing, as discussed in the last chapter) should be distinguished from a more fundamental and important investment principle called asset allocation. This principle recognizes the many types of assets available to investors, not just common stocks. Alternatives include bonds, cash, real estate, real estate investment trusts (REITs), and commodities. These alternatives often furnish attractive ways to store and build wealth. Their relative attractiveness is potentially greatest when stock markets do not appear to offer prices lower than values, a prudent time to consider investing in these asset classes. Alternatives also include any mix of these asset classes invested in tax-advantaged vehicles such as individual retirement accounts (IRAs) and 401(k) plans.

Most investors tend to end up with a diversified mix of these different asset classes: home ownership, some cash on hand, a retirement vehicle, and a stock and bond mix. Those who do not should try to do so. Diversity across asset classes is important as a way to preserve wealth. If 100% of wealth were allocated to stocks and the stock market overall dragged for a decade, total wealth would erode. If a portion of the wealth were stored in bonds and the bond market performed favorably over that time, much of the wealth would be preserved.

One problem with investments made through tax-advantaged plans is a lack of diversification in the asset classes offered. Many plan menus are weighted disproportionately toward stock funds. Many people simply elect an even allocation between the items on the menu. Many others simply allocate 100% to the stock funds. Either way, assets are allocated heavily toward stocks. Heavy stock weighting may be prudent for very young people and even for older people, but only so long as other (non-plan) assets are in different classes.

Putting all your eggs in the stock market basket is imprudent asset allocation. Once you have allocated your assets across different classes, the portion you allocate to stocks need not be diversified. In short, asset diversification is far more important than stock portfolio diversification.

Beyond asset preservation, the ultimate issue in asset allocation—as in investing in general—is the prior and larger question of opportunity cost. You want to invest your money in the assets most likely to produce the greatest return in future periods. The general principles for evaluating that likelihood are pretty much the same across asset classes. The form of the asset itself guarantees nothing about its relative attractiveness, a question that depends on its context. That said, there are plenty of exotic asset classes that most people are better off staying far clear of, ranging from innocuous-sounding instruments such as convertible bonds to the more mysterious zones of private equity and hedge funds (more on this below).

The business analysis mind set is just as important in assessing these alternative asset types as it is in investing in common stocks. While each asset type warrants attention to the peculiar issues associated with it (the price of silver depends on supply and demand for the metal, for example), a mind-set trained in thinking as a business analyst about common stocks can easily adapt itself for application to these other asset classes (that is why this book concentrates on common stocks).

INCOME ALLOCATION

Asset allocation is less important than income allocation, but most people get this backward too. People focus on how much they make but less on how they allocate income between investment and consumption. The result is a national savings rate around zero.

But if you save more of what you make, it is easier to meet investing goals since more assets are at work. Those who save relatively smaller portions of their income are more easily tempted by speculative impulses that make intelligent investing more difficult.

Everyone with income faces the question of income allocation. You have to decide how much of your income to allocate to housing costs, food and clothing, entertainment, transportation, education, and so on. Some people also have the unfortunate chore of deciding how to allocate income to pay for past consumption in the form of cumulated credit card debt, automobile or personal loans, and mortgages on real estate.

It should be a no-brainer that the high-interest-expense items in this category should be paid down to zero before an allocator even thinks about investing in common stocks. If you are carrying a balance on your credit card accounts that requires you to pay something like 10 to 18% interest annually, you are wasting your money. Pay those debts down to zero and you will automatically earn the rate you otherwise would be paying—guaranteed (something that is never possible with stocks). The same holds true even for less expensive obligations such as automobile loans (with average interest rates of around 8 to 12%): Paying them down to zero with your extra cash guarantees you that return. It can even be true for home mortgage loans in some cases: Paying down 6 to 8% debt locks in that rate in a way that no common stock can ever guarantee.

MARGIN TRADING

The growth in the number and size of margin accounts for stocks—especially among day traders—suggests that many people foolishly neglect these simple truths. From 1996 to 1999, margin debt rose nearly fivefold at on-line brokerage firms and doubled among NYSE member firms. During the decade of the 1990s, margin debt as a percentage of total consumer debt quadrupled from 4% to 16%. Yet many people do not understand that margin loans are not like other consumer loans.[7]

Margin traders borrow from their brokers at rates ranging around 9 to 11% in order to buy stocks with the borrowed money. They think they can leverage those loans by using the proceeds to buy stocks whose price rises plus dividends yield greater returns. In euphoric markets those people may win, getting returns higher than the cost of the money. In gloomy markets they get crushed.

When the balance in your portfolio falls so that your margin loans are equal to about half or more of that amount, you have to put cash in to pay down that debt (your broker gives you a "margin call"). If you don't have the cash, your broker will sell some of your shares—with or without your cooperation. Add the interest expense and the trading costs to a reversal of Mr. Market's euphoria to count your losses; then multiply that by the number of overextended margin traders and you have the acute slope of a downhill market before you.

The big margin traders might as well be high-rolling in Monaco on borrowed money. Look no further than the poster boy of marginized day trading to see the stupefying risk of this strategy. The most vocal proponent of this high-stakes game is Barry Hertz, the impresario of a company called Track Data Corporation. Its marketing pitch gleefully enthused that investing was easy ("you don't have to be a pro to trade like one"), and Hertz advised his customers to day trade, using borrowed funds.

Hertz at least took his own (bad) advice to double speculate. So on Q day (April 14, 2000, when markets plunged), his own brokers called him to say they needed over $45 million to shore up his margin account. To do so, Hertz had to pledge over 50% of his shares of Track Data.[8] Heed the advice of those like Hertz if you like what happened to him.

FINANCIAL GAMBLING

You would also do well to remember the tragedy of 28-year-old Nick Leeson, the so-called rogue trader working for the Singapore branch of Barings. He funded his trading with millions of dollars of borrowed money, and when the market turned against him, he brought down Barings, the oldest bank in England and the one that financed the Napoleonic wars and the Louisiana Purchase!

Leeson ostensibly was doing arbitrage trading, focusing on differences in prices of Nikkei 225 futures contracts listed on the Osaka Securities Exchange (OSE) in Japan and the Singapore Monetary Exchange (SIMEX). He bought futures on one market and simultaneously sold them on the other. This was a low-risk strategy, since the two positions offset.

Its success led Leeson to another move, a straddle where he

simultaneously sold put options and call options on Nikkei 225 futures. This was a medium-risk strategy, very effective in stable markets but dangerous in volatile ones.

An earthquake that rocked Kobe, Japan, in January 1995 plunged the Nikkei and terrorized Leeson. As the market roiled, Leeson acted like a heroin addict and adopted the high-risk strategy of buying more Nikkei futures in the vain hope of propping up the fallen market.

When the dust settled, Barings's exposure on the futures contracts ran to a staggering $1 billion, far in excess of Barings's total capital. The bank fell to its knees. Investigators discovered that Leeson's positions had been covered by Baring's margin accounts while he was trading, but after the crash—and after Leeson fled Singapore for Germany—they were not.

During his trading, Leeson told Barings's main branch in London the plausible story that he was hedging his long futures positions with private contracts and was also making hedged trades on behalf of a client of the bank. In fact, the client did not exist but was a fictitious name given to an account that Leeson invented earlier for his own use.

Leeson allegedly funded that account with proceeds from other trades and used those funds to maintain the margin account balance. He apparently used the fictitious client account to convince Barings in London to provide additional firm capital, which Lesson in turn used to shore up the margin account. In the end, none of that was enough.[9]

The Leeson lesson is admittedly an extreme psychological case tripped up in a mix of exotic securities, excess margins, and fraud. But the drama is a memorable warning that margins and exotica can get you in over your head and that mixing them can get it handed to you on a platter.

OPTIONS

A final warning on exotica takes us back to Ben Graham's opinion on options. Even before stock option awards to managers became commonplace, Graham disparaged the instruments on more general grounds.

Options originally were attached to bonds and by the 1920s had expanded as part of other financial innovations Graham regarded as abusive. When they reappeared more widely in the 1960s, Graham regarded "stock option warrants" as they were then called, as "a near fraud, an existing menace, and a potential disaster." He believed they created value out of thin air, had no excuse for existing except to mislead people, and should be prohibited by law or at least capped at a minor part of a company's total capital.

The major negative effects of options are dilution of existing shareholders' ownership interest in the company—including existing earnings per share, sharing in future growth, enjoying dividend payments, voting for managers, and other major corporate changes such as mergers and (a bit ironically) new option plans. Graham could see no purpose in options generally other than to "fabricate imaginary market values." In short, Graham condemned stock options as criminal, a monstrous and "wanton creation of huge paper-money."[10]

Buffett echoes the point less vociferously by saying that "the business project in which you would wish to have an option frequently is a project in which you would reject ownership. (I'll be happy to accept a lottery ticket as a gift—but I'll never buy one.)"[11] The lesson for investors is clear. Stay away from options and stay as far away as possible from companies in which options constitute a significant portion of total capital.

ALCHEMY

Stock market bubbles occur when aggregate capital invested in equity securities exceeds the amount of profitable deployment opportunities so that prices exceed values by terrific multiples. They result from the hope that the stocks people pick will turn out to be the ones that enjoy the profits. But if, say, $100 billion is allocated to ventures that can only give returns from profitable investments on $10 billion, then $90 billion in disappointment is going to come— 90% of the dollars will be left standing without chairs to sit in when the music stops.

The main difference between the musical chairs of market speculation and the activity at the typical racetrack is that horse races take only about two minutes to separate the gambler from her money. What horse betting and the stock market do have in common, however, is that those who study the horses or businesses and who bet seldom are more likely to be winners than are those who bet on every race or stock.[12] In the early stages of a boom that may bubble, if you can find the cinch stock at a low price and load up on that stock, it is reasonably likely that you will win; if you bet on everything that comes down the track, it is most certain that you will lose.

Those who bet on everything coming down the track add hot air to the bubble. It is a large-scale version of the mania that leads to around-the-block lottery lines during hefty jackpots. What creates most bubbles is the whiff of great riches from something new that excites people and leads them to irrational behavior or at least herd-like behavior.

The wildfire of excitement is spread by unchecked rumors of champagne and caviar dreams come true—stories of riches, reinforced by greed. The frenzy spirals, but ultimately breaks. In reality, only one person wins the lottery jackpot and the multitudes experience the most expensive case of "monkey see, monkey do."

Edwin LeFèvre put it nicely: "The appeal in all booms is always frankly to the gambling instinct aroused by cupidity and spurred by pervasive prosperity. People who look for easy money invariably pay for the privilege of proving conclusively that it cannot be found on this sordid earth."[13]

Real investors are not the same people who wait in long lottery ticket lines. They realize that "get rich quick" usually means "get poor quicker."

For a bit of déjà vu, consider Graham's observation from the late 1960s: "The speculative public is incorrigible. In financial terms it cannot count beyond 3. It will buy anything, at any price, if there seems to be some 'action' in progress. It will fall for any company identified with 'franchising,' computers, electronics, science, technology, or what have you, when the particular fashion is raging."[14]

In Yogi Berra "it's déjà vu all over again" style, note this similar vintage Graham lament: "Bright, energetic people—usually quite young—have promised to perform miracles with 'other people's money' since time immemorial. They have usually been able to do it for a while—or at least to appear to have done it—and they have inevitably brought losses to their public in the end. . . . [I]t is probably too much to expect that the urge to speculate will ever disappear, or that the exploitation of that urge can ever be abolished."[15]

The urge to speculate endures, with vast numbers of people seeming to accept the declaration of hyperventilating venture capitalists and day traders that the new economy of the late 1990s and early 2000s means that the old rules of the game no longer apply. An extraordinary statement of these times was uttered by the chief economist of a prominent investment research firm who announced to *The New York Times* that "we no longer think we know how to value companies" (to be kind, that confused confessor shall go unnamed in this book).

Valuation has always been difficult, but how much harder now can it be than it was before? Cash is the ultimate economic payoff. If you can't get to the point of figuring out how long it takes to get cash and what risks may reduce the amount or value of it, then it is not that you don't know how to value companies anymore but that the things you are trying to value are not worth trying to value.

Proponents of financial alchemy shrink from the mind-set of business analysis discussed in this book, presumably deeming its tools conventional, maybe even boring, dull, and old-fashioned. When people want to be rich now, they relegate the idea of a nest egg grown with patient discipline to the dustbin of the older generation's history, alien territory to freshly minted paper millionaires and their envious contemporaries.

Unfortunately, this attitude leads to day gambling on stocks using credit card debt and a "buy now, pay later" myopia that neglects the inevitable day of reckoning. It also leads to the popularity of techniques that enable false positive answers to key questions about a business when traditional tools give negative answers.

In the biotechnology industry in the early to mid-1990s, for example, fewer than 10% of companies generated earnings and few even generated positive cash flows from their operating businesses. But those companies needed new investment. Since the traditional measures of business analysis could not tell a convincing story, they turned to unorthodox measures. The most striking was a measure of so-called performance known as "cash-burn." This was the rate at which a business was "able" to spend cash on new research projects. The more burn, the better the management and the more desirable the investment. Crazy?

It is not much crazier than the similar move made in the Internet and high-technology industries of the late 1990s and early 2000s. These financial entrepreneurs jettisoned the traditional metrics of performance and value based on earnings and cash in favor of new ways to look at these questions. Take market share, for example.

Entrepreneurs say, "Look, we have 60% of the market in selling flowers (or whatnot) over the Internet, and you should give us credit for that." Or, more optimistically yet, "We have 10 million 'hits' on our Internet site every month. Even though we don't make money, that's 20 million (or so) eyeballs, so we must be good, we must have value, and you should invest with us."

People do in droves, following a monkey see, monkey do mentality. For most—though not all—of those businesses, the flood of funds is unjustifiable in a business analysis mind-set. (The next growth industry is likely to be Internet bankruptcy law firms.)

Every frenzy is accompanied by rational-sounding new rules that attempt to explain the irrationality. In the last century alone, a "New Era" bull market culminated in the 1929 crash (fueled by the spread of wonderful new technologies such as cars, electricity, vacuum cleaners, washing machines, radio, and talking movies), a "Second New Era" flamed out in 1962's "New Panic," and a "New Performance Phenomenon" preceded the implosion of markets and mutual funds in the late 1960s. The stock market bubble in Japan in the 1980s was fueled by the widespread belief that Japan had created a "new" economic model that defied the historical principles of economics. Market share was king, and companies were rewarded if they had it and rewarded more if they got it at the price of having no or low profits, much as in 1990s–2000s U.S. markets.[16]

This is not to say that market share is irrelevant. Market share is a standard and useful indicator of the relative performance of Coke compared to Pepsi, for example, and something both these companies pursue aggressively in their competition in the beverage marketplace. And it is significant that Cisco has 80% of the router market and 30 to 40% in network switches and that DuPont dominates global markets in nylon and Lycra. That kind of market scale enables a company to lower the cost of sales and general and administrative expenses, which translates into higher profits.

But Coke, Pepsi, Cisco, and DuPont make money in their markets. A larger share of a profitable market is certainly desirable and a good indicator of strong business performance. The same can hardly be said for a larger share of an unprofitable one. On the contrary, the greater your share is, the more money you lose.

Aggressive accumulation of market share can be perfectly disastrous for a business. Look at what happened to the airline industry after deregulation. Intense competition for market share drove nearly all the profits out of that business. The same thing occurs in the submarkets where Coke and Pepsi compete, driving profits at bottlers for those brands close to zero in some places.

Nor is this to deny that technological changes from the 1980s to the 2000s produced significant shifts in the economy. Rising oil prices, for example, historically throttled the economy, sponsoring the recessions of 1973, 1980, and, to a lesser degree, 1990. Yet when oil prices more than doubled during the late 1990s and early 2000s, inflation remained quite low and no threat of recession loomed. Part of the reason was a shift to natural gas and greater use by major oil consumers (such as airlines) of hedging contracts that reduced their exposure to such price increases.

But a major part of the reason is econographic shifts from oil-consuming manufacturing operations to oil-independent service businesses, including those run on the Internet. Manufacturing operations as a percentage of the economy shrank from 22% in 1977 to 17% twenty years later. The share of gross domestic product (GDP) allocated to oil purchases fell from 8.5% in 1981 to about 3% in the late 1990s. The Internet is surely part of this shift, as it enables the conduct of sales and distribution businesses at far lower cost than traditional means.[17]

Even so, oil prices above some level will still trigger such macroeconomic problems. Indeed, the plunge in the Dow by nearly 4% in March 2000 was led by a 30% drop in the stock price of Procter & Gamble. That company issued a warning that its quarterly earnings were going to be way lower than those in the same quarter of the prior year and much lower than analysts expected. The company cited as one cause of that disappointment the rising cost of oil, which it uses in many of its products.

Another part of the shift is surely the increasing value attached to intellectual as opposed to physical capital. Businesses producing and selling software or on-line services can grow more quickly and at lower cost than can those producing and selling automobiles or oil. Far less investment in factories, plants, and equipment is required.

There is no reason to believe, however, that those companies as a whole can grow any faster than the economy overall is growing. In the end, the old-fashioned companies (the so-called old economy companies) are the major customers (and beneficiaries) of the tech upstarts (the so-called new economy companies), so how much faster can the latter group grow than the former? Some companies might, but not forever or just because they have in the past (indeed, the bigger you get, the harder it is to grow). Even if outsized growth is possible, it cannot be guaranteed.

Even with these shifts, the new economy does not change the

basic facts of business life that call for investing based on an understanding of a company's business climate; some key ratios must be in the tool box of all smart investors. Even if some of the new economy business metrics are used, they should be analyzed critically. Ignoring losses is foolish, but ignoring signs of endurance is downright stupid.

If you accept growing market share as an indication of future value, for example, you also have to recognize that slowdowns in customer growth are a sign of reduced future value. You must agree that when revenues per new customer fall while costs per new customer climb, you go from uncertain to bad. These facts are characteristic of many Internet companies whose stock prices actually rise on this kind of news. These companies include some of the best names in the "space," giving reason to think that the new economy may just be a wolf in sheep's clothing. After all, something that seems too good to be true usually is.

People talk of the new millennium and the unmatched pace of technological change, but this impression is mistaken. If you comb through the annals of economic and investment writing over the centuries, you will discover repeated periodic references to the rapid pace of technological change and declarations that nothing like it has ever been seen (historians dubbed the late 1890s and early 1900s the Age of Optimism, imbued with technological excitement that makes centennial turns seem the natural apotheoses of exuberance). Just pause to consider the printing press, the agricultural and industrial revolutions, the assembly line, television and radio, and now computers and the Internet.

Even the sober Ben Graham felt constrained to report on the sense of his time, writing in the relatively recent period of the early 1970s that: "the rapid and pervasive growth of technology in recent years is not without major effect on the attitude and the labors of the security analyst. More so than in the past, the progress or retrogression of the typical company in the coming decade may depend on its relation to new products and new processes."[18] To repeat what Graham was fond of saying, *plus ça change, plus ça la même chose.*

THE LONG RUN

The attitude that drives any mania is as shortsighted as it is shortlived. Investors need to look long down the road of years rather than the path of days when thinking about business and returns. How far will vary with the person's age and needs, but a minimum time frame for anyone serious about investing is four years—and way longer for most of us.

It is customary to call people with a long-term view "long-term investors" and to say that such investors adopt a "buy-and-hold" strategy. Apart from using redundant vocabulary (an investor, by definition, is always dealing in the long term), these characterizations are imprecise.

One reason to look at the long term is to realize that while early investing is better, no one needs to make an investment every day or even every year. As Warren Buffett says, using a baseball analogy, there is no such thing as a called strike in investing—no penalty for sitting back and waiting for your pitch to come in. If a characterization of this style of view is necessary, it is more apt to call it the "wait-and-see" approach than the "buy-and-hold" approach.

Either of these approaches, however, is superior to the promiscuous practices of speculative traders. It is true, to an extent, that today's rookie companies are tomorrow's classics, but it is false, to a fault, that day traders and their ilk act on this insight. The average holding period for the top 50 Nasdaq stocks in late 1999 was less than 30 days, and for Nasdaq stocks as a whole it was about 150 days (compared to about 730 days in the late 1980s).[19] That kind of turnover means the speculators are neither picking stocks carefully (a wait-and-see approach) nor buying them for the long term (a buy-and-hold approach).

Keynes famously quipped that in the long run we are all dead. But he wasn't talking about stock picking. Keynes made that comment in the context of persuading policy makers to focus on short-term needs that could be met, he believed, only by governmental rather than market actions. Indeed, the phrase makes no sense in the stock-picking context, since it is always better to be rich later than to be poor sooner and most of us will leave family survivors.

Ben Graham expressly referred to stocks when he said that in the short run the market is a voting machine, while in the long run it is a weighing machine. This means that the market is risky in the short run for its wild pricing gyrations but gets relatively stable and safer over the long run. But what does it mean to say that the market will eventually price an asset correctly? Doesn't it mean that the market is sometimes correct—that it must, as Alice said in Wonderland, "sometimes come to jam today"? Not exactly.

Milton Friedman's rejoinder to Keynes was that the long run is just a series of short runs linked in succession. Thus the long run is simultaneously with us (it was the long run four years ago) and ahead of us (four years from now). Market price today reflects the value of a business as long ago as four years, and the price today is a guess about business productivity and returns some four years from now. If your guess is better than the market's, then while four years from now the market may be getting today's value of that business right, you will be that much ahead.

That is the sense in which the market may get it right in the long term: Four years from now the market will get correct what Starbucks is doing today; if you are able to assess that performance better than today's market crowd is doing, you will reap outsized returns. The hard question, of course, is how to make that determination with high success rates.

Warren Buffett takes Keynes seriously, adopting the "till death do us part" standard. He invests only in businesses he would be happy to hold forever. It is a commitment not unlike the one you make to your spouse. The consequence is the same: be patient and picky in your search.

PART II

SHOW ME
THE MONEY

CHAPTER 6

APPLE TREES AND EXPERIENCE

If market price is the last thing an investor or manager should look at in determining the value of a business or an ownership interest in it, the first thing to consider is its fundamental economic characteristics. There are so many approaches to appraising those fundamentals that many people use the relatively lazy metric of market price as a guideline in valuation, but that is a mistake. Of all the approaches to appraising business value, just a few do virtually all the hard work, and those are the ones you need. A parable will illustrate the basics, and the rest of this part will fill in the details.[1]

FOOLS AND WISDOM

Once there was a wise old man who owned an apple tree. It was a fine tree, and with little care it produced a crop of apples each year which he sold for $100. The man wanted to retire to a new climate, and he decided to sell the tree. He enjoyed teaching a good lesson, and he placed an advertisement in the business opportunities section of *The Wall Street Journal* in which he said he wanted to sell the tree for "the best offer."

SOME RED HERRINGS

The first person to respond to the ad offered to pay $50, which, he said, was what he could get for selling the apple tree for firewood after he cut it down. "You don't know what you are talking about," the old man chastised. "You are offering to pay only the salvage value of this tree. That might be a good price for a pine tree or even this tree if it had stopped bearing fruit or if the price of apple wood had gotten so high that the tree was more valuable as a source of wood than as a source of fruit. But you are obviously not competent to understand these things, so you can't see that my tree is worth far more than 50 bucks."

The next person who visited the old man offered to pay $100 for the tree. "For that," she opined, "is what I would be able to get for selling this year's crop of fruit, which is about to mature." "You are not as out of your depth as the first one," responded the old man. "At least you see that this tree has more value as a producer of apples than it would as a source of firewood. But $100 is not the right price. You are not considering the value of next year's crop of apples or that of the years after. Please take your $100 and go elsewhere."

The third person to come along was a young man who had just dropped out of business school. "I am going to sell apples on the Internet," he said. "I figure that the tree should live for at least another 15 years. If I sell the apples for $100 a year, that will total $1,500. I offer you $1,500 for your tree." "Oh, no, dot-commer," lamented the man, "you're even more ill informed about reality than the others I've spoken with."

"Surely the $100 you would earn by selling the apples from the tree 15 years from now cannot be worth $100 to you today. In fact, if you placed $41.73 today in a bank account paying 6% interest, compounded annually, that small sum would grow to $100 at the end of 15 years. So the present value of $100 worth of apples 15 years from now, assuming an interest rate of 6%, is only $41.73 not $100. Pray," advised the beneficent old man, "take your $1,500 and invest it safely in high-grade corporate bonds and go back to business school and learn something about finance."

Before long there came a wealthy physician who said, "I don't know much about apple trees, but I know what I like. I'll pay the market price for it. The last fellow was willing to pay you $1,500 for the tree, and so it must be worth that."

"Doctor," advised the old man, "you should get yourself a knowledgeable investment adviser. If there were truly a market in which apple trees were traded with some regularity, the prices at which they were sold might tell you something about their value. But not only is there no such market, even if there were, taking its price as the value is just mimicking the stupidity of that last knucklehead or the others before him. Please take your money and buy a vacation home."

The next would-be buyer was an accounting student. When the old man asked, "What price are you willing to give me?" the student first demanded to see the old man's books. The old man had kept careful records and gladly brought them out.

After examining them, the accounting student said, "Your books show that you paid $75 for this tree ten years ago. Furthermore, you have made no deductions for depreciation. I do not know if that conforms with generally accepted accounting principles, but assuming that it does, the book value of your tree is $75. I will pay that."

"Ah, you students know so much and yet so little," chided the old man. "It is true that the book value of my tree is $75, but any fool can see that it is worth far more than that. You had best go back to school and see if you can find a book that shows you how to use your numbers to better effect."

A Dialogue on Earnings

The final prospect to visit the old man was a young stockbroker who had recently graduated from business school. Eager to test her new skills, she too asked to examine the books. After several hours she came back to the old man and said she was prepared to make an offer that valued the tree on the basis of the capitalization of its earnings. For the first time the old man's interest was piqued, and he asked her to go on.

The young woman explained that while the apples were sold for $100 last year, that figure did not represent the profits realized from the tree. There were expenses attendant to the tree, such as the cost of fertilizer, pruning, tools, picking apples, and carting them to town and selling them.

Somebody had to do those things, and a portion of the salaries paid to those persons ought to be charged against the revenues from the tree. Moreover, the purchase price, or cost, of the tree was an expense. A portion of the cost is taken into account each year of the tree's useful life. Finally, there were taxes. She concluded that the profit from the tree was $50 last year.

"Wow!" The old man blushed. "I thought I made $100 off that tree."

"That's because you failed to match expenses with revenues, in accordance with generally accepted accounting principles," she explained. "You don't actually have to write a check to be charged with what accountants consider to be your expenses. For example, you bought a station wagon some time ago and used it part of the time to cart apples to market. The wagon will last a while, and each year some of the original cost has to be matched against revenues. A portion of the amount has to be spread out over the next several years even though you expended it all at one time. Accountants call that depreciation. I'll bet you never figured that in your calculation of profits."

"I'll bet you're right," he replied. "Tell me more."

"I also went back into the books for a few years and saw that in some years the tree produced fewer apples than it did in other years, the prices varied, and the costs were not exactly the same each year. Taking an average of only the last three years, I came up with a figure of $45 as a fair sample of the tree's earnings. But that is only half of what we have to do to figure the value."

"What's the other half?" he asked.

"The tricky part," she told him. "We now have to figure the value to me of owning a tree that will produce average annual earnings of $45 a year. If I believed that the tree was a 'one-year wonder,' I would say 100% of its value—as a going business—was represented by one year's earnings."

"But if we agree that the tree is more like a corporation in that it will continue to produce earnings year after year, the key is to figure out an appropriate rate of return. In other words, I will be investing my capital in the tree, and I need to compute the value to me of an investment that will produce $45 a year in income. We can call that amount the capitalized value of the tree."

"Do you have something in mind?" he asked.

"I'm getting there. If this tree produced entirely steady and predictable earnings each year, it would be like a U.S. Treasury bond. But its earnings are not guaranteed, so we have to take into account risks and uncertainty. If the risk of its ruin was high, I would insist that a single year's earnings represent a higher percentage of the value of the tree. After all, apples could become a glut on the market one day and you would have to cut the price, thus increasing the costs of selling them."

"Or," she continued, "some doctor could discover a link between eating an apple a day and heart disease. A drought could cut the yield of the tree. Or the tree could become diseased and die. These are all risks. And we don't even know whether the costs we are sure to incur will be worth incurring."

"You are a gloomy one," reflected the old man. "There could also be a shortage of apples on the market, and the price of apples could rise. If you think about it, it is even possible that I have been selling the apples at prices below what people would be willing to pay and that you could raise the price without reducing your sales. Also, there are treatments, you know, that could be applied to increase the yield of the tree. This tree could help spawn a whole orchard. Any of these would increase earnings."

"The earnings also could be increased by lowering costs of the sort you mentioned," the old man continued. "Costs can be reduced by speeding the time from fruition to sale, managing extensions of credit better, and minimizing losses from bad apples. Cutting costs boosts the relationship between overall sales and net earnings or, as the financial types say, the tree's profit margin. And that in turn would boost the return on your investment."

"I am aware of all that," she assured him. "The fact is, we are talking about risk. And investment analysis is a cold business. We don't know with certainty what's going to happen. You want your money now, and I'm supposed to live with the risk.

"That's fine with me, but then I have to look through a cloudy crystal ball, and not with 20/20 hindsight. And my resources are limited. I have to choose between your tree and the strawberry patch down the road. I cannot buy both, and the purchase of your tree will deprive me of alternative investments. That means I have to compare the opportunities and the risks.

"To determine a proper rate of return," she continued, "I looked at investment opportunities comparable to the apple tree, particularly in the agribusiness industry, where these factors have been taken into account. I then adjusted my findings based on how the things we discussed worked out with your tree. Based on those judgments, I figure that 20% is an appropriate rate of return for the tree.

"In other words," she concluded, "assuming that the average earnings from the tree over the last three years (which seems to be a representative period) are indicative of the return I will receive, I am prepared to pay a price for the tree that will give me a 20% return on my investment. I am not willing to accept any lower rate of return because I don't have to; I can always buy the strawberry patch instead. Now, to figure the price, we simply divide $45 of earnings per year by the 20% return I am insisting on."

"Long division was never my strong suit. Is there a simpler way of doing the figuring?" he asked hopefully.

"There is," she assured him. "We can use an approach we Wall Street types prefer, called the price-earnings (or P/E) ratio. To compute the ratio, just divide 100 by the rate of return we are seeking.

If I were willing to settle for an 8% return, that would be 100 divided by 8, which equals 12.5. So we'd use a P/E ratio of 12.5 to 1. But since I want to earn 20% on my investment, I divided 100 by 20 and came up with a P/E ratio of 5:1. In other words, I am willing to pay five times the tree's estimated annual earnings. Multiplying $45 by 5, I get a value of $225. That's my offer."

The old man sat back and said he greatly appreciated the lesson. He would have to think about her offer, and he asked if she could come by the next day.

A DIALOGUE ON CASH

When the young woman returned, she found the old man emerging from behind a sea of work sheets, small print columns of numbers, and a calculator. "Delighted to see you," he said, enthralled. "I think we can do business.

"It's easy to see how you Wall Street smarties make so much money, buying people's property for less than its true value. I think I can get you to agree that my tree is worth more than you figured."

"I'm open-minded," she assured him.

"The $45 number you came up with yesterday was something you called profits, or earnings that I earned in the past. I'm not so sure it tells you anything that important."

"Of course it does," she protested. "Profits measure efficiency and economic utility."

"Fair enough," he mused, "but it sure doesn't tell you how much money you're getting. I looked in my safe yesterday after you left and saw some stock certificates I own that never paid a dividend to me. And I kept getting reports each year telling me how great the earnings were. Now I know that the earnings increased the value of my stocks, but without any dividends I couldn't spend them. It's just the opposite with the tree.

"You figured the earnings were lower because of some amounts I'll never have to spend, like depreciation on my station wagon," the old man went on. "It seems to me these earnings are an idea worked up by the accountants."

Intrigued, she asked, "What is important, then?"

"Cash," he answered. "I'm talking about dollars you can spend, save, or give to your children. This tree will go on for years yielding revenues after costs. And it is the future, not the past, we need to reckon with."

"Don't forget the risks," she reminded him. "And the uncertainties."

"Quite right," he observed. "If we can agree on the possible range of future revenues and costs and that earnings averaged around $45 the last few years, we can make some fair estimates of cash flow over the coming five years: How about that there is a 25% chance that cash flow will be $40, a 50% chance it will be $50, and a 25% chance it will be $60?

"That makes $50 our best guess if you average it out," the old man figured. "Then let's just say that for ten years after that the average will be $40. And that's it. The tree doctor tells me it can't produce any longer than that.

"Now all we have to do," he finished up, "is figure out what you pay today to get $50 a year from now, two years from now, and so on for the first five years until we figure what you would pay to get $40 a year for each of the ten years after that. Then, throw in the 20 bucks we can get for firewood.

"Simple," she confessed. "You want to discount to the present value of future receipts including salvage value. Of course you need to determine the rate at which you discount."

"Precisely," he concurred. "That's what my charts and the calculator are for." She nodded as he showed her discount tables that revealed what a dollar received at a later time is worth today under different assumptions about the discount rate. It showed, for example, that at an 8% discount rate, a dollar delivered a year from now is worth $.93 today, simply because $.93 today, invested at 8%, will produce $1 a year from now.

"You could put your money in a savings account that is insured and receive 5% interest. But you could also buy U.S. Treasury obligations with it and earn, say, 8% interest, depending on prevailing interest rates. That looks like the risk-free rate of interest to me. Anywhere else you put your money deprives you of the opportunity to earn 8% risk-free. Discounting by 8% will only compensate you for the time value of the money you invest in the tree rather than in Treasuries. But the cash flow from the apple tree is not riskless, sad to say, so we need to use a higher discount rate to compensate you for the risk in your investment.

"Let's agree to discount the receipt of $50 a year from now by 15%, and so on with the other deferred receipts. That is about the rate that is applied to investments with this magnitude of risk. You can check that out with my neighbor, who just sold his strawberry patch yesterday. According to my figures, the present value of the expected yearly profit is $268.05, and today's value of the firewood is $2.44, for a grand total of $270.49. I'll take $270 even. You can see how much I'm allowing for risk because if I discounted the stream at 8%, it would come to $388.60."

After a few minutes of reflection, the young woman said to the old man, "It was a bit foxy of you yesterday to let me appear to be teaching you something. Where did you learn so much about finance as an apple grower?"

The old man smiled. "Wisdom comes from experience in many fields."

"I enjoyed this little exercise, but let me tell you something that some financial whiz kids told me," she replied. "Whether we figure value on the basis of the discounted cash flow method you like or the capitalization of earnings I proposed, so long as we apply both methods perfectly, we should come out at exactly the same point."

"Of course!" the old man exclaimed. "The wunderkinds are catching on. The clever ones are not simply looking at old earnings but copying managers by projecting cash flows into the future. The question is which method is more likely to be misused.

"I prefer my method of using cash rather than earnings because I don't have to monkey around with costs like depreciation of my station wagon and other long-term assets. You have to make these arbitrary assumptions about the useful life of the thing and how fast you're going to depreciate it. That's where I think you went wrong in your figuring."

"Nice try, you crafty old devil," she rejoined. "You know there is plenty of room for mistakes in your calculations too. It's easy to discount cash flows when they are nice and steady, but that doesn't help you when you've got some lumpy expenses that do not recur. For example, several years from now that tree will need serious pruning and spraying that don't show up in your flow. The labor and chemicals for that once-only occasion throw off the evenness of your calculations."

"But I'll tell you what," she bellied up. "I'll offer you $250. My cold analysis tells me I'm overpaying, but I really like that tree. I think the delight of sitting in its glorious shade must be worth something."

"It's a deal," agreed the old man. "I never said I was looking for the highest offer but only the best offer."

LESSONS

The parable of the old man and the tree introduced a number of alternative methods of valuing productive property, whether a single asset or an entire business enterprise. The original $50 bid was based on the tree's salvage value, also sometimes called its scrap value. This valuation method will virtually always be inappropriate for valuing a productive asset, business, or share of stock (though many bust-up takeover artists of the 1980s popularized the opposite claim).

The $100 bid was based only on one year's earnings and ignores the earning power over future time. The Internet apple maven's $1,500 overvaluation ignored the concept of the time value of money by simply adding together the raw dollar amounts of expected earnings over future years. Neither of these approaches even qualifies as an appropriate valuation method.

The doctor's bid drew on a market-based valuation technique that considers what other willing buyers had offered. But that technique will be helpful only if the property under consideration or similar properties are regularly traded in reasonably well developed markets. Even then, it is circular because it uses the question (What's it worth, according to others?) to get the answer (What it's worth, according to others).

The deal was ultimately sealed when the buyer and the old man agreed that the two methods they used—capitalizing earnings and discounting cash flows—made the most sense (noting that these two techniques, if perfectly applied, give the same answer). The buyer preferred to use earnings because accounting rules regarding earnings are intended to reflect economic reality pretty well. The old man had less confidence in those rules principally because they call for deducting from revenues accounting depreciation, which he was not sure accurately reflected economic reality.

Although reasonable people can differ, both methods show that valuation is not a fool's game. The buyer and the old man both wisely and rightly acknowledged the importance of keen judgment in business analysis. As the type of investment you consider becomes more uncertain, your judgment must become proportionately more razor-sharp.

Picking an index fund or even a mutual fund requires the least amount of knowledge or judgment; picking a classic stock a bit more, a vintage stock much more, and a rookie stock the greatest. In terms of apples, the apple tree the old man just sold is much like a classic business, a GE, say, or DuPont or United Technologies. It is mature and productive and has an extensive track record.

At the other extreme might be a dot-com start-up business whose only record is on paper—a business plan that is the apple tree equivalent of a bag of seeds. Even if the ingredients are there, the execution is entirely in front of you. You may still have a basis for gauging the probable future—the quality of the seeds, soil, fertilizer, and farmer—but you are leaving more to judgment than in the case of the mature tree.

A few additional morals of the parable: Methods are useful as tools, but good judgment comes not from methods alone but from experience. And experience comes from bad judgment. Listen closely to the experts and hear the things they don't tell you. Behind all the sweet sounds of their confident notes there is a great deal of discordant uncertainty. One wrong assumption can carry you pretty far from the truth. Finally, you are never too young to learn.

HORSE SENSE

The old man and his ultimate buyer shared a business analysis mind-set. That mind-set focuses on individual businesses but must be formed against the backdrop of a few general conditions—what economists call macroeconomic conditions: interest rates, taxes, inflation, and the time value of money (or compounding).

COMPOUNDING

A powerful and intuitive introduction to the time value of money is given by this characteristically witty vignette by a 32-year-old Warren Buffett:

> I have it from unreliable sources that the cost of the voyage Isabella originally underwrote for Columbus was approximately $30,000. This has been considered at least a moderately successful utilization of venture capital. Without attempting to evaluate the psychic income derived from finding a new hemisphere, it must be pointed out that . . . the whole deal was not exactly another IBM. Figured very roughly, the $30,000 invested at 4% compounded annually would have amounted to something like $2,000,000,000,000. . . .

That is $2 trillion—based on a quite modest 4% rate of return. Not only nothing to sneeze at but something to be joyous over. Buffett called this vignette "The Joys of Compounding."

It explains the apocryphal story of Buffett riding up a crowded office building elevator. All heads were staring up at the floor numbers lighting across the top, while Buffett was scouring the elevator floor. As he walked out, Buffett stooped down and picked up a penny lying on the floor. The doors closed behind him, smirks crossed some passengers' faces, and one rider remarked, "That is the start of the next billion."

If you think a penny today does not amount to a hill of beans, consider how much it will grow to over time! That is the joy of future values of money—they get higher the more compounding there is. You get compounding in two ways. You can put money away earlier rather than later, and you can get returns (interest or dividends) paid more frequently and reinvest them too. That is why building wealth calls for saving early and often, though investing only when the price is right.

Investors grasp the joys of compounding, for it is a useful tool to evaluate competing opportunities quickly. A handy reference for making the comparisons gauges how long it takes a given amount of money to double at varying compounded rates of return (or interest rates).

Called the *rule of 72s*, it says that dividing 72 by the rate of return gives the approximate number of years it takes for an amount of money to double. For example, an investment yielding a compounded rate of return of 9% will double in about eight years (72 divided by 9 equals 8) and one yielding 6% will double in about 12 years (72 divided by 6 equals 12).

The rule of 72s can show all sorts of variations on the relationship between money in hand now and money to be gotten in the future. For example, it can determine what required rate of return is necessary for a certain sum to grow to a desired sum in the future. Or if you know what rate of return is available or possible, it can figure how much money someone needs today in order for it to grow to a desired level at some future time.

Take an example. If the available average rate of return on money from now until 40 years from now is 9%, how much money does a 25-year-old person need today in order to retire as a millionaire at age 65 without saving another cent over that time? Work backward from ending up with $1,000,000 at age 65. Since money earning a compound rate of return of 9% doubles approximately every 8 years, at age 57 she'd need to have $500,000; at age 49 she'd need to have $250,000; at age 41 she'd need to have $125,000; at age 33 she'd need to have $62,500; and today, at age 25, she'd need to have (only) $31,250!

If this illustrates the joy in compounding, take another use of the rule of 72s to illustrate the joy of slightly higher rates of return. Assume that instead of being able to earn about a 9% rate of return over the next 40 years, our 25-year-old can only reasonably expect a 6% rate of return. Now her money will double approximately only every 12 years rather than every 8. So 12 years hence at age 37 she'd have $62,500; at age 49 she'd have $125,000; at age 61 she'd have $250,000; at age 73 she'd have $500,000; and she'd have to reach the ripe age of 85 to end up with a million!

INTEREST RATES

A subtle but most important lesson of the apple tree parable is the pivotal role interest rates play in the value of assets. The old man mentioned that U.S. Treasury instruments provide a risk-free rate of interest. That benchmark interest rate is a major determinant of the value of any other asset in the economy, including the value of whole businesses and shares of stock in them. The risk-free rate sets the standard of value of assets with risk. The higher the risk-free rate, the lower the values of riskier assets; the lower the risk-free rate, the higher the values of riskier assets.

As Warren Buffett reflected in a rare public commentary prepared for *Fortune* by Carol Loomis, when the risk-free rate was very high in the late 1960s and 1970s, for example, the average price of stocks was depressed.[2] The Dow hardly moved an inch in price from the early 1960s to the late 1970s because for investors to buy stocks, they had to get a return that exceeded the sky-high risk-free interest rate. When the risk-free rate was very low from the mid-1980s to the early 2000s, in contrast, average stock prices shot up. The Dow enjoyed the greatest bull market in history because the risk-free rate was so low that it was relatively easy for investors to get a risk premium (returns above the risk-free rate).

TAXES

The only thing more mind-boggling about amateur day trading than the outright losses that are racked up is how many among the trading winners neglect how much they are losing to tax payments both outright and in terms of the time value lost by the payments.

Suppose you buy an investment that pays 15% per year for 30 years and keep that investment compounding yearly until the end of that time without being obligated to pay taxes on it. Suppose also that you are taxed on your income from that investment at the end of that thirtieth year at a rate of 35%. This means your after-tax annual rate of return on that investment was about 13.3%. Hard to beat.

Suppose instead that your 15% per year investment for 30 years pays you that 15% annually and subjects you to tax of 35% each year you get it. Your annual after-tax return suddenly shrinks to about 9.75%. Not a bad net return, you say, but that is over 3.5% less than the tax-deferred position. And now we are talking about huge sums, with that 3.5% difference compounding over periods such as 30 years.

The same is true at every level of return differentials and remains quite substantial even at lower rates of return. A 10% pretax return with taxes due only at the end of 30 years gives you an after-tax return of about 8.3%, compared with about a 6.5% after-tax return if you had paid taxes on that income each year. Again, that kind of 2% difference compounded over a few decades works out to be lots of dollars.[3]

INFLATION

Our parable's business school dropout did not know that the value of money across time is nonlinear. Inflation often differs from returns, and returns differ from each other. Annual inflation of 4% means that a basket of goods that can be bought for $100 on January 1 costs $104 on December 31. But if during that year you put $100 in a savings account paying 8%, your balance at the end of that year would be $108. Left uninvested, that $100 would decline in purchasing power to about $96, whereas the invested amount gives you a purchasing power of about $104 (the $108 you have less the impact on its buying power of the 4% inflation).

These macroeconomic factors bear on value. Tax and inflation in particular determine how much your gross return will give you in increased purchasing power. Changes in interest rates require revising any valuations made under different interest rate assumptions. Operating as a business analyst requires knowledge of these things but not their prediction. As Buffett says, "We do not have, never have had, and never will have an opinion about where the stock market, interest rates, or business activity will be a year from now."[4] Still, you can't avoid eating a little spinach in the enterprise of investing. Those who dine on the business investor's rigorous diet emerge more muscular and fit from the meal. Course two is served up next.

CHAPTER 7

YOUR CIRCLE OF COMPETENCE

Investors avoid stocks outside their circle of competence; those who buy stocks outside their circle of competence are gamblers, speculators, or fools. If you lack the grounds for understanding a business—grounds ultimately for estimating a gap between value and price—but make a purchase anyway, you may as well be at a Las Vegas or Atlantic City blackjack table or a local poker party. All you are really doing is guessing, hoping, maybe even praying that things work out your way. Yet there is little reason, other than dumb luck, to think they will.

The first thing you must do before investing in any business is make sure you have a basic understanding of that business. This requires some familiarity with its products, customers, selling environment, and so on—in short, its operating climate.

It is quite a different proposition to understand businesses, such as Procter & Gamble, that make and sell a wide variety of familiar consumer products such as peanut butter, soap, and toothpaste than it is to understand businesses, such as Applied Materials, that make and sell a wide variety of highly technical materials for the semiconductor industry such as expitaxial and polysilicon deposition, etch, ion, implantation, and metrology (understand?).

Getting the information necessary to determine whether a business is within your circle of competence before making an investment decision is easy. Check out the SEC-maintained Free-Edgar.com Web site or contact the SEC at its Washington, D.C., or various regional offices. Or check out each company's Web site directly. You can even search the SEC Edgar database on lots of other Web sites, including 10kwizard.com, Edgarspace, and Edgaronline.

Find the section in the company's annual report called management's discussion and analysis of the business. This is a narrative assessment of the business that should help and test your understanding of it. Another useful source to consult is the chairman's or CEO's letter, as much for what it says as for what it does not say about the business. You will learn an enormous amount by reading just a few of these reports, and the more you read, the better able you will be to evaluate them.

THE INITIAL CIRCLE

Circles of competence should be drawn according to your ability and willingness to understand a business and its operating climate. Your circle's boundaries are defined by your knowledge and aptitude; its contents are companies about which you can make an intelligent investment decision in light of those boundaries. Omit from your circle businesses that are too hard for you to understand or that change too rapidly for you to keep up with.

To define your circle of competence, start with your own industry. Retail store managers probably have a head start in understanding CVS, Walgreen's, Gap, and Home Depot; restaurant employees, in understanding McDonald's. People in the energy business tend to know that business and will have a leg up on Exxon-Mobil, Enron, and Texaco. Engineers and scientists will have a better shot at understanding Dow Chemical and DuPont, and telecommunications devotees have a good shot at MCI, AT&T, and Lucent. Doctors should certainly have an edge in evaluating pharmaceutical concerns such as Eli Lilly and Pfizer. Farmers may be able to evaluate John Deere better than the average Wall Street banker can.

Think also about the things you buy and use and how you do so. You may know more about companies such as American Home Products, BMW, Federal Express, and Sony than you think, or at least you may be able to understand them better than you think. Try Hershey's and Nestlé if you are a chocolate lover, Anheuser-Busch or Heineken if you drink a lot of beer, and Tiffany's if diamonds are your best friend.

Do the same with regional companies in your area. Public utilities such as ConEd in New York and Black Hills in the Rocky Mountains (South Dakota, Wyoming, and Montana) and regional banks such as First Oaks in Chicago, Wilshire in Los Angeles, and Alabama National in the Southeast (Alabama, Georgia, and Florida) should be easy and interesting to examine for people living in those areas. So too are similarly located larger companies, say, Boeing in Seattle,

Coca-Cola in Atlanta, Kimberly-Clark in Dallas, and Johnson Controls in Milwaukee.

How do the companies which seem a natural fit for your circle of competence relate to less obvious ones that fit just as well? If you are in retail, what about apparel companies such as Gucci, Polo Ralph Lauren, and Hèrmes International? Up-and-comers such as Kenneth Cole? Sports fans may enjoy learning more about Nike; musicians, Steinway. The examples pour out if you identify the sector your business or interests are in and comb through lists of companies in that sector published by all the major investment banking firms and available on many reputable Web sites.

To sharpen your boundaries after you've identified one or a few companies and industries you know something about, evaluate whether a particular company qualifies for admission by asking yourself a series of commonsense questions about that business. If you can answer them, the company probably qualifies; if you can't, pick another one that stands a better chance and ask the same questions. Here are the key questions.

What products does the company sell or services does it provide? There is a big difference between razors (Gillette) and computer chips (Intel) and cruises (Carnival). Do you understand these products and how they are used?

Does the company make products that people need? Razors and chips almost certainly, but that's less true of luxury goods such as cruise vacations. Will these products probably be needed for the indefinite future? There are big differences between toothpaste (Colgate-Palmolive), paper (Mead), and pet rocks (who made them?). Big differences can arise between today's needs and tomorrow's (razors can become obsolete with an explosion of electrolysis or laser removal, and computer chips may be displaced by chemical-driven substitutes now in the research stage).

How distinctive is the company's product compared to possible substitutes for it? The difference between Coke and Pepsi may be slight, but do consumers think it matters? Product differentiation in the beverage industry, as in many other consumer product businesses, can be remarkably successful.

Asked another way, how likely is it that this company can raise prices on its products without losing unit volume in sales? Carnival might be able to do that with its cruises more easily than Mead can with its paper. The ability to raise prices without hurting sales is called economic goodwill. Some companies get more of it by distinguishing their products in the consumer's eye as having distinctive traits that make them worth buying even at higher prices. Bang & Olufsen did this successfully in upgrading its image to a maker of stereos and other sound systems at the "high end" of audio technology.

Proceed with similar sorts of questions about the product market. What is the company's target customer and/or client base? Is it teens and preteens (say, electronic music) or retirees (medical devices), male or female (sporting goods, clothing, cosmetics)?

Does the company depend on one or a few customers for a major portion of its revenues, as might a manufacturer or wholesaler such as Procter & Gamble (13% of sales go to Wal-Mart)? Does it have millions of customers, or does it depend on a handful? (Coca-Cola has over 14 million customers who sell in turn to the ultimate consumer!)

How much does any dependency matter—how sturdy is a major customer? Even businesses with well-known and time-tested products can suffer enormous economic damage from policy changes by their major customers. Mattel (with its venerable Barbie line) and Hasbro (with powerful branded products such as Star Wars and Pokémon figures) both took major financial beatings when one of their largest customers—Toys-"R"-Us—forced major inventory control changes that shifted much of the cost of carrying inventory from the store to the manufacturers.

How does the company sell its products? Direct mail (say, Dell) and storefronts (say, Starbucks) are quite distinct modes of distribution, and each differs again from sales over the Internet (say, Amazon.com) or sales by industrial manufacturers to their industrial clients (say, Johnson Controls and General Electric).

What is the company's geographic market? An economic downturn in Asia can severely impair profits at multinational companies that do significant parts of their business there, as the crisis in 1998 showed for venerable companies such as Procter & Gamble and Coca-Cola. Yet both also had such global reach, they survived with no long-term damage.

Has the company led or at least adapted quickly to changing economic and business conditions? Companies able to maneuver quickly to join their old economy businesses with new economy strategies—such as General Electric—deserve credit for that deftness. Can you judge which ones can do this?

These commonsense questions can go on and on to include questions such as the following: What is the company's supply situation like? Its employee relations? Does it operate in regions subject to ordinary or extraordinary risks of political or economic instability?

Grappling with these questions should be enough to test whether a company is within your circle of competence. Again, if you can answer these questions, the company probably qualifies; if you can't, try one you are more familiar with.

Graham advised: "The field of choice is wide; the selection should depend not only on the individual's competence and equipment but perhaps equally well upon his interests and preferences."[1] Buffett echoes the point: "You don't have to be an expert on every company, or even many. You only have to be able to evaluate companies within your circle of competence. The size of that circle is not very important; knowing its boundaries, however, is vital."[2] If you have to choose between a large circle and a thick boundary, choose the latter. But a bigger circle will give you more opportunities, so work on enlarging it.

THE NURTURED CIRCLE

The boundaries of your circle must change over time. If you leave them the same, some companies will simply disappear. If you are a master of the fashion industry today—say you work in New York City's garment industry or are a buyer for a large retail chain such as Sak's Fifth Avenue—you know that to remain a master five years from now you will need to learn new things over that period. Indeed, particularly in the fashion industry, you need to keep up daily, since fashion is (by its very name) a business that swiftly and constantly evolves. Colors, hemlines, cuts, and who's in and who's out change by the season. To stay on top, you must change.

If you simply took what you knew about an industry you worked in ten years ago and used that knowledge to evaluate a company in that industry today, you would be at a severe disadvantage. Take the business of book publishing, which has changed rapidly in that period. In the distribution channels, for example, first the rise of chain booksellers such as Barnes & Noble and Borders eclipsed much of the power of the old-fashioned independent booksellers; then the rise of on-line booksellers such as Amazon.com altered the dynamic again. And the entire book publishing industry has consolidated substantially and become part of a broader entertainment industry.

Anyone in the publishing industry during that period needed to constantly stretch her knowledge of that industry and in doing so redefine her investment circle of competence. If an editor, publisher, or other industry member simply stuck with only what she knew in the beginning, she risked losing not only power in her job but investment insight into her industry as well. If you stop learning now, you will know less as the world changes. And as the world changes, you need to know more just to stay in the same place.

Those who can discern trends in their industries are better able to ascertain which businesses in an industry are likely to remain or emerge as leaders. Equally important is recognizing that industries you know can be affected by other industries about which you know less. In book publishing, putting 4-pound, 3-inch volumes on tape or compact disc (CD) created competition for the music industry—people listen to books in their cars and even at home instead of listening to music. Turning multivolume encyclopedia sets into the single-disc CD-ROM format sucked a huge chunk of the profit out of the traditional print encyclopedia business.

To maintain your circle of competence in the face of invasions and forced change from other industries thus requires that you know something about those other industries. That calls not merely for a commitment to maintain your circle of competence as the things in it change but for constantly stretching your circle of competence to include things that might affect it.

Some people were raised in tech environments and know more about computers, digitalization, and the Internet than they know about fashion and publishing. Companies in those industries may dominate their initial circle of competence. However, sticking to those industries alone is dangerous. A tech company's value will be affected by how its products are used by other industries, such as fashion and publishing.

Likewise, those who work in industries such as fashion and publishing may know more about those fields than about anything tech-related, and their initial circle of competence will be filled with companies in that cohort. But if they don't learn something about the tech businesses that drive changes in fashion and publishing, they will know less about fashion and publishing too.

All companies and industries are exposed to change from outside forces. Among those forces are globalization, computerization, and the rise of the service sector in the United States and of e-business globally. Keeping up with such developments helps gauge their probable impact. Other external forces are much harder to measure, such as war, trade disputes, oil price spikes, and earthquakes. This calls for a delicate balance.

Graham advised that "there are other factors outside the control of the company that are perhaps equally important in their influence on the value of its securities. The outlook for the industry, general business and security-market conditions, periods of inflation or depression, artificial market influences, the popular favor of the type of security—these factors cannot be measured in terms of exact ratios and margins of safety. They can only be judged by a general knowledge gained by constant contact with financial and business news."[3]

Buffett appreciates this too but emphasizes selecting businesses that will prosper despite these things, and never indulging the fantasy of being able to see into the crystal ball:

> We will continue to ignore political and economic forecasts, which are an expensive distraction for many investors and businessmen. Thirty years ago, no one could have foreseen the huge expansion of the Vietnam War, wage and price controls, two oil shocks, the resignation of a president, the dissolution of the Soviet Union, a one-day drop in the Dow of 508 points, or treasury bill yields fluctuating between 2.8% and 17.4%
>
> But, surprise—none of these blockbuster events made the slightest dent in Ben Graham's investment principles. . . . Fear is the foe of the faddist, but the friend of the fundamentalist.
>
> A different set of major shocks is sure to occur in the next 30 years. We will neither try to predict these nor to profit from them.[4]

All companies—whether classic, vintage, or rookie—are subject to change in character and quality. Classics with rising sales and earnings can face contractions and reversals from competitors, new entrants, downturns in important markets, or changes in the way their customers or suppliers do business in the face of changes. Rookies with low sales and no earnings can come to dominate an industry, throttle the competition, and ultimately generate enormous earnings and value. Vintage companies can go either way.

Even if all businesses change, some businesses enjoy one thing that does not change: the reasons their customers keep coming back. Companies like that in your circle deserve careful attention; they are so rare and valuable that Buffett calls them the Inevitables.[5]

In maintaining and stretching your circle of competence, note how changes that affect industries and companies follow certain pretty well defined paths. Business change is not unpredictable, only hard to predict. There are myriad types of business changes and patterns that they follow, but the infinite potential variation can be organized pretty simply to enable you to think about those changes in a profitable way. The chief patterns that matter relate to products and their degree of brand or commodity characteristics, the sources and costs of supply, the chain of distribution, customers' habits and tastes, and business and organizational design.[6]

Take the brand-commodity pattern. Some businesses are able to transform a commodity product into a branded product, as Clorox did with bleach and Frank Perdue did with chicken. Those branded products can be retransformed back into commodity products, going the way of the Model T and the Hoover vacuum, or at least have the franchise value of the brand reduced, as occurred with the Xerox machine and Campbell's Soup. Knowledge of a company's brand position is important, but more important is knowing its commitment and ability to promote, protect, and expand that position.

Supply patterns either reduce or enlarge the amount of inventory a company has to maintain. Companies that reduce their inventory end up decreasing their costs and boosting profits. Dell developed close relationships with its suppliers that enabled it to pretty much eliminate carrying inventory of any of the computer components it uses. IBM and Compaq have had less success in doing that.

Distribution patterns are always important and got a huge amount of attention during the dawn of the Internet. The direct seller of products has come and gone over the years. The Fuller brush salesman, the milkman, and the Avon lady used to give a good profit advantage to their companies, but the shift to suburban living and the proliferation of cars, highways, shopping centers, and malls changed all that. Some of that changed again as direct sellers re-emerged to bring computers, books, and even groceries direct to the home.

Customers' tastes obviously relate to distribution patterns, though the causality is not always certain. As they say in marketing, if you make it, people will come (and if you deliver it, people may take it). But consumer tastes and habits are equally obviously an enormous driver of profits and a determinant of where the profit centers are. It is useful to distinguish here, however, between fad patterns and longer-term patterns.

Silly products that capture the temporary imagination of the masses may generate some short-term profit (hula hoops, yo-yos), but the typical pattern is that those tastes evaporate and the profit in them moves to the collectors and dealers (Pez candy dispensers). The patterns of endurance give rise to longer-term profit centers, as with the trend toward low-salt and low-fat foods that companies such as Nabisco took advantage of.

Business organization and design move around a lot with changes in the context in which companies operate and compete:

- Globalization led many companies, such as Procter & Gamble and Xerox, to reorganize their management structures—from having heads of different parts of the world to having heads of various product lines throughout the world.
- The rise of the Internet and e-commerce led many to create entire new dimensions of their businesses to market product on-line or to redirect major chunks of their businesses to take advantage of the lower costs and wider reach of Internet sales—in GE's case, the company did both.
- The move toward service profit centers and the ability to unleash greater profits with fewer hard assets led many companies to operate parts of their businesses as managers under contract rather than through outright ownership, the way Barnes & Noble entered the college bookstore market.

Companies that adapt organizational structure and business design to meet changing needs and opportunities are good companies to keep an eye on. If you notice a company that constantly readapts itself in this way, try to learn more about it. Even if those companies don't make it into your circle of competence, you can enlarge it with the knowledge you gain from studying them. Coca-Cola and Disney are good examples.

Coca-Cola's main business is selling beverages globally, principally gallons of concentrates and syrups that constitute the Coke brand but also Minute Maid and nearly two hundred others. Coca-Cola devotes most of its resources to marketing its brands to promote consumer awareness and maintaining and expanding its bottling operations through a mix of independent bottlers and wholly or partly owned bottlers. Coca-Cola reinvented itself in the 1980s to see its chief customers not as those who actually drink Coke and the other brands but the distributors around the world who carry product to those end consumers (this transformation was led by

Coca-Cola's late CEO, Roberto Goizueta, who is discussed further in the final chapter of this book).

Disney's segments are mainly creative content (films, animation, books), broadcasting through the American Broadcasting Corporation (ABC) and ESPN, and theme parks and resorts. A unique thing about Disney is that going to Disneyland and Disney World (with children or grandchildren especially) is an incomparable experience. And Disney constantly reinvigorates its business by expanding into television, building blockbuster products that can be sold in multiple forms (film, record, tape, theme park, apparel, and souvenirs), and so on, and by exploiting the Internet to broaden both its content and its distribution channels.

By no means an exhaustive list of patterns, these are the kinds of important trends that alter and reshape circles of competence and that must be looked after to expand your circle. To sharpen your idea of what you should know about companies in order for them to qualify as members of your circle of competence, let's take a closer look at some candidates.

A FULL CIRCLE

Take one company from each of the categories mentioned in the beginning: the classic General Electric (GE), the vintage Microsoft, and the rookie Amazon.com. These are all important companies and are widely discussed in the financial press, but they differ in age, products, and financial and business characteristics.

GE operates through numerous divisions in a wide range of industries. The most important divisions are appliances such as refrigerators, lighting such as lamps and bulbs, the National Broadcasting Corporation (NBC), aircraft engines, capital services (itself a widely diversified group of about thirty businesses engaged in various consumer and commercial financing activities worldwide), plastics used in a wide range of applications from cars to CD-ROMs, and industrial, medical, power, and transportation systems (including products and business solutions such as factory automation, surgical diagnostics, gas turbines, and locomotives, respectively).

Understanding all of GE is a tall order that calls for some appreciation of the basics of finance, broadcasting, consumer, and industrial businesses. But if you read its annual report for the last few years and pay special attention to the excellent letters written by

CEO Jack Welch (discussed in Chapter 14), you will gain a good sense of the company and how it operates. Indeed, Welch argues that understanding GE is not a tall order at all, and after you read Chapter 14, you may agree.

One thing that immediately jumps out at you is that GE got to where it is through Welch's declaration 20 years ago that the company would remain in any business only if it were the number one or number two player in that business. Businesses that did not achieve that rank were fixed, sold, or closed. The company has ended up the business equivalent of a magnificent art collection, Jack Welch, curator.

Founded in 1975, Microsoft is a relative newcomer compared to the century-old GE. It develops, manufactures, licenses, and supports a range of software products, including operating systems, server applications, worker productivity applications, and software development tools. Microsoft's success would have been hard to predict in the middle to late 1980s, when the dynamic of the software industry was uncertain. As that decade came and went and the 1990s confirmed the power and importance of that industry, the company's dominant position became easier to predict.

Yet pervasive and widespread Internet use in the late 1990s might have posed a threat to Microsoft's business, though a threat it managed to navigate (excuse the pun, but it is an apt characterization) through its aggressive entry into and forceful presence in the Internet browser industry. While it is a somewhat older business than Amazon.com, its relative youth compared to GE makes its future (wholly apart from its legal and regulatory environment) harder to predict than that of its classic elders.

Still, you can learn from its annual report that Microsoft's Windows operating system is installed on more than 300 million Intel-based personal computers (PCs), making it the world's leading PC software company. It is also a leader in PC application tools and has grown rapidly to rank among the top networks on the Internet. Its properties receive over 40 million unique monthly visitors to sites such as Hotmail, MSNBC, Carpoint, and MoneyCentral. If these computing and Internet operations are up your alley, read about Microsoft's stuff in its annual report and CEO Bill Gates's books or annual letters to shareholders.

Amazon.com is a business infant begun in 1994, retailing on-line books, CDs, and videos and offering some 5 million titles. Its business model, while interesting, is hard to pin down because it constantly and rapidly evolves. Amazon.com started as a bookseller but quickly expanded into a wide range of product lines such as toys, electronics, home improvement, and even a joint venture with Sotheby's auction house. It attracts an average of as many as 12 million unique monthly visitors to its site.

Amazon.com buys inventory from suppliers on a just-in-time basis, thus minimizing its inventory and warehousing costs, and takes orders on its state-of-the-art Web site for shipping by its warehouse teams. Whatever one thinks of this business model, it depends entirely on the continuing success and proliferation of the Internet as an important way of doing consumer shopping.

While so far so good, the Internet's brief history makes forecasting the future of Amazon.com and other e-businesses more difficult for most people than it is to forecast the future of companies such as GE and even Microsoft. Indeed, it is also difficult because Amazon.com has never generated a profit. The book business is mature, slow-growing, and fiercely competitive and has low profit margins; Amazon.com's expansion into other businesses poses huge start-up costs that will deepen those losses further in the short run, though they may come roaring back in the form of huge profits in the future.

Amazon.com's growing diversity of businesses can fragment managerial attention (much as your diversified portfolio can distract you). If well managed, though, they could be as successful a group as GE's varied lot. Despite the uncertainties, Amazon.com's business is intriguing. Those with the ability to learn more about it and an aptitude for understanding it would be foolish not to look a little harder.

DECISION MAKING

Assessing information about a business and its industry and related industries enables you to make rational judgments about the probable payoffs versus the probable losses. Anything less is simply a toss of the dice. Conservative decision makers take the position that no option should be pursued without a high level of positive evidence and information. To put a number on it, they might argue that you must have a degree of confidence in your judgment of, say, 90% (you are 90% sure of the outcome and 10% unsure).

Less conservative people believe that the level of evidence required for a particular decision varies with the probable payoff from being right compared to the probable loss from being wrong.[7] If the payoff from being right is very high compared to the loss from being wrong (say, gaining $99 versus losing $1), this view says you can reduce the required confidence level substantially—maybe to as low as 1%. People who buy lottery tickets reflect this kind of decision making.

If the gain-loss matrix goes the other way (say, gaining only $1 versus losing $99), then you would insist on a much greater confidence level—maybe nearly 100%. These are the sure bets in life. And as even the most steadfast gambler knows, there is no such thing as a sure bet.

Your risk appetite will determine the sort of decision maker that best suits your own psychology. Losses are inevitable. If they make your misery index soar, stick with conservative approaches; if you can tolerate them, a more aggressive approach is defensible. (Beware: most people weigh losses more heavily than gains by a factor of about 2.5.)

Buffett is a conservative decision maker. Explaining Berkshire's conservative financial policy of using little debt, Buffett says that if there were a 99% probability that higher leverage would produce something good and a 1% chance of a surprise that would produce something between anguish and default, he would not bite that bullet: "We wouldn't have liked those 99:1 odds—and never will. A small chance of distress or disgrace cannot, in our view, be offset by a large chance of extra returns."[8]

Graham was also cautious, warning investors to avoid ventures with little to gain and much to lose.[9] He advised forming judgments on the basis of knowledge and experience, not on the basis of optimism (valuable in many settings but not in investing; Buffett calls optimism the "enemy of the rational buyer").[10]

Graham and Buffett's views reflect contemporary social psychology. Research in this field shows that in any decision-making process, the cognitive weaknesses shared by most people produce subconscious errors of judgment. The main cognitive biases in reasoning that investors need to worry about are the following:

• *Overconfidence and superiority*: believing you are certain when you are only pretty sure (or believing you are pretty sure when you are uncertain) and believing you are better than average (the Lake Woebegon syndrome).

- *Confirmation and resistance*:   skewing your interpretation of new information to support earlier beliefs and being slow to update those beliefs.
- *Vividness and pattern seeking*:   weighing dramatic information too heavily and overreacting to a series of similar sorts of news items in the belief that they show a pattern.[11]

Of these, the most potentially damaging cognitive biases are overconfidence and superiority. As Buffett advises: "What counts for most people in investing is not how much they know, but rather how realistically they define what they don't know. An investor needs to do very few things right as long as he or she avoids big mistakes."[12]

There are three simple strategies to help investors avoid these reasoning errors. The first is to recognize them. The second is to insist on a justification, something you can do by writing a memo to yourself about why you are making a decision. (Beware of the traps of this strategy, which Buffett illustrates by quoting Ben Franklin: "So convenient a thing it is to be a reasonable creature, since it enables one to find or make a reason for everything one has a mind to do."[13] Many people do not have articulable reasons for many of their decisions. In investing decisions, if you don't have one, don't try to make one up.) The third, and related, strategy is to have clear guidance in your decision making. For investing, this includes the ideas discussed in this book.

CHAPTER 8

RECOGNIZING SUCCESS

What makes an investment attractive? A price substantially lower than value. Estimating value requires making judgments about probable future performance, but the only available basis for prognosis is the record of the past. The historian Daniel Boorstein likened planning for the future without knowing some history to planting cut flowers.

Investments cannot be made on the basis of such temporary gardens either but require a look at the history of business. If accounting is the language of business, numbers are its history. Just as history is complex, broad, and replete with contradictions, so too are the numbers of business history. If you focus on a few key numbers, however, the road map to good investment selection becomes clear.

Start with the management's discussion and analysis of the business. In addition to a narrative assessment of the business, this summarizes the most important numbers in the company's financial statements. So you don't have to go to the trouble of doing the calculations—just look them up. This discussion also interprets the meaning of those numbers from management's perspective. So you also don't have to become an expert in accounting to make sense of this stuff.

Beware of using secondhand databases. Lots of Web sites give you a chance to employ screening tools to search through 12,000 or more different businesses with dozens of different variables of the kind described below. These tools operate as filters to give you a limited number of businesses to examine more closely. In principle, this is precisely the kind of technique that is sensible to use.

However, you cannot be sure the search engines are working with data of integrity. The data do not usually include information about a company's accounting policies, footnote information, or management's discussion and analysis. The data are not always updated or corrected, may have embedded errors that arise in the transmission process, and may be the product of aggregating information that is dissimilar or noncomparable. This is not to say that these systems are worthless, only that you should exercise care in using them.[1]

BUSINESS FUEL

Every business has debts coming due every day which require resources to meet. The difference between short-term needs and resources is called working capital. It is a bit like fuel in an engine; it is better to have a full tank, but overfilling can be dangerous. Too little working capital can pose a threat to the ability of a company to operate in the ordinary course over the immediate future, but too much working capital can mean that resources are not being deployed in optimal ways.

The right level of working capital varies across businesses. One way to determine how much working capital is needed and assess its adequacy is to compare the working capital to sales. Typically, a retailing business that generates substantial sales of low-cost items, such as a supermarket, needs less working capital per dollar of sales (perhaps around 10 to 15%) than does an industrial manufacturer of high-ticket items such as airplanes (perhaps around 25 to 35%). A manufacturer of consumer goods—say, Carnation or Clorox—might require some level in between.

Other businesses can operate with low or even negative working capital. Companies in the restaurant business, McDonald's, for example, often operate with negative working capital because of the cash nature of the business. This system provides direct liquidity, and payment terms with suppliers usually permit payment after product is both received and used in the business to generate cash. Companies in other industries can benefit from the same combination, as Amazon.com aptly demonstrates by operating sometimes with negative working capital without apparent impairment of its ability to meet obligations as they come due.

In the oil and gas industry, a principal source of cash is proved reserves that are produced in the ensuing year. While they cannot be reported as working capital on the balance sheet under generally accepted accounting principles, they are turned into cash. Companies in other industries sometimes fund new construction by issuing short term obligations such as commercial paper that is later refinanced with long-term obligations such as bank loans. This can also produce low or negative working capital while not posing any threat to the company's short-term ability to meet its obligations.

Ben Graham put it this way in his marvelous little book published in 1937, *The Interpretation of Financial Statements*:

> The proper amount of working capital required by a particular enterprise will depend upon both the amount and the character of its business. The chief point of comparison is the amount of working capital per dollar of sales. A company doing business for cash and enjoying a rapid turnover of inventory—for example, a chain grocery enterprise—needs a much lower working capital compared with sales than does the manufacturer of heavy machinery sold on long-term payments.[2]

CURRENT AND QUICK RATIOS

Evaluating the working capital position is achieved by comparing the relationship between current assets and current liabilities in relative terms. Known as the *current ratio*, this relationship shows how many dollars in cash or other assets likely to be turned into cash within a year are available to pay debts that are due within that year. As a rule of thumb, for most businesses the ideal current ratio is around 1.5, but the range of current ratios across companies and industries is broad.

A current ratio substantially higher—say, 3 or 4 or more—is a sign of potential problems, not with respect to liquidity but with respect to efficiency. It implies that there are financial resources that could be freed up and put to better use: Inventory could be reduced, receivables could be collected more quickly or sold, or payables could be aged a bit more before being paid.

At the other extreme, a current ratio of 1 or less (i.e., negative working capital) is often a warning signal that a company may face difficulties in paying its debts as they come due in the short term. As the ratio gets close to 1 or below it, therefore, investigate the liquidity question further.

Recently the average current ratio of the companies in the S&P 500 was about 1.5, about the same as for the conglomerate segment of that index, of which GE is a part. The current ratio in the computer industry tends to be higher, closer to 2.75 (with Microsoft right around that average). Specialty retailers, including Amazon.com, had higher current ratios than these, around 3.5, with Amazon.com's fluctuating from negative to 4.5, depending on its borrowing levels for investment in new businesses.

This range of ratios reflects different corporate needs as well as unique funding situations (called the net trade cycle, or the relationship between desired investment in inventory compared to the relationship between credit extended and credit taken). Amazon.com has at times operated with negative working capital, which, given the retail nature of its business with low inventory and low accounts receivable, is safe and indeed a good indicator of value from managing working capital. Microsoft's relatively high ratio is due in large part to the fact that it generates enormous amounts of cash in its operations. GE and its peers exhibit the usual characteristics of relatively mature businesses, though GE constantly tries to reduce the amount of working capital it requires to zero.

You can fine-tune your analysis even more by looking only to highly liquid assets, excluding assets such as inventory and prepaid expenses. This leaves cash (liquidity itself) and assets such as accounts receivable that are due in shorter periods (say, within three months). This more refined test is known as the *quick ratio* and sometimes (equivalently) as either the *liquidity ratio* or the *acid test ratio*.

Rules of thumb still apply. A minimum quick ratio of 1 is desirable, and higher ratios are generally better—up to a point. This is useful to know because of what it reveals about the relative level of the current ratio. For example, a current ratio within a seemingly satisfactory range (say, between 1.4 and 2) could actually be high largely as a result of excessive inventory levels. Since a business cannot pay debts with inventory, there is reason to worry about a company's ability to pay its debts as they come due if it has a low quick ratio even while sporting a high current ratio.

Conglomerates such as GE tend to have a relatively wider gap than do other businesses between the current ratio and the quick ratio. As a segment, the conglomerate current ratio of around 1.5, compared to a quick ratio of about .8, reflects the fact that most of the current assets are neither cash nor short-term accounts receivable. The band is tighter in the more liquid businesses of computers and on-line retail sales, where there are speedier assets in the current ratio (2.75 and 2.6 in the computer industry and about 3.5 and 2.5 in the specialty retailer segment). These variations reflect the range of operating environments in these businesses and also show that neither GE, Microsoft, nor Amazon.com is all that different from its segment in terms of liquidity needs or how they are being met.

DEBT

Check out a company's ability to attract additional financing; this is particularly important when a company has negative working capital from issuing short-term obligations such as commercial paper. This is done by using the *debt-to-equity ratio*. In its most general formulation, the calculation is the ratio between the total debt of a company, including short-term debt as well as long-term debt, divided by the amount of owners' equity.

The ratio measures the relative borrowing capacity and debt-paying ability of the enterprise over the long term. Businesses with relatively high debt-to-equity ratios are characterized as "highly leveraged," meaning that the debt level in relation to the investment level of the owners in the business (the shareholders) is very high. What levels of debt-to-equity ratios are normal has varied historically, in accordance with economic conditions and collective beliefs about credit.

During the 1980s, for example, debt-to-equity ratios in the range of 7:1 or higher were common, whereas during the early 1990s the typical ratios were closer to 4:1. At the turn of the twenty-first century, the debt-to-equity ratio of the S&P 500 averaged just about 1:1, reflecting a decade in which most business financing was done using equity rather than debt.

Conglomerates still are relatively debt-heavy, however, with the segment average of about 3:1 and GE above that segment average with a debt-to-equity ratio of around 4:1. That level reflects the relatively more mature stage of these companies, particularly compared with the far leaner computer industry. Microsoft, for example, funds all its operations with internally generated cash, enabling it to operate with no debt whatsoever, and the average debt-to-equity ratio for the computer industry as a whole is a staggeringly low .2:1. Amazon.com weighs in between these levels, reflecting both its need to finance its expanding operations and warehouse construction projects and its relatively lesser ability compared with Microsoft to generate sufficient cash to satisfy those needs.

Leverage reflected in a relatively higher debt-to-equity ratio can be desirable. If a company borrows at rates below what it can earn on its capital, borrowing is profitable. Shareholders benefit. There is a limit to the benefit, however, for even relatively cheap money must be repaid and too great a debt burden could be crushing during periods of depressed returns.

A way to gauge these trade-offs is to examine the coverage ratio—a comparison of earnings to interest obligations on debt. For most industrial companies, an interest coverage ratio in the range of 3 to 4 is considered prudent and implies a relatively safe level of borrowing. In light of the relatively low levels of indebtedness and relatively high levels of profitability of corporate America at the turn of the twenty-first century, the average interest coverage ratio among the S&P 500 soared to nearly 11.

Conglomerates remained closest to historical norms, with GE's coverage ratio at about 2.5 and the segment at about 4.5. At nearly the other extreme, Microsoft enjoys total coverage because it is simply debt-free. Amazon.com is an interesting case: Its coverage ratio is negative because it is losing money (has negative profits), as low as −4. That kind of situation calls for looking more closely at other fixed charges, which in Amazon.com's case include leases on various warehouses that also have to be paid. Its fixed charge coverage ratio is therefore even worse, making its ability to generate additional funds to cover its increasing expansion all the more important.

MANAGERS UNDER THE MICROSCOPE

Three simple tools clue us into managerial effectiveness. They center on the efficiency of inventory and receivables management and the thickness of profit margins. Some companies report the speed of inventory and receivable turns and the levels of profit margins directly in their periodic reports, and some even highlight this in the chairman's letters—usually signs of good or at least honest management. In other cases, you have to dig for it (not a good sign). Putting managers under the microscope this way helps gauge the prospects for future business performance—whether the maximal profits are being squeezed from the business or whether there is room for more.

INVENTORY TURNS

While inventory is considered a current asset in that it is expected to be realized in cash within one year, you can be more precise about its relative liquidity by measuring the speed of its sale. Inventory speed, or turns, is measured by the relationship between the cost of goods sold (COGS) during a period and the average level of inventory during that period:

$$\frac{\text{Current year's cost of goods sold}}{(\text{Beginning inventory} + \text{ending inventory})/2}$$

Inventory turn levels are reliable indicators of the quality of inventory management. The longer inventory sits around without being sold, the less value it adds to the business, since it could be converted into cash deployed for more productive uses. High inventory levels also increase the risk of obsolescence or spoilage, require large amounts of either cash or bank borrowing to finance, and pose the risk of loss if the market price at which they can be sold declines materially.

GE is well known for its inventory turn management, and its long-time CEO, Jack Welch, regularly reports this in his annual letters. GE boasts inventory turns of a robust 8 amid a conglomerate average inventory turn of about 7 though shy of the S&P 500 average inventory turn of about 10. Microsoft manages inventory well too, right along with the rest of the computer industry, with turns of about 15; this is larger than GE in part because of the vastly different products these businesses sell.

But Amazon.com is superefficient in inventory management, at a breakneck pace of around 20. Amazon.com is a specialist in just-in-time inventory, a key management strategy developed in the last couple of decades that Amazon.com has taken to new levels. Stock doesn't sit idle in Amazon.com's warehouses, and this swift turnover lowers costs. That enables the business either to charge lower prices to its customers (hence Amazon.com's aggressive pricing discounts) or to continue to charge the market price but generate more profit.

RECEIVABLE TURNS

A company's credit policies can be its Achilles' heel or a driver of efficiency. Too many sales on credit or too many delinquencies or uncollectible accounts can crush cash flows. Speedy collection enhances liquidity and can enable a company to get its customers to finance its business. Receivable turns are measured by credit sales (or total sales if those sales are not broken out separately) during a period divided by the average accounts receivable outstanding during the period:

$$\frac{\text{Credit sales}}{(\text{Beginning accounts receivable} + \text{ending accounts receivable})/ 2}$$

To gauge the speed of receivables collection, in turn, divide the number of days in a year by the number of turns. The result gives the average number of days the receivables are outstanding. Compare that average to the business's credit policies to see how well managers are running the credit part of the business. There is trouble if the average is greater than the policy (say, collections average 70 days but billing calls for payments to be made within 30 or 60 days).

GE displays considerable skill in receivables management, turning them about eight times per year, meaning they are collected on average within 45 days. That compares dramatically well to a conglomerate industry average of three turns, or 120 days. Microsoft is also a speedy collector, turning receivables about 11 times a year, or just over 30 days—perhaps as a result of its no-paper policy under which all bills (and invoices) are completed electronically—routing a slower computer industry average that looks more like that of GE (about eight turns, averaging 45 days).

Again, the exceptional case is Amazon.com, a standout in this category, with about forty turns, or a mere nine days outstanding. That means Amazon.com's customers are funding a substantial part of Amazon.com's operations! They provide funds well ahead of the company's obligations to pay its creditors, particularly its suppliers, whose trade terms extend up to 60 days.

PROFIT MARGIN

The key to business efficiency is the profit per dollar of sales, which is called the *profit margin*. To calculate it, divide operating income by the total net sales (i.e., sales after returns, discounts, and so on) and express the result as a percentage. (Two alternatives to this standard profit margin calculation are also often made: A more general one called *gross profit margin* divides *gross* profit on sales by total net sales, and a more specific one called *net profit margin* divides *net* income by total net sales.) The standard way is as follows:

$$\frac{\text{Operating income}}{\text{Net sales}}$$

There is tremendous variation in profit margins across industries. Average profit margins in the automotive and banking industries, for example, are way lower (often around 10%) than they are in the computer, pharmaceutical, and food industries (as high as 40% in the case of Microsoft). The S&P 500 average profit margin is about 17.5%, right around where GE stands, while other conglomerates show margins of around 13 to 14%. Again, companies without earnings, such as Amazon.com, have negative profit margins.

Profit margins can be squeezed or expanded, depending in large measure on whether a business has a special franchise that gives it market power or competes in a commodity market where branding and product differentiation are harder. Coke and Pepsi constantly pursue product differentiation to exploit the possibility of raising prices without hurting unit volume, with varying degrees of success in various economic climates.

Amazon.com invests heavily in this kind of product differentiation, with a state-of-the-art Web site that includes patented features such as "one-click" and distinctive formatting. Yet competitors, including barnesandnoble.com and buy.com, easily mimic much of this would-be differentiation, quickly eroding profit margins.

The competition results in constant efforts to innovate and advance technology, whether in hamburger stands, on-line booksellers, or the beverage industry. Such innovation tends to hurt rather than help commodity businesses but benefits franchise businesses enormously. That is why Microsoft so jealously guards the code to its Windows operating system. It is why GE spends so many advertising dollars on campaigns such as "We bring good things to life," in which it highlights all dozen or so of its businesses without pitching particular products such as a washing machine or x-ray diagnostic equipment.

When a company develops a superior production system for a commodity product (such as oil), the bulk of the savings from that system goes to consumers rather than to the company. In contrast, a company that improves branded goods—those on which prices can remain high or be raised—reaps most of the upside from that innovation. Profit margins are driven up or down depending on the degree to which any business—whether GE, Microsoft, Amazon.com, or any other company—can differentiate its products to earn branded pricing and innovation power or else be left to bear the cross and costs of innovation.

A warning on profit margins is in order. Very high profit margins may seem desirable and often are, but they also invite competition that could destroy them. Very low profit margins are worth their level. Something in between, toward the high end, is ideal.

BANG FOR THE BUCK

"Returns" are a measure of the bang a business gets for its buck. The bang is always measured in terms of earnings. There are three bases (or bucks) against which to measure the bang: equity, investment, and assets.

In each measure, it is smart to gauge the return over a relatively long period of time—say, five to ten years—rather than over short periods to get a perspective that tracks a business's ability to weather the downsides and reap the upsides.

RETURN ON EQUITY

Return on equity is the amount a business earns on the capital owned by its shareholders. Shareholder capital is equal to the total assets minus the total liabilities. If a business earns $10 million on shareholder equity of $100 million, its return on equity is 10%.

Returns on equity were relatively high in the late 1990s and early 2000s. The S&P 500 average return on equity is around 22%. Below that average are specialty retailers (15%, other than Amazon.com, whose losses rather than profits give it a negative return on equity). At or somewhat above the average are GE (about 27%) and the conglomerate sector (about 25%) as well as the computer industry at about 25%. Leading the pack is Microsoft (about 34%).

RETURN ON INVESTMENT

Return on investment is the amount a business earns on both the capital owned by its shareholders and the capital supplied by lenders on a long-term (over one year) basis. A business may borrow capital rather than issue equity if it needs capital and believes it will generate greater returns on the capital than the costs of borrowing it.

Suppose a business with $100 million in shareholder equity borrows $50 million from long-term lenders and then generates earnings of $15 million on that total capital. Its return on investment will be 10% (15/150). But this leveraging boosts the business's return on equity—earnings of $15 million on shareholder equity of $100 million means a return on equity of 15%.

Using debt to boost return on equity is common but by no means imperative. Some companies generate sufficient cash from their operations to enable high returns on equity more cheaply than they could by borrowing. As was noted earlier, Microsoft is debt-free, generating returns on equity of nearly 34% and returns on investment that are just about the same (a similar near 1:1 ratio holds across the computer industry).

The norm among the S&P 500 is to use debt, driving the average return on equity to about 22% while return on investment is about 14%. GE exploits leverage with more spectacular results, with returns on equity of nearly 27% tripling return on investment of just above 9% (similar results hold across the conglomerate sector).

RETURN ON ASSETS

Return on assets is the amount a business earns on all its resources—not only shareholder equity and long-term borrowing but short-term resources generated by effective management of working capital. A business may seek short-term, low-rate loans or buy goods on credit that it resells for cash, thus increasing the assets available for deployment at low or no cost. Those assets contribute to incremental increases in earnings, boosting both return on equity and return on assets.

Suppose a business maintains an average amount of short-term assets of $20 million over a year (by continually repaying the obligations as they come due and incurring new ones as rollovers). That could increase incremental annual earnings by, say, $2 million. Thus, a company with shareholder equity of $100 million and long-term debt of $50 million, carrying that additional $20 million in the short term and earning $17 million, generates a return on assets of 10% (17/170). This deployment boosts return on investment to 11.3% (17/150) and return on equity to 17% (17/100).

Return on assets is thus the toughest measure of performance based on returns, as it reveals the results of deploying all the assets at management's disposal. Starting with a high return on assets should yield a high return on investment and hence on equity. (Some analysts calculate a "financial leverage index" equal to the return on equity divided by the return on assets.)

Higher returns on assets are achieved by squeezing earnings out of fewer or smaller asset bases. Microsoft starts off with a return on assets of 25%, suggesting a relatively low level of asset intensity, freeing it from dependency on debt and enabling it to generate returns on equity of nearly 10 points more. At the other extreme, GE starts off with a return on assets of just 3%, meaning it must manage its capital structure to use debt skillfully and deploy assets efficiently in order to get the higher returns on equity of about 27% that it achieves.

Microsoft is asset-nonintensive, whereas GE is quite asset-intensive. The earnings of many companies (Amazon.com maybe) are driven by brand names and/or inventory and distribution systems far more than by the plants and other physical resources that make up their balance sheet assets. Microsoft relies more on fixed and other assets but also is able to extract prodigious earnings from its brand name and market position. GE's asset-intensive business requires heavy investment in plants and equipment even as its products enjoy enormous brand recognition ("We bring good things to life").

It is too soon to tell how Amazon.com will fare in the contest for high returns on assets. Certainly its business model is designed to minimize asset intensity. Its brand name and Internet presence are the key drivers of sales and hence earnings. It minimizes its fixed asset needs by avoiding the bricks-and-mortar store operations to which Barnes & Noble and other traditional retailers devote resources.

Amazon.com's just-in-time inventory management is designed to reduce the carrying costs of inventory. Its trade terms with customers and suppliers drive incremental earnings by superior short-term working capital management—it receives revenues from customers as products are ordered but usually need not pay its suppliers for those goods until some 30 to 60 days later. Internet customers base purchases on pictures and images on the Internet screen, moreover, meaning Amazon.com does not suffer from books damaged by customers thumbing through them. Bricks-and-mortar bookstores incur losses from such damaged books (though they have the right to return damaged books to publishers, the result is often a lower discount on purchases from them). These characteristics of low asset intensity are extremely favorable to Amazon.com, though it remains a hard business to assess given its relative youth and negative earnings.

THE FULL TOOL CHEST

This tool chest of ideas helps you assess a company's liquidity, efficiency, and performance. The tools can be adapted from the basic metrics outlined here to deal with special situations and more advanced analysis.

A few examples of measures that help further gauge various aspects of a company's relative and probable future success are as follows. *Quality of income* (cash flows provided by operating activities divided by operating income) tells you what portion of income is actually turning into cash to gauge the liquidity position. The amount of annual *depreciation expense* can be a good proxy for future capital investment needs. *Sales per employee* helps evaluate overall productivity.

A company's key ratios vary with time, and any trends are important guides to managerial efficiency and performance. Therefore, you might look at all the expenses on the income statement over several years. There is no reason to automatically assume that any particular ratio or trends will continue, but history does help define probabilities for the future.

Suppose, for example, you see a large reduction in an expense for research and development. That would significantly increase income in a period. But growth in income resulting from the reduction in such an expense would not mean that the business is being managed more efficiently. It could even mean that there are reasons to worry about its prospects for growth in the future.

Or take receivables turns. Suppose the average number of collection days during a period increases materially in relation to the credit terms. Maybe part of any sales growth during the period is due to a relaxation in credit collection policies rather than to business efficiency. If those accounts are more likely to go uncollected, the sales growth might look good today but there'll be hell to pay tomorrow.

We could go on and on but don't need to.[3] Get acquainted with the key ratios mentioned above and you'll instantly be miles ahead of the crowd in your ability to distinguish strengths and weaknesses in numerous businesses within your circle of competence. Focus on the strong ones and keep looking—they might have the value you want, especially if they pass the tests in the next chapter.

CHAPTER 9

YOU MAKE THE CALL

A business is worth the present value of the future cash flows it generates from now until doomsday. Present value is in the eye of the beholder, for its realization is entirely in the future. People will disagree at virtually every step of the process of figuring present value, including the methods used and the different answers they yield.

Gazing into the cloudy crystal ball of valuation, you can never be sure of the accuracy of forecasts when you make them. Yet since your future wealth is at stake, you do not want to fly blindfolded even if you cannot predict the future. What you can do is minimize the hazards of your errors.

What drives cash flows are assets and earnings. These factors and historical cash flows are the best gauges for thinking about probable future cash flows. You could figure value based just on assets (something called book value), based just on earnings (what the earnings stream is worth), or from the cash flows (the worth of the dividends paid out to shareholders).

However, none of these separate valuation tools in itself is usually sufficient to determine the value of a business. Not only is none of them definitive, all of them together remain imperfect, for all share the inevitable and irremovable infirmity in any valuation exercise: using current and past information to forecast future cash flows. You'll need information about all these things to aid your judgment.

Some valuation tools are more useful for certain businesses than for others. For example, GE generates earnings and pays cash dividends, Microsoft generates earnings but does not pay cash dividends, and Amazon.com does neither. Obviously, you can value all three companies by using asset measures; you can value GE and Microsoft based on earnings, and GE based on dividends.

Less obviously, you could use all these tools—but in different ways—for all three companies. That is, estimated future earnings and dividends can be made for all three (relatively easy for GE, less so for Microsoft, and very hard for Amazon.com).

If these companies are within your circle of competence, you can do it. You can do it even if you are nervous about using the huge number of valuation techniques that are discussed in innumerable books or below because none of them will enable you or anyone else to pinpoint with precision what the value of any business is.

At best, these techniques produce a range of values that depend on your interpretation of history and prognosis for the future. These acts expose you and everyone else to risks of error, and those risks are precisely why Ben Graham insisted on getting a thick margin of safety between the price paid and the value one could reasonably expect to get. Every star investor follows that principle.

In the most famous chapter of *The Intelligent Investor*, Graham wrote: "In the old legend the wise men finally boiled down the history of mortal affairs into the single phrase, 'This too will pass.' Confronted with a like challenge to distill the secret of sound investing into three words, we venture the motto, MARGIN OF SAFETY."[1] Commenting on this passage over 40 years later, Warren Buffett said he still believes those are the right three words.[2]

Getting a wide gap between the price you pay and the value you buy is the cornerstone of intelligent investing because as Buffett says, while "intrinsic value can be defined simply," its calculation "is not so simple."[3] Graham invoked the margin of safety principle to avoid the risk of error in calculating intrinsic value. And while Charlie Munger—Buffett's business partner and alter ego—has quipped that he has never seen Buffett do an intrinsic value calculation, the principles that follow are part of the mind-set that enables him not to.

ASSETS

The book value of a company is the excess of its total assets as set forth on the balance sheet over its total liabilities and any outstanding preferred stock, also as set forth on the balance sheet. The book value per share of a common stock of that business is simply that amount divided by the number of common shares outstanding.

This use of the word "value" is misleading. Balance sheets list assets at their cost when acquired rather than their current value (or in some cases at current market values if lower). The balance sheet report of the carrying amount of assets does not reflect increases in value under current market conditions. And while the long-term assets are shown less the depreciation on them, that is only an approximation of what it would cost to replace them rather than an exact figure.

The range of book values per share is as broad as the range of businesses itself, and all those values reflect historical acquisition costs rather than current values. The book value per share of our sample illustrates this. GE's is about $12; Microsoft's, about $6; and Amazon.com's, about $2.[4]

These numbers correctly suggest that the usefulness of book value decays when more productive activity is performed with fewer rather than more tangible assets (as more production is generated not by, say, steel mills and other factories but by information technologies and Internet distribution systems). The fact that GE's book value per share is six times Amazon.com's may reflect more the greater asset intensity of GE's business compared to Amazon.com's than the value of those businesses.

For a whole range of businesses, the current accounting system based on historical cost is handicapped in appraising present and future values. For example, GE's property, plant, and equipment if sold at current market prices would fetch a substantial multiple of the book value per share; Amazon.com's might fetch only about what the book value says, chiefly because all its assets were acquired within the past few years.

Not only does this cost principle mean that some assets listed on a balance sheet are worth far more than their listed amount, it also means that the opposite is true. Even if book value purports to reflect the amount for which a company could be sold (its liquidation value), it cannot reflect the circumstances under which a sale is held. A business liquidation conducted under or caused by adverse conditions may lead to assets such as inventory and equipment and machinery being sold at a loss compared to their balance sheet carrying amounts.

For some companies, losses on major assets such as plants and warehouses can be enormous. If Disney were liquidated, for example, there is reason to doubt that its theme park fixed assets—an important part of its book value—could be sold at their book value.

Perhaps more obviously, if Coke were liquidated, its inventory of syrup and concentrate would undoubtedly fetch far less in a fire sale of those goods than the amount at which they are carried as inventory on its balance sheet.

This does not mean that the balance sheet is useless. It is a starting point for analysis. All the historical numbers can be adjusted to reflect prevailing economic conditions. On the upside, inflation and appreciation in market values can be acknowledged to arrive at a current measure of the financial value of assets. Guides to this adjusting of old numbers to new conditions include sales prices of similar property and increasing asset amounts based on changes in the consumer price index.

On the downside, the historical amount of assets recorded on a balance sheet can be reduced to the amount they could be sold for in a fire sale upon liquidation of the business. How much to reduce the amounts for things such as inventory and accounts receivable would depend on their respective turnover rates. Amazon.com's inventory, for example, turns so quickly (24 times a year) that even in a fire sale the company would probably be able to get rid of it at pretty close to cost (the amount listed on its balance sheet). Some of GE's inventory, which turns only eight times per year, might have to be sold at a loss.

Even those adjustments may not serve as an accurate basis for financial valuation, however, because of another accounting principle: the principle of economic or monetary exchange. A business enterprise may have financial value derived from intangible assets that are not recorded in the financial statements because they were not attributable to any discrete economic exchange. For example, only the cost of development of intellectual property (such as patents, trademarks, and copyrights) is recorded as an asset on the balance sheet even if the property is worth billions of dollars in the form of brand recognition or customer loyalty.

You undoubtedly recognize the GE brand name, for instance, and collective consumer recognition is certainly valuable, but you will not see any line item for GE's brand names and associated intellectual property on its balance sheet. The same is true for company know-how, employee capital and education, and similar items increasingly crucial to many companies in a wide variety of businesses, particularly but not exclusively companies such as Microsoft and Amazon.com.

These sources of value are referred to as economic goodwill, a bundle of intangible assets that enable a business to generate superior returns on equity, investment, and assets. They can, as was noted before, create a franchise or branding power that enables a business to increase prices without hurting total sales volume. Disney, for example, can raise ticket prices to Disneyland without hurting attendance.

Another sort of goodwill is called accounting goodwill. This is a record of prices paid for businesses a company acquired at a premium to book value. The economic value of accounting goodwill is even trickier to appraise. If the purchase was a prudent one, the value of the economic goodwill obtained is usually greater than the amount of accounting goodwill. That is especially true because another accounting rule requires that accounting goodwill be amortized—reduced annually by specified amounts over future decades. But again, if the businesses were smartly bought, the goodwill value should rise over those years rather than, as the amortization suggests, fall.

Sidestepping the need for these adjustments to the balance sheet, an old-fashioned rule of thumb championed by Ben Graham says that a common stock carries a sufficient margin of safety if it can be bought at a price equivalent to less than the company's net current assets,[5] that is, a price equal to per share working capital. This means that the buyer would pay nothing for the business's fixed assets. Such companies are so rare today that this tool in its pristine form is of little use.

But a modest variation retains the old rule's conservative rigor while still catching some fish. A business still qualifies if it can be bought for its net current assets plus, say, half the original cost of its fixed assets. Thus, the investor pays for net working capital at the stated value and gets a 50% discount for all the other assets. In the case of most companies today this would still be quite a low figure, but some companies—particularly smaller ones—end up in your nets.[6]

The potential trouble with these approaches is that they relegate you to being a bottom fisher—the person trolling for very low priced businesses. That is fine, but you need to be careful not to buy a dying fish. Bargain hunting leads to disaster if all you get is a burst of economic return but nothing in the long term. Prudent investors hunt for stocks with fair rather than cheap prices and strong rather than modest economic characteristics. As Warren Buffett advises, it is better to buy a great business at a fair price than a fair business at a great price.

A neophyte investor's mistake, in any event, is to assess business value solely on the basis of the balance sheet, even after overcoming the limits imposed by accounting principles. Unless you are indeed valuing a company for purposes of liquidating it, what you really want to know is not what its assets could sell for but what earnings and cash they spin off.

Graham recognized the limits of a balance sheet. Noting that it is quite useful with respect to working capital position, Graham cautioned that it is of less use concerning the carrying amount of fixed assets, which he said "must not be taken too seriously," and the figure at which intangible assets are listed, to which he said "little if any weight should be given."[7] He advised:

> It is true that in many individual cases we find companies with small asset values earning large profits, while others with large asset values earn little or nothing. Yet in these cases some attention must be given to the book value situation, for there is always a possibility that large earnings on the invested capital may attract competition and thus prove temporary; also that large assets, not now earning profits, may later be made more productive.[8]

Accordingly, Graham concluded that "book value is of some importance in analysis because a very rough relationship tends to exist between the amount invested in a business and its average earnings," where the real money is.[9]

EARNINGS

Earnings refer to accounting earnings as reported on the "bottom line" of an income statement. These figures are separated into basic earnings per share and diluted earnings per share. Basic earnings per share are the total earnings divided by the average number of common shares outstanding during the period.

Diluted earnings take account of the possibility that some convertible securities and stock options could increase the number of common shares outstanding. This reduces the earnings per share by taking into account the conversion or exercise of those instruments. Focus on the diluted earnings per share (and bear in mind that even that figure does not always reflect full dilution or cost of stock options issued to managers, as we will see later).

In assessing what the enterprise can do for you in the future, you only have present and past earnings available. How can present and past earnings guide an assessment of future earnings? Or which of various prior year earnings or which combination is the "right" level of earnings?

In GE's case, four recent annual diluted earnings per share were $2.16, $2.46, $2.80, and $3.22; in Amazon.com's, negative $.06, .$24, $.84, and $2.18 per share.

Perhaps you should use only the most recent period. But what if, as with GE and Amazon.com, there is significant change in that year compared to the prior years? One issue is, of course, why that change occurred. Was it due to extraordinary factors that are unlikely to recur?

If that is the case, using the prior periods might seem appropriate, though a more precise gauge for companies that periodically experience such extraordinary occurrences is to lengthen the period to seven to ten years to iron out those bumps. Alternatively, perhaps the business is experiencing a steady positive or negative trend in its earnings. In these cases, averaging the earnings over the last four years makes sense. In GE's case, that is about $2.66 (in Amazon.com's, negative $.83).

All these issues obviously entail judgment, and on top of that you must recognize that the estimate is about future earnings. Taking the average earnings over the past four years and projecting them forward to the next four years requires a further forecast of the earnings growth in the future period. Despite steadily rising losses, Amazon.com's management expects profits within a few years (as apparently do thousands of its stockholders, who at one point in the early 2000s drove its market capitalization to over ten times the combined totals of its profit-making archrivals Borders and Barnes & Noble!).

GE's earnings growth rate was about 12 to 15% in the late 1990s. You might cautiously expect similar or slightly slower growth in the early 2000s. Taking a conservative view of the future could justify a 10% growth rate—roughly $3.50, $3.90, $4.30, and $4.75, or an average of about $4.10.

In estimating earnings, note again the limits of accounting records. Accounting earnings result from subtracting cash expenses plus noncash expenses such as depreciation and bad debt reserves from gross revenue. This sounds simple, but the exercise entails making a number of decisions about how various events are accounted for. Accounting earnings are affected by a host of accounting conventions, including, for example, the method of computing the cost of goods sold, the method of depreciating fixed assets, and policies concerning allowance for bad debts.

But imperfect accounting rules are still effective. With respect to earnings (as distinguished from, say, book value), accounting rules work when properly and consistently applied. Even if depreciation expense for fixed assets such as computers is not a perfect gauge of the future costs of replacing them when they wear out, for example, it does capture a minimum reasonable amount that must be reinvested in the business to maintain its sales level and competitive position in the future.

Once a representative earnings figure is selected, the earnings must be discounted. Doing this requires a suitable discount rate (conventionally called the capitalization rate or cap rate). It is the rate of return required to compensate for the risk of making the investment, and so it is equal to the risk-free rate (that available on U.S. Treasury obligations) plus an additional amount to reflect the particular risk of the business.

Assume you determine that GE's expected earnings over the next four will be about $4.10 per share. The price you are willing to pay for the right to that $4.10 per share in the future is a function of the rate of return necessary to compensate for the risk that the $4.10 per year will not materialize. It will equal the risk-free rate—say, 3%—plus a premium to induce you to take the risk of owning GE stock.

A robust debate centers on what the right cap rates are for different businesses and types of investments. In general, the lower the risks involved in a particular type of business, the lower the cap rate. For example, if there is a high degree of certainty that a business will continue to perform as it has in the past, a cap rate in the range of around 10% is appropriate. For businesses that present moderate degrees of risk, a cap rate in the range of 15 to 25% is better. For particularly risky businesses, those where uncertainty about future success is great, an appropriate cap rate could range from 30 to 40% up to 100%.

Businesses whose earnings fluctuate widely in the ordinary course may be seen as subject to a greater risk that estimated earnings will vary. For example, banks and insurance companies whose assets consist largely of cash or investments are more exposed to cycles of economic change and may warrant a discount rate in the range of 8 to 12%. Consumer products businesses—those selling foods and detergents, for example—tend to remain more stable during periods of both boom and bust and thus generally warrant a lower-risk cap rate in the range of, say, 6 to 8%.

In addition to depending on the risk-free rate of interest, an appropriate cap rate takes into account the rate of economic growth in the overall economy. During periods of steady economic growth and industry expansion, risks are relatively lower. During economic downturns, growth is less likely, even steady earnings are less likely, and there is a greater likelihood of overall earnings contractions. In such an environment, risk rises, and you should choose higher cap rates.

Therefore, the rules of thumb for cap rates have to be set according to the risk-free rate, the risks of a particular business, and those of industry in general. Equally important, we must adjust the cap rate to allow for future variations. If interest rates rise or the economy slows, for example, the cap rate will have to be increased, and vice versa.

The difficulties in estimating earnings and selecting a cap rate relate back to your circle of competence. Just as an appreciation of economic history is essential, knowledge of the operating context is indispensable for the forecasting exercise. GE, Microsoft, and Amazon.com all look exceptionally well managed, with Amazon.com even scoring some knockout points in the key ratios, though GE and Microsoft also make money from good management.

GE is a money machine, particularly in its capital financing division. It delivered steady earnings increases throughout nearly all its 100 years and every year during the last 20. Its diverse businesses and leadership in virtually all of them suggest a reasonable basis for forecasting continued steady earnings generation in the future, though that is never free from doubt because of evolving economic environments. With GE's distinguished performance, however, a modest cap rate is perfectly reasonable.

Let's assume GE warrants a risk premium just above the risk-free rate—say, 5%—and apply it to our estimate of average future earnings of about $4.10. An estimate of GE's value can be made simply by dividing the earnings estimate by the cap rate, in other words, $4.10 divided by .05, which equals $82 per share.

If we took a slightly more aggressive guess about GE's earnings prospects, our valuation would look different. Suppose, for example, we forecast the earnings at $5.00. Still using the cap rate of 5%

would give us a value per GE share of $100 (5.00/.05). If you go further and deem a lower cap rate of, say, 4% more appropriate given GE's prowess and current business opportunities and conditions, the value per share shoots up to $125 (5.00/.04).

This play with the numbers gives a valuation for GE with a fairly wide range of $82 to $125. The range is broader yet if we take a more pessimistic view. If you use only the average earnings of the past four years of $2.66 and stick with our original discount rate of 5%, the valuation is about $53. If you believe the road ahead is riskier than the road just traveled so that a cap rate of, say, 6% is more suitable, the value becomes $44 per share, generating a "Texas range" from $44 to $125.

The selection of your earnings estimate and discount rate is crucial to this exercise. (A plausible range of values for Amazon.com, for example, starts from zero and goes to a few hundred dollars!) But even if you make those selections ruthlessly, your result cannot be the "answer" to the question of what a share of such stock is "worth." After all, there are plenty of steps in the process where your judgment could turn out to be wrong.

SILVER BULLETS AND THE MARGIN OF SAFETY

Most people agree that discount rates are driven by the risk-free rate of interest in effect from time to time, usually that available on U.S. government bonds that are deemed free of any default risk. This could range from the prevailing rate of about 3%, to the historical average of about 3.5%, to the present rate on inflation-protected government bonds of about 4%. Some people use bonds of shorter durations (such as 30 days instead of 30 years), but since equities are inherently long term (i.e., corporations have perpetual duration), it is probably better to use the long bond.

After settling on a risk-free rate, you then add a premium for your stock. The tendency is to look at the average rates of return on equities overall for long periods of time, which has been roughly 7%. That gives you an average risk premium of 3 to 3.5%, which must be tailored to the individual stock you are investigating. The rules of thumb mentioned above get you a long way here, though you should know that many try to be very precise about these matters.

Believers in the modern finance stories discussed earlier, for example, multiply the market risk premium by a stock's β to come up with an appropriate discount rate.

All this disagreement and the examples we've just gone through show you that there is plenty of play in the valuation enterprise. Tiny variations in your assumptions take the bottom line in widely different directions and magnitudes. A 1% change in your guess about the market premium, for example, throws off an appropriate level for the S&P Index by about 200 points (and more if you also play around with your estimate of future earnings growth rates).

Your best approach remains artistic judgment rather than scientific precision. Phil Carret made it one of his investing commandments to "ignore mechanical formulas for valuing securities."[10] Sorry to disappoint you if you expected magical solutions and think you haven't gotten them. In a sense, though, magic *is* what you get.

Graham delivered the silver bullet of investing when he said the three most important words in investing philosophy are "margin of safety." Recognizing that it is essentially impossible to pinpoint the precise intrinsic value of a business and that the best you can do is compute reasonable ranges of value based on reasonable assumptions, Graham thought you should give yourself a break by making sure the price you pay is way lower than the low end of your valuation estimate.

Graham called the margin of safety the central concept of investment because its essential function is to render an accurate estimate of the future unnecessary. In using it, you need not stress or struggle over the precise way to define the "right" risk premium, earnings, or discount rate so long as you have a reasonable approximation of what makes sense. Its secondary function is to absorb the effect of error in your assumptions—and remember, even tiny errors cause huge effects—as well as the effect of plain bad luck.

Graham observed that most investing errors are made not so much by paying too high a price for high-quality stocks as by buying low-quality stocks during times of economic prosperity (much as in early 2000s America). Indeed, Graham repudiated a strategy that overemphasizes what the fashion plates of finance call growth stocks. If you can get the same margin of safety by carefully estimating the future of growth stocks, more power to you, but the danger is that growth stocks tend to be favorites and favoritism in stocks is measured by high prices that steal safety margins.[11]

Graham said the margin of safety principle ultimately served as the touchstone in distinguishing between investing and speculation. Those who deny the difference between price and value or fail to get a margin of safety take their seats at the roulette wheel. Place your bets!

CASH

The same judgment can be applied to the cash a company is expected to generate and pay to shareholders in the future. The cash dividend–based approach to valuation was championed by John Burr Williams, who argued as follows:

> Earnings are only a means to an end, and the means should not be mistaken for the end. Therefore we must say that a stock derives its value from its dividends, not its earnings. In short, a stock is worth only *what you can get out of it*.
>
> In saying that dividends, not earnings, determine value, we seem to be reversing the usual rule that is drilled into every beginner's head when he [or she] starts to trade in the market; namely, that earnings, not dividends, make prices. The apparent contradiction is easily explained, however, for we are discussing permanent investment, not speculative trading, and dividends for years to come, not income for the moment only.
>
> Of course it is true that low earnings together with a high dividend for the time being should be looked at askance, but likewise it is true that these low earnings mean low dividends *in the long run*. On analysis, therefore, it will be seen that no contradiction really exists between our formula using dividends and the common precept regarding earnings.[12]

Williams indicates that dividend discounting and earnings capitalization give the same answer (or range of answers) to the question of what a share of stock is worth.

This is the case because dividends are a subset of earnings. A corporation can deploy its earnings either by paying them out to shareholders as dividends or retaining them for reinvestment in the business. If the retained earnings generate a return equal to the cap rate, the value you get from capitalizing the earnings stream will be the same as the value you get from discounting the dividend stream.

Indeed, valuation by discounting dividends is analytically identical to the capitalization of earnings technique. An assumed dividend payment is divided by an assumed discount rate, just as an assumed earnings level was divided by an assumed cap rate. In each case, the questions are (1) What does the expected stream look like in terms of amount and growth? and (2) What is the risk that the amount and growth will not be realized?

The conceptual difference between the two techniques is that in discounting dividends you assume that the value of a share of stock is the present value of the expected dividend payments on it from now until doomsday. This makes sense because the value of the stock consists of the payment stream it yields while it is owned and when it is sold.

The only reason there will be a gain on sale is that some other investor wants to buy the payment stream, and so on. These investors may or may not be correct or even rational in that determination, but it is precisely differences in valuation judgments that lead to such exchanges anyway. As a result, the value of a share of common stock resides solely in its expected stream of cash dividends.

Discounting dividends is just as difficult as capitalizing earnings because both require selecting a highly sensitive discount rate. For dividend discounting, many people try to minimize this difficulty by using the subject's weighted average cost of capital. But that is not a uniquely correct number, and calculating it requires just as much judgment as they are trying to escape.

Calculating the weighted average cost of a company's indebtedness is relatively easy: It is the average interest rate on all long-term obligations weighted according to the various amounts of principal outstanding on each type of debt. Figuring out the cost of a company's equity capital is far harder.

The cost of equity is usually defined by what the market expects the annualized return on the stock to be, combining price appreciation and dividend payout. But what are we really doing here? In determining a stock's value, we are trying to figure out what the return is going to be. If your key variable in that figuring is what the market expects, you are begging the question. You are assuming the answer rather than analyzing the question.

You are better off forming your own value judgment. There is no formula to tell you the answer, as these examples emphasize. Your only friend at that point is the Graham-Buffett margin of safety, not Mr. Market (you may be fallible; we know Mr. Market is).

MARKET CIRCULARITY

The greatest deficiency in using market metrics for valuation is the problem of circularity. To say that a share of Exxon-Mobil is "worth" what the stock last traded for tells you nothing about how that last trade was valued. Of course we know how it was priced: by the forces of supply and demand in the stock market. We also know from Part I that those forces are far from rational; are infected by emotion, psychology, and noise; and may even be chaotic.

But that is all we know. None of this tells you whether the price is a product of analysis or hope or fear, is a product of discounting expected future earnings or cash flows, or is based on a determined multiple of book values or on hunches and guesses.

You can try to penetrate the problem of market circularity by remembering John Burr Williams's point that the value of any asset is the amount of cash flow it will generate in the future, discounted by the probability that those flows will materialize. You could argue that a collection of comparable assets yields a particular return and use that comparable return as the discounting factor. But not only are you left with the challenge of defining comparable assets, you still have not determined the basis on which those comparable assets have been valued (other than, again circularly, by the market's collective judgment).

Countless books and articles have been written about how interest rates and other returns are determined by the market, but no one knows for sure. Interest rates vary according to people's collective inclination to borrow for immediate consumption or invest for future consumption (say, at retirement). These inclinations are shaped not only by roughly quantifiable conditions such as productivity and returns and the supply of money but by behavioral and psychological conditions that are virtually impossible to measure and in any event are highly unstable.

People undoubtedly have specific expectations about returns from assets, but those expectations vary widely. Current survey data show that people who lived during or in the aftermath of the Great Depression now expect average annual returns on stock portfolios that are in line with their averages in the postwar period of close to 10% while younger people with only history lessons rather than personal memories of that period expect returns in line with those of the 1990s of closer to 20%. (A similar gap has existed in other periods, such as the late 1960s.)[13]

Neither of these groups is correct, for it is logically impossible to say that any person is correct about the future. But these sorts of expectations—founded in the infinitely complex map of human psychology and experience—furnish the underpinnings of the returns the market generates. Great expectations are inherently unreliable, and the circularity of market metrics remains impenetrable.

Once you have made the call about value, you have to go to Mr. Market to see what prices he is offering. While there, compare your estimation of value to a few price ratios before making a final decision.

There is no guarantee that stocks with low price ratios offer value higher than their price, but they are a good place to look. Nor do high price ratios automatically mean a stock is unattractive, since price still may be lower than value.[14] Businesses with attractive operating climates, liquidity and performance measures, and earnings records deserve a close look, particularly but not exclusively if all the price ratios are low and the return on equity is high.

PRICE/BOOK RATIO

The relationship between a company's stock market price and its book value is called the *price/book ratio (P/B ratio)*. It is equal to the market price per share divided by book value per share.

Comparing the P/B ratio of one business with its peers is a way to gauge how investors regard that business compared to others or the industry average. Higher P/B ratios mean that investors regard the stock more favorably.

The average P/B ratio for publicly traded stock in the early 2000s is around 2 to 3.5, with older, industrial companies (such as steel companies) sometimes trading at P/B ratios near or below 1 and newer, technology-oriented companies (such as computer software manufacturers) sometimes trading at P/B ratios as high as 20 or more.

In our crop, Amazon.com's P/B ratio leads the league at above 40, with Microsoft at about 15 and GE at 10. While none of these fits the bill, if you find a stock trading below a P/B ratio of 1, you can buy that stock for a price below the company's net worth. Such stocks are rare and certainly warrant further investigation.

PRICE/SALES RATIO

For most companies, a strong relationship between a company's value and its sales levels should exist. Sales drive growth. More sales mean more earnings. A company cannot grow faster than its sales, but it can grow more slowly with poor management, which will be reflected in poor efficiency and performance ratios.

The sales figure is also less affected by accounting conventions. Since it is the top-line number on the income statement, pretty much the only accounting rules affecting sales relate to the timing of their recognition. While that can be manipulated to an extent (this is discussed further in Chapter 10), it is far purer than the bottom-line earnings number, which can be affected by scores of accounting conventions.

Calculate the *price/sales ratio (P/S ratio)* by dividing the stock price by the sales per share (this is not commonly reported in financial statements but is an easy calculation to make). Alternatively, you can follow the conventional but equivalent method of dividing the total market capitalization (price times shares outstanding) by the total sales. Either way, if you can buy a stock for a price that is equal to or less than the company's sales, you are on your way to getting a good margin of safety.

In our group, Microsoft is richly priced compared to its sales at a P/S ratio of about 20, with Amazon.com also heftily priced at about 15, and GE at about 5. No bargains exist on these numbers, but again, if you can find a company with a low P/S ratio, particularly one that also has high profit margins, you are getting good value for money.

PRICE/EARNINGS RATIO

Investors commonly use market prices to compare businesses by relating trading prices to earnings per share. This is called the *price-earnings ratio (P/E ratio)*, and it is computed by dividing the market price of a share of common stock by the company's earnings per share. The limitations of using the earnings multiple for valuation and the ruthlessness required to specify a cap rate explain the popularity of P/E ratios as guides for selection.

In general, higher P/E ratios suggest that investors are more optimistic about a company's prospects than they are about comparable businesses with lower P/E ratios. The historical breakpoint for high and low P/E ratios has been 15—above that was high, and below it was low. Very high P/E ratios (anything above 50) imply loads of optimistic investors swooning over a company's prospects. However, the relative levels of P/E ratios also vary with a company's growth outlook, industry, relative maturation (rookie, vintage, or classic), and accounting policies used in calculating net income. Don't count on P/E ratios being comparable across companies.

The P/E ratios of our group of companies fluctuated wildly during the 1990s and early 2000s, along with the volatile overall market. But suppose the market price of a share of common stock sits between 25 and 50 and suppose its average earnings per share are around $1.00. The P/E ratio thus has ranged from 25 to 50. The *implied cap rate* hovers between 2% and 4%. Does that mean you should use such rates? Why would it? But suppose a stock had a P/E ratio of 5. Now that sounds like a deal with a thick margin of safety.

ECONOMIC VALUE ADDED

Consider an all-industry metric created (and trademarked!) by a business consulting firm that apparently has realized that the marketplace is thirsting for new tools to justify all kinds of crazy ideas.[15] The tool has been cleverly named "economic value added" (EVA). It says that a company's performance can be evaluated in terms of whether returns on capital are higher than costs of capital. If they are, value is being added.

Though the components of the EVA calculation are simple to state—the company's return on capital minus its weighted average cost of capital—we already know that pinning down the latter is a lot harder than it sounds.

For EVA, the weighted average cost of capital could be defined simply as the appropriate discount rate at which to value the company, but that doesn't escape the circularity trap. Or it could be the cost of the company's indebtedness—the average interest rate paid on its debt during the measured period. But if that is all it is, then EVA is just another name for leverage.

If it includes a mixed measure of the cost of debt and the expected return on equity, the measure not only still has the problem of circularity but also gets nonparsimonious. All it really tells you is by how much a company beat expectations. If return on equity last year was 10% and the market this year expects the same 10% but the company actually has delivered 12%, EVA says it increased value by an additional 2%—but you don't need a name like EVA to tell you that.

Worse, part of the motivation to develop tools such as EVA was to overcome earnings management techniques: managerial manipulation of revenue recognition timing, restructuring charges, and others discussed in the next chapter. These techniques proliferate in proportion to investor emphasis on (or obsession with) whether a company meets analysts' earnings expectations. EVA exacerbates rather than solves the problem, because it applauds managers only when they exceed expectations.

Moreover, if EVA is intended to measure a company's ability to generate profits for shareholders on the amount of their invested capital, it potentially suffers from the same weaknesses of traditional financial ratios: They all rely on the integrity of the underlying accounting data used to calculate profit. EVA tends to increase rather than reduce pressure on managers to manipulate (or make up) numbers.

None of this denies the underlying insight of EVA: assessing performance based on how much extra return is generated from a dollar of investment. Indeed, in evaluating managerial performance, we should deduct from reported results a charge for the capital employed in producing them (something rarely done, especially in connection with reports and rewards of stock options tied to returns, a subject discussed in Part III). For some companies—Coke under Roberto Goizueta, for example—returns on capital are so impressive that even with difficulties in pinning down the cost of capital, there is no question that returns exceed costs by impressive distances.[16]

Obsession with EVA puts a false premium on precision, just as the tools of modern finance discussed earlier do. Though he believes in the basic idea underlying EVA, Warren Buffett often says he prefers to be approximately right than precisely wrong. Speaking publicly at the Berkshire Hathaway 2000 annual shareholders meeting, Charlie Munger put it more epigrammatically with a characteristically ungloved denunciation of EVA: "bullshit."

Graham's comments on market price and business value are worth memorizing:

> The accepted idea that a common stock should sell at a certain ratio to its current earnings must be considered more the result of practical necessity than of logic. The market takes the trend or future prospects into account by varying this ratio for different types of companies. Common stocks of enterprises with only slight possibilities of increasing profits ordinarily sell at a rather low price-earnings ratio (less than 15 times their current earnings); and the common stocks of companies with good prospects

of increasing the earnings usually sell at high price-earnings ratio (over 15 times the current earnings). . . .

When neither boom nor deep depression is affecting the market, the judgment of the public on individual issues, as indicated by market prices, is usually quite good. If the market price of some [stock] appears out of line with the facts and figures available, it will often be found later that the price is discounting future developments not then apparent on the surface. There is, however, a frequent tendency on the part of the stock market to exaggerate the significance of changes in earnings both in a favorable and unfavorable direction. This is manifest in the market as a whole in periods of both boom and depression, and it is also evidenced in the case of individual companies at other times.

At bottom the ability to buy [stocks] successfully is the ability to look ahead accurately. Looking backward, however carefully, will not suffice, and may do more harm than good. Common stock selection is a difficult art—naturally, since it offers large rewards for success. It requires a skillful mental balance between the facts of the past and the possibilities of the future.[17]

CHAPTER 10

MAKING (UP)
NUMBERS

Accounting shenanigans have plagued bookkeeping since it was invented by Luca Pacioli in 1494, and there is no reason to expect that the next 500 years will stray from the historical pattern. No amount of rule making—from accounting, auditing, or elsewhere—can ensure the integrity of financial reporting. Rules cannot eliminate managerial discretion, and there will always be the possibility of imaginative, unorthodox, creative, and even fraudulent financial reporting.

Investors and managers should expect it and, instead of wishing it away, take pains not to be its victims or accomplices. Just think of the notorious accounting frauds of relatively recent memory—from Leasco, National Student Marketing, and Penn Central in the late 1960s and early 1970s to Cendant, MicroStrategy, and Sunbeam in the late 1990s and early 2000s. These frauds sting investors, and managers who engage in them should know they will be caught, punished, and made to pay (though investors will not profit in the process).

The nonfraudulent cases are often the trickier to deal with. They consist of a variety of *smoothing techniques* designed to massage the whole range of financial numbers, from the ratios discussed previously to income itself. Income smoothing, also known as earnings management, exploits the flexibility of generally accepted accounting principles to classify transactions or allocate them by time period to achieve favorable financial reporting.

PERENNIALS

SEC Chairman Arthur Levitt delivered a series of major speeches in the late 1990s and early 2000s identifying several long-standing accounting issues that are hallmarks of earnings management. These techniques are as old as accounting itself and have been used to full advantage (sometimes appropriately, often not) by managers over the centuries. Yet the contemporary problems are heightened, according to Levitt, by a managerial obsession with meeting consensus earnings estimates formulated by the increasingly influential profession of investment analysis.

This dizzying obsession with "making numbers" is documented by the accounting professors David Burgstahler of the University of Washington and Ilia Dichev of the University of Michigan.[1] They show that about one in ten managers facing small declines in earnings manage to show earnings increases, and that about four in ten facing negative earnings manage to report positive earnings! The obsession with "making numbers" leads managers to make them up.

Levitt singled out five issues of particular concern, giving each a catchy phrase intended, one supposes, for both poetic and mnemonic value.

- *Big bath.*   Big bath accounting is a particularly aggressive version of earnings management that is sort of a financial face-lift. It lumps major events adversely affecting income in current periods to facilitate improved financial appearances in succeeding periods. It is particularly common in, but by no means limited to, costs occasioned by acquisitions, divestitures, reorganizations, and other extraordinary organic business changes. These transactions call for numerous accounting judgments in regard to both timing and classification. Managers often expense as much of the potential cost of a transaction at the time it is consummated as possible. It's also tempting to give current earnings a "big bath" in one year to create a brighter-looking future when the year is so dismal anyway that investors have written it off (this happens all the time, even at otherwise reputable companies).
- *Merger magic.*   This describes a subset of creative accounting in acquisitions. If a business buys another business for a price higher than the seller's book value, the buyer in most cases must record an asset called accounting goodwill (discussed in the last chapter) and amortize that account as an expense over future decades. That reduces earnings over that period. To minimize the reduction, a buyer's manager can allocate some or a lot of that excess to other things, most notoriously to in-progress research-and-development

(R&D) costs. Accounting rules require such R&D costs to be expensed when incurred (rather than amortized), and so many buyers allocate that excess as a one-time expense at the merger time even when that allocation defies business reality.

* *Cookie jar reserves.*   This entails the overestimation or underestimation of things such as sales returns by publishers, probable loan losses of lending institutions, and warranty obligations for manufacturers. The incorrect estimation enables managers to adjust and smooth out earnings as actual earnings vary from expected earnings period to period.

* *It's not material.*   The materiality principle requires the reporting of items that are material and allows the nonreporting of items that are not. Materiality is not an absolute concept but entails making judgments. A standard legal formulation for public corporations under federal securities laws is whether an item would be important to an investor in making an investment decision about a security (the accounting rule similarly asks whether it would influence a reasonable person's judgment). Judgments concerning materiality are often guided by rough rules of thumb. One rule of thumb accountants and auditors often use in determining materiality is whether a particular item entails more than, say, a 5% impact on a company's earnings. But applying such a simple rule could lead to excluding things that are meaningful to a user of the financial statements in a qualitative sense.

* *Wine before its time.*   This image of popping open a bottle of wine before it matures reflects the premature recognition of revenue. For instance, a toy manufacturer may tag goods in a warehouse as "sold" even though they are not and may never be sold, or a distributor of cell phones may record revenue for merchandise that it shipped and received payment for but that is subject to free return by the buyer for a period of, say, 90 days.

To address these manipulations, the SEC called for immediate and coordinated action, seeking nothing less than a fundamental change in American corporate culture. Levitt articulated a multifaceted program, beginning with instructing the SEC staff to scrutinize financials for abuses of restructuring accounting and accruals for losses and reserves. He asked the American Institute of Certified Public Accountants (AICPA) to clarify auditing rules concerning purchased R&D, large acquisition write-offs, and revenue recognition. He also instructed the SEC staff to focus on materiality not solely in quantitative terms but also in qualitative terms, reject the notion that materiality can excuse minor errors, and promulgate new standards on revenue recognition.

Levitt also called on private standard-setting organizations to join the cause, particularly asking the Financial Accounting Standards Board (FASB) to reconsider the definition of liabilities under generally accepted accounting principles. He encouraged the Public Oversight Board to review and intensify its focus on the audit committees of boards and recruit more members with financial backgrounds (as opposed to legal, marketing and public service backgrounds). He envisioned audit committees meeting more often and asking tougher questions—what he called a "private sector response." He impaneled a blue ribbon commission to report on ways to enhance the audit committee's role and ultimately called upon management itself and Wall Street to revitalize integrity in financial reporting by cooperating and supporting these initiatives.

This program emboldened the SEC to prosecute scores of enforcement actions against companies engaged in earnings management of the sort Levitt highlighted. The SEC adopted tougher rules governing audits, including a requirement that quarterly financial statements be reviewed by auditors, and materiality rules that expressly deal with qualitative and quantitative dimensions.[2]

Audit committees must now review and vouch for the accuracy of financial statements, provide a report in proxy statements concerning whether they signed off on the financial statements, state whether a written charter spells out the committee's duties, and submit any such charter to the SEC every three years. The stock exchanges adopted rules requiring listed companies to disclose whether members of the audit committee are independent of management and requiring audit committee members to have a financial background.[3]

Levitt's ambitious crusade is ongoing, and investors should support those who carry it out. No amount of effort, however, can eliminate the inevitable flexibility that generally accepted accounting principles provide or the temptations or capitulations to which they lead. It remains for the intelligent investor to monitor financial reporting with measured skepticism and stay alert to the possibility of distortion. While the past is no guarantee of the future, it certainly is prologue, and as early as 1936 Ben Graham lampooned corporate

America for its abuses of financial reporting, as have many since, most notably City University of New York accounting professor Abraham Briloff.[4]

SATIRE

Graham satirically hypothesized a phantom US Steel Corporation adopting "advanced bookkeeping methods" to report "phenomenally enhanced" earnings without any cash outlays or changes in operating conditions or sales. To update that illustration of accounting chicanery, consider how a phantom company might today achieve the same results by using techniques like those Levitt denounces. Its press release and accompanying financial reports might look like this:

E-America Dot.Com Announces Positive Earnings

E-America Dot.Com today announced positive earnings, stunning Wall Street analysts whose consensus view estimated continued negative earnings for the start-up that went public last year. Its stock price shot up 40% on the news. Though this response is usually reserved for companies that report negative earnings, we believe it is justified for the same sort of reasons—none.

Rather than taking any action to increase sales or improve its products, marketing strategy, distribution channels, or customer service, the earnings increase was due to improvements in the manner in which the company's economic activity is recorded in its books. These new bookkeeping methods report profits of $50 per share instead of the $25 loss per share that otherwise would be reported. The accounting improvements consist of the following steps:

- Modifying revenue recognition policies
- Adjusting reserves and treatment of returns
- Recording the value of market share as an asset
- Recording the amount of cash we "burn" as an asset
- Reporting in a different currency
- Refining the concept of materiality

The Board of Directors of E-America Dot.Com, in collusion with their auditors, reached the following conclusions in adopting this program in a resolution unanimously approved at its board meeting this week:

The Board of Directors and its Independent Outside Auditors, after careful study and review, determined that the accounting policies and practices the company used since its recent initial public offering ten months ago are outdated and do not reflect the kind of performance managers of the company expect or predict.

The Board and its Auditors, aided and abetted by a special audit committee, determined that many other companies obtain a competitive advantage in the capital markets by reporting accounting results in terms of innovative, cutting-edge techniques and that the company was penalized for failing to follow these best practices, referred to as the "New Accounting."

Adopting the New Accounting will neutralize this disadvantage and enable the company to increase its market capitalization without the need for disbursing cash or changing any of its operating activities. The changes adopted by the Board, with the attestation of its Auditors, are as follows:

MODIFYING REVENUE RECOGNITION POLICIES

Competitive conditions in our industry lead us to give generous credit terms to our customers. These include giving them the right to return goods to us for a full refund if they cannot resell them to the ultimate consumer within 180 days. We formerly deferred recognizing the revenue in connection with such transactions until after that 180-day period passed on the grounds that no sale was complete until then.

But this old economy policy substantially reduced the amount of reported sales reflected on our income statement. The Board decided to treat those transactions as sales right away, on the grounds that our sales team put tireless effort into generating them and should get credit. (We can make adjustments for returns later, but for now we would rather report the good news in the short term and defer the bad news for the long term.)

In particular, we will occasionally "park" inventory with our customers, to whom we give unconditional return rights either orally or in "side letters" kept separate from the sales documents. As a result of this scheme, we will report much higher sales revenue and dramatic increases in earnings. If adjustments must be made to smooth those earnings, we will restate past earnings in subsequent quarterly reports and disclose that these resulted from a problem with the "collectibility" of our accounts receivable.

ADJUSTING RESERVES AND TREATMENT OF RETURNS

In the financing arm of our business, we intend to reduce the amount of reserves we record for delinquent and uncollectible accounts by reporting them as current. To do so, we will in some cases simply extend the due dates of our customers' obligations. In others, we will assume that we can repossess the items secured by these delinquent loans whether or not that is feasible. This enables us to record far lower reserves in our allowance for credit losses, thus increasing our net income.

Similarly, in all of our businesses, we will record customers' returns of merchandise as purchases of goods rather than charging them against our reserves for returns. Another benefit of this new policy is to increase our receivable turns, making our operations look speedier and more efficient.

RECORDING THE VALUE OF MARKET SHARE AS AN ASSET

A hot trend in the marketplace for traders and speculators is to assign a value to Internet companies based on the percentage of their product market their sales levels represent. This is necessary to justify the stratospheric prices being paid for stocks of these companies in initial public offerings and in exchange trading. After all, most of these companies do not generate any earnings or even positive cash flows. Staying ahead of the stampede, we are moving one logical step further by listing the value of this market share on our balance sheet as an asset.

Every quarter we will gauge the amount of value the market is giving us based on our market share and record that in an asset account called market share. This may seem like a "belts-and-suspenders" policy given that our other New Accounting changes will enable us to report actual earnings and actual cash flows which otherwise would be negative. Nevertheless, we believe that this is what shareholders and market players want, and we are just trying to cooperate.

RECORDING THE AMOUNT OF CASH WE "BURN" AS AN ASSET

Companies with negative cash flows sometimes get credit for the amount of cash they raise and spend on researching new products. This is especially true in the biotechnology industry, but we see no reason why the logic of that approach should not extend to our businesses as well. Speculators and traders give substantial valuation credit for this cash burn.

Beginning today, we will treat the amount of our cash burn as an asset on the balance sheet rather than as an expense on the income statement. On the other hand, because of the significant impact that the treatment of disbursed cash as an expense or an asset has on our earnings, we reserve the right from time to time to alternate between these treatments, depending on the trend in reported earnings from quarter to quarter.

REPORTING IN A DIFFERENT CURRENCY

We sell many of our products and conduct a clearinghouse operation for other businesses in a barter exchange Web site on the Internet. In lieu of trading (or bartering) such goods and services directly, however, exchange members use our trademarked "dot-com dollars," issued to them by us for the purpose of bartering. These dot-com dollars have a face value far greater than the U.S. dollar and we propose to record certain of our assets and sales transactions in dot-com dollars rather than U.S. dollars, thereby substantially increasing the amounts of reported assets and income (we are not fools, however, so expenses and liabilities, of course, will continue to be reported in U.S. dollars).

REFINING THE CONCEPT OF MATERIALITY

Lawyers and auditors often place great weight on whether some economic event is material to our company or not. They define materiality in terms of what a reasonable investor thinks about its impact on the business or financial condition of the company. In the past, this led us to report in our financial statements details that don't really seem to matter very much to the managers at our company or to other owners of options on our stock.

To reconcile managerial needs with the requirements of financial reporting, the board adopted a new rule of materiality. Under it, no economic activity is material to the company unless it impacts our earnings by at least 5%. This rule is more definitive and reliable than the old rule and will result in greater certainty in our bookkeeping department. By applying this approach to materiality, we can ignore a variety of burdensome reporting questions, thus saving (material) basketfuls of money.

As satire, the report from E-America Dot.Com reveals how atrocious and distorted aggressive accounting and earnings management can be. (Most of the examples are based on actual cases.) However, you will never see the kind of candor expressed in this news release coming out of corporations. That kind of honesty is inconsistent with the goals underlying the shenanigans.

Accordingly, you will not recognize financial disingenuousness, recklessness, aggressiveness, deception, or fraud when you see it unless you know how to look. You will find the following examples of recent financial chicanery helpful and will benefit from constant perusal of the reports of financial deception chronicled virtually daily in newspapers, newsletters, and reputable Web sites.

In thinking about such charades, note that many frequently criticized techniques are not always unlawful and do not necessarily violate generally accepted accounting principles. Often, however, they impair the integrity of financial reporting. Worse, a corporate or financial reporting culture that condones aggressive practices creates the risk of degradation of financial reporting: What starts as merely aggressive can create pressure that leads reporting over the line and into the fraudulent.

There is always pressure to engage in accounting shenanigans. Many scandals suggest that irregular accounting is especially acute at businesses with poor economic characteristics and those facing tough competitive conditions. A company's contractual profile may increase pressure for aggressive or irregular accounting. Many loan agreements, for example, contain promises by the borrower to maintain certain financial ratios, including debt-to-equity ratios and the others discussed earlier, and can lead managers to meet those promises by finessing.

Incentive compensation agreements triggered by meeting sales or earnings targets may encourage accounting games. Similar pressures emerge from settlement agreements, consent decrees, and the other legal obligations a company faces. Planning for additional financing can produce pretty pictures despite dismal performance. More generally, in an investment climate obsessed with short-term results, as Levitt cautioned, there is invariably pressure to sustain steady increases in earnings growth.

CHARADES

There are lots of aggressive accounting techniques and opportunities for difficult judgment calls, and so it would be surprising for any two scandals to be identical.[5] However, most accounting scandals have a simple common denominator: Earnings are inflated. One of the most common ways to inflate earnings is to treat as an asset or liability something that should be treated as an expense. This deception hides the costs of doing business on the balance sheet so that they never burden the income statement.

Dissecting most accounting scams requires only a rudimentary understanding of simple bookkeeping rules and their relationship to financial statements. Double-entry bookkeeping requires a debit and a credit in equal amounts for every transaction. The double entries keep a balance sheet equalized (assets always equal liabilities plus net worth) and reflect the direct relationship between income (revenue minus expenses) and net worth.

More particularly, increases in asset or expense accounts require debits, and decreases in them require credits; increases in liability or revenue accounts require credits, and decreases in them require debits. These bookkeeping rules are invariant, and so short of making up or not recording transactions, the trickery involves classifying transactions as assets or expenses or as liabilities or revenues.

PEARSON/PENGUIN

Consider how the Pearson conglomerate accounted for book sales through its Penguin publishing division. Sales made on credit require two entries in equal amounts: a debit to Accounts Receivable, the asset account, and a credit to Sales, the revenue account. Subsequent receipt of the cash payment requires a debit to Cash and a credit to Accounts Receivable.

Penguin began granting 10% discounts off its list price to selected buyers who paid their accounts early. Following bookkeeping rules, receipt of those early cash payments called for a credit to Accounts Receivable equal to 100% of the list price. Since the buyer received a 10% discount on the price, the debits should have been made to Cash for 90% of the list price, with the other 10% going to an expense account. Adding it up, those 10% discount expenses would have reduced reported earnings.

Instead of following these standard bookkeeping rules, Pearson apparently recorded receipts of early payments as a debit to Cash for 90% of the list price and a credit to Accounts Receivables for 90% of the list price, and so the 10% discount never showed up as an expense. It simply remained part of the asset account—Accounts Receivable—and artificially inflated reported earnings.

While Penguin's 10% individual discounts given on a per customer basis may at first seem like small change, they aggregated over six years to $163 million. Pearson's management eventually discovered the buried discounts when integrating Penguin and Pearson's newly acquired Putnam Berkley publishing house. Dirty bookkeeping then turned into housecleaning.

MERCURY FINANCE

In January 1997 Mercury Finance announced that it had overstated earnings for the first three quarters of 1996 and for the whole of 1995 by a total of more than 100%. All corporate hell broke loose at Mercury Finance, a company in the business of lending to consumers with weak credit ratings. Its CEO and controller both left, a turnaround specialist was recruited, and pending deals with the Bank of Boston and Salomon Brothers were terminated. It lacked cash to meet its maturing commercial paper obligations and teetered on the edge of bankruptcy.

The company and the consumer finance industry made headlines every other day. Some commentators correctly noted that many companies in high-risk businesses like Mercury Finance's use "aggressive accounting techniques"; other so-called experts incorrectly stated that accounting in finance companies is "extraordinary complex." It is not all that complex.

To lenders, loans are assets even though some loans are unlikely to be repaid. Bad loans are an expense—a cost of doing business. Expenses reduce net income. Estimating the amount of bad loans may involve complex judgments, but the accounting is simple. The portion of loans deemed uncollectible is recorded as an expense (a debit). The credit is to an account called Allowance for Doubtful Receivables.

Instead of treating all bad loans as expenses, Mercury Finance apparently decided that even if a borrower was not going to pay, somehow the company would recover the money (by repossessing the borrower's car, for example). In the bookkeeping, a debit was made to an asset account called Other Assets to reflect the right to repossess rather than to an expense account to reflect that the loan probably was never going to be paid. With fewer reported expenses, Mercury Finance reported far higher earnings.

A bright red flag flew over Mercury Finance's financial statements. The Other Assets account on its balance sheet rocketed from $24.6 million at the end of 1994 to $121 million a year later. Even if the account included other assets besides repossession rights, the striking increase should have seemed peculiar to anyone with a little accounting sense (or even common sense).

AMERICA ONLINE

America Online's asset- and expense-flipping imbroglio resulted from treating disbursements for developing a subscriber base not as a cost of doing business (an expense) but as an investment in the business (an asset). While this is exactly what was done in the National Student Marketing scandal of the late 1960s and early 1970s, there was a judgment to make here.

One could liken on-line services to newspapers and follow that industry's practice of expensing these costs, or one could analogize to direct mail order companies and follow that industry's practice of capitalizing them—treating them as assets whose cost is allocated over future accounting periods.

In choosing between these treatments, the accounting issue is whether the disbursements will contribute reliably to revenue generation in future periods. As it turned out, America Online could not gauge for how long its new subscribers would remain customers, and so there was no basis for saying the disbursements would increase future revenue.

Maybe it was reasonable for AOL's managers and auditors to make the judgment they made. After the horrible press coverage and class action shareholder lawsuit that resulted, however, you can be sure they regret it.

As with Mercury Finance, a telltale red flag flew high: AOL's balance sheet showed an unusual asset called Deferred Subscriber Acquisition Costs. Mushrooming to $385 million between August 1995 and October 1996, it became the largest asset on AOL's balance sheet. Angry shareholder agitation forced AOL to abandon the practice in the fall of 1996 and restate its earnings, wiping out about 80% of owners' equity.

FABRI-CENTERS

Judgment plays a critical role in corporate accounting decisions, enabling managers to persuade auditors and directors to accept their position when choosing to expense or capitalize a transaction or make other accounting decisions. Even when the managerial decision is accepted, full disclosure about the judgment should be included in the company's financial statements but isn't always.

If you have any doubt about the need for disclosing these difficult judgment calls, consider the enlightening story behind the settlement of SEC charges against Fabri-Centers, an operator of over 900 retail stores, including the JoAnn Fabrics chain. Fabri-Centers knew the daily sales figures at its stores but could not determine the cost of goods sold or the profit margin until it conducted an annual inventory, and so it estimated them, using the so-called gross profit method of applying the prior year's actual profit margin to calculate quarterly profits for the succeeding year.

During several quarters, however, heavy price competition substantially eroded the margin. Before the erosion was reported or publicly disclosed, the company effected a public debt offering. The SEC charged Fabri-Centers with inadequate disclosure about price competition and its estimation practice in that offering.

Under Fabri-Centers' inventory system (it has since been modernized), a judgment about quarterly profit margins was necessary. But those involved in the debt offering—aware that the quarterly financial statements were unaudited and prepared in anticipation of the offering—should have paid greater attention to the role that accounting estimates played.

SUNBEAM

Sunbeam committed a distinct but all too common type of accounting fraud. Its widely publicized accounting machinations boiled down to a series of so-called bill-and-hold transactions. During the winter months, it recorded charcoal grill sales even though the grills were not to be shipped until the spring. This manipulative maneuver enabled it to report higher sales in the winter.

The accounting shenanigan took place near the end of the reign of the self-proclaimed turnaround king Al Dunlap. Upon taking the helm at Sunbeam—which was floundering from a substantial business downturn—Dunlap fired half its workers and closed or consolidated more than half its facilities. Boasting that he aimed to "attack" his company, Dunlap declared that his plan was as carefully plotted as the invasion of Normandy. (Alas, Dunlap is no Churchill, and all his plans for Sunbeam failed miserably.) With that kind of siege mentality driving the company, accounting irregularities might not have been inevitable, but they were certainly made more likely.

MICROSTRATEGY

Sunbeam's travails of revenue recognition have spread through other businesses, especially the computer software companies that Levitt singled out for special illustration. One of the most dramatic examples of the potential fallout occurred at the software company MicroStrategy.

MicroStrategy entered into several unusual contracts under which it bought and sold something from the other party. The dual deal enabled MicroStrategy to record revenue much earlier than accounting rules permit and to obscure that accounting from the auditors reviewing its books.

Pressure from journalists compelled the company and its auditors to scrutinize those contracts, and they ultimately decided the earlier accounting had been incorrect. Shazam! When the company finally came clean, its stock price plunged from $245 to $87 per share (over a 60% wipeout). Who lost? Popeyed shareholders.

CENDANT

Obfuscatory language in corporate disclosure signifies brewing trouble. This is only one of the scores of lessons learned from the notorious accounting scandal that unfolded in the late 1990s at Cendant Corporation, a company formed by the merger in late 1997 of CUC International and HFS Inc.

CUC operated a members-only discount shopping service that

generated revenue through membership dues. On average, membership clubs like these earn greater profits from long-term members than from short-term members. Indeed, the tendency is to make zero profit from members enrolled less than a year because they are typically entitled to a cancellation refund of dues.

As early as 1989, CUC met with some accounting embarrassment for its practice of recognizing as revenue the total amount of each membership payment in the period it was received while expensing amounts allocable to each membership over a three-year period. In bookkeeping terms, it debited revenue while crediting both an expense account and some liability account, a mismatching that boosted reported earnings.

Although CUC retreated from that position after harsh criticism by financial analysts and others, it continued practicing aggressive accounting in other areas. Chief among these practices was its reporting technique for membership flow and annual renewal rates—important information for gauging company prospects given that newer members contribute little or nothing to the bottom line while the real value is in long-term members.

Among new members enrolled at the end of a given year, 70% renewed, but the way CUC reported this in its disclosure made it seem as if 70% of all members who joined during the year renewed. Thus, if 100 members were in and out during the year but 10 remained members at year end, the 70% figure meant that 7 renewed even though it looked like 70 renewed—a tenfold difference in the company's prospects.

This misleading disclosure represents only one egregious example of numerous irregularities at the company, as a subsequent $2.8 billion settlement of an investor lawsuit and a forensic accounting report later made clear. The report emphasized that these practices manifested an overall culture of pernicious accounting practices. Others included manipulating books relating to the percentage of refundable membership dues, cash management, and even how the merger between CUC and HFS that created Cendant was accounted for.

CODA

Aggressive or irregular accounting is not a sign of business promise. The trouble is, it is often hard to detect. Buffett quipped: "It has been far safer to steal large sums with a pen than small sums with a gun."[6] Steering clear of such robbery requires attention to managers, who shape corporate culture. Some corporate cultures encourage laudable accounting practices, while others—as these chicaneries illustrate—encourage what Ben Graham called "prestidigitation" or magical numbers.[7] From National Student Marketing to Cendant, the question is the tone of trust at the top, which raises the subject of the next part of this book.

PART III

IN MANAGERS WE TRUST

CHAPTER 11

GOING GLOBAL

Warren Buffett repeatedly emphasized the importance of investing only with people you "like, trust, and admire" (the phrase appears over a dozen times in *The Essays of Warren Buffett: Lessons for Corporate America*). Ben Graham deemphasized this managerial factor in investment selection, but not because he did not think it was important.

Graham's trouble was the difficulty in measuring the management factor. He believed that until "objective, quantitative, and reasonably reliable tests of managerial competence are devised and applied, this factor will continue to be looked at through a fog."[1] The best Graham thought an investor could do to gauge the management factor was to look at historical financial performance as it is reported in financial statements.

At the same time, one of Graham's key principles of investing as business analysis focused squarely on integrity. Graham implored investors not to entrust wealth to someone else unless either (1) the investor could supervise that person or (2) the investor had "unusually strong reasons for placing implicit confidence in his integrity and ability."[2] Graham was expressly talking about investment advisers, but the point applies equally to managers. After all, whether an investor uses an intermediary or not, her wealth is in the hands of business managers.

A fog still clouds the view of managerial ability and trustworthiness, but consider two important points. First, the corporate governance field has blossomed since Graham wrote, and many people argue that it now contributes clearer ways of thinking about and measuring managerial integrity and effectiveness. Second, Graham implicitly noted the importance of managerial trustworthiness when he deferred to the financial record as a gauge of managerial ability. As we just saw, the reliability of historical financial statements depends on managerial trustworthiness.

While managerial ability and trustworthiness may not warrant an increase in your estimate of a company's value, the weakness or absence of these qualities certainly justifies the opposite. As Buffett says: "Investors should pay more for a business that is lodged in the hands of a manager with demonstrated pro-shareholder leanings than for one in the hands of a self-interested manager marching to a different drummer."[3]

To set the stage for examining managerial integrity and ability, it is first useful to consider the standards of behavior managers are held to both in the United States and around the industrialized world. Much rhetoric characterizes discussion of these conventions, but the reality is often at odds with it. Let's take a brief tour of the world stage of corporate governance before zeroing in on specific indicators of pro-shareholder management.[4]

THE TWO-WORLD STORY

Customarily, it is believed that corporations in the United States and the United Kingdom (U.K.) operate primarily for the benefit of shareholders. This contrasts with corporations in Japan, Germany, and other Continental European countries, where managers are thought to operate for the common good—for the benefit of shareholders, workers, creditors, and communities. At an abstract level both generalizations are correct, but on closer inspection neither is.

This comparison describes the U.S./U.K. approach as a shareholder market model. In it, two internal groups constitute and regulate a corporation: managers and shareholders. Shareholders own the corporation's equity, the value of which fluctuates with the fortunes of the corporation. Managers consist of both the daily operators of the corporation (the officers) and those who oversee and supervise those operations (the directors).

The key problem in U.S. and U.K. corporate governance is the separation of ownership from control that results from the shareholder-manager dichotomy. Two broad sets of mechanisms address the issues raised by this problem. Monitoring mechanisms either impose duties on managers or empower shareholders to take action against them. Exit mechanisms include, most importantly, the free transferability of ownership interests, which enables shareholders to sell their stock and thus exit the corporation at will; this often is called the Wall Street rule.

Monitoring and exit mechanisms reinforce the financial and labor markets, and vice versa. Shareholders can oust inferior managements because a market for managing and controlling corporations exists. The free transferability of ownership interests—an exit mechanism—has contributed to the development of deep, liquid, and active (if not efficient) capital markets. Disclosure laws in the United States, which promote the transparency of corporations' performance, have substantially aided these market forces.

Corporate transparency, coupled with the U.S./U.K. tradition of at-will employment, also facilitates reasonably well-functioning labor markets. For example, if managers perform poorly, corporate transparency makes it more likely that shareholders will vote to oust them and other corporations will not hire them readily.

At the same time, however, managers can contract and expand the employee base to enhance performance. Of course, labor unions often gain substantial power through collective bargaining agreements which contract and federal labor laws protect. That power does not derive, however, from externally imposed regulation but instead is the product of voluntary arrangements.

Consumer product markets also contribute to the discipline of corporate managerial performance by registering preferences which eventually lead to corporate profits. Nonetheless, in the end, labor markets are far from perfect, and it is not uncommon to see senior executives earn staggering compensation despite mediocre or subpar performance.

The great American pastime of litigation reinforces these monitoring mechanisms. Shareholders are equipped with a vast arsenal of legal claims, procedural devices, and legal and equitable remedies to protect their interests. They benefit from a specialized group of lawyers who not only bring direct, derivative, and class action suits under both state and federal law but also identify and communicate the bases for such actions and even finance them.

The rights of other constituencies in a U.S. corporation differ from those of shareholders. Contracts set employee, supplier, creditor, and customer rights. The primary rationale for this treatment is that in bankruptcy, shareholders are last in line after the claims of all the other groups are paid off. This means that when managers act for the shareholders they indirectly protect the interests of all those claimants.

The central finance characteristic of this market model is fragmented ownership of equity securities in corporations. An underlying cultural aspect of the fragmented ownership structure generates an entrepreneurial spirit which encourages widespread participation in equity investment in terms of both those who demand it (start-ups and expanding enterprises) and those who supply it (venture capitalists and investors generally).

This ownership structure also rests on a cultural aversion to concentrations of power. The best examples are the Sherman and Clayton antitrust acts that shut down trusts such as Standard Oil in the climate of Theodore Roosevelt's trust-busting populism. Another is the Glass-Steagall Act, the Depression-era law that segregated the industry of investment banking from that of commercial banking. The repeal of that act in 1999 may reflect a degree of change in U.S. attitudes, though it at least equally likely reflects the globalization of the world economy, in which power is greatly diffused already; the governmental efforts waged against Microsoft under the antitrust laws suggest that such concerns remain prevalent.

Contrast all this with the so-called bank/labor model used to describe Japanese, German, and other Continental European corporate systems. Instead of the shareholder market model's fragmentation of ownership, the central finance features of the bank/labor model are ownership concentration and substantial investment intermediation.

Banks act as financial intermediaries by accepting individual deposits and compiling them for investment in corporations. Only a relatively small number of these investing entities exist. This concentration of ownership and debt holdings reduces the pressure for the development of actively functioning, deep, and liquid capital markets. Moreover, nothing like the Glass-Steagall Act has prevented the commercial and investment bank unity that mitigates this concentration of investment ownership.

This centralization results in a small and powerful body of shareholders and debt holders whose dual position requires few regulatory governance mechanisms compared to the array of tools used to define the rights of various interests in U.S./U.K. corporations. Because a single bank acts as both primary shareholder and debt holder, there is less pressure to choose between models that favor either shareholders or other constituencies of the corporation.

Also, less need exists for regulating governance mechanisms because of traditions that have put labor at the center of the governance structure rather than as a participant with contractually defined interests. European nations are deeply committed to worker protection, as evidenced by wage-setting policies and laws that make firing workers difficult (in contrast to U.S./U.K. at-will employment). These sorts of forces also explain why the disparity in compensation levels between senior executives and ordinary laborers is relatively narrower under the bank/labor model than it is under the market model.

In terms of formal governance, the German and Dutch version of this model formally elevates labor as a third key participant in the leadership of a corporation. These corporations operate with worker councils which management must consult on a variety of matters concerning corporate policy. German corporations generally have a two-tiered board system which consists of a management board and a supervisory board.

The management board (*Vorstand*) manages the corporation, represents it in third-party dealings, and submits regular reports to the supervisory board. The supervisory board (*Aufsichtsrat*) appoints and removes the members of the management board and oversees the management of the corporation. Under German law, employee-elected and shareholder-elected representatives are represented on the supervisory board in equal shares. While it cannot make management decisions, the supervisory board may determine that certain actions or business measures contemplated by the management board require its prior approval.

The German dual-board structure is based on the concept of codetermination (*Mitbestimmung*). According to this view, because labor and capital codetermine a corporation's future, labor should protect its interests from within the corporate governance system through formal representation on the supervisory board rather than through contract or governmental regulation. Banks, which occupy the unique positions of debt holder and shareholder, constitute the other half of the supervisory board. Consequently, the separation of ownership from control, a defining characteristic of the shareholder market model, is expressly absent in the bank/labor model.

In the bank/labor model, even sole shareholders may lack the power to remove or replace management. This lack of power is especially pronounced under the two-tiered board structure prevalent in Germany and the Netherlands, in large part as a result of the work council regulations that have been adopted across Europe. The European Union (EU) mandates that all members except the United Kingdom require most of their corporations to establish procedures for employee consultation and worker council formation.

Many Continental European countries have gone beyond the EU mandates to require that virtually all corporations establish and maintain worker councils. Management must consult with these councils on major corporate policies affecting labor interests, including layoff proposals and in many cases potential changes of control. Galvanizing this labor element in the corporate governance model, the EU also requires that employment contracts follow business assets when sold as a going concern so that a buyer of such assets remains subject to those agreements by operation of law.

Compared to the European model, the Japanese variation deepens the roles of both labor and lender banks in the governance structure. As in Europe, banks tend to own the vast bulk of the debt and equity of industrial companies. The distinguishing factual characteristic is the Japanese production model that is called horizontal coordination. Workers are generalists when it comes to the production process and engage in a substantial amount of information sharing and training throughout production. Limited specialization, however, requires high corporate investment in labor markets to develop the necessary human capital.

Japanese corporations thus face a higher risk of loss on investment from worker defection than do European and American corporations. However, workers face the risk of acquiring nontransportable, firm-specific skills. Corporations and workers have addressed these risks by developing a system of lifetime employment. This policy provides workers with permanent job security and affords corporations a concomitantly restricted labor market.

No binding contract guaranteed this mutual security system, and so the Japanese model turned to corporate cross-ownership to provide the necessary structural protections. Industrial corporations in Japan own substantial percentages of the securities of other industrial corporations. The resulting ownership concentration is even more centralized than it is in the European model, and it causes a commensurate dilution of capital market disciplining power.

ILLUSIONS OF DUTY

So much for these polar stories. Reality suggests far more overlap and universal looseness across advanced economies in regard to the real beneficiaries of managerial duties—an important point for investors to understand.

Corporate social responsibility remains an important dimension of U.S. corporate governance. Direct efforts to improve the lot of nonshareholder constituencies supplement the simple argument that shareholder-based profit maximization helps all the other participants.

Scores of organizations promote this direct approach in response to the needs of corporate constituencies on a variety of issues, including affirmative action, child labor, downsizing, the environment, fair wages, privacy, sexual harassment, and the balance between work life and family life. These organizations operate through employee training and assistance programs, mission statements, and social responsibility audits.

Social responsibility has reached the large organizational level. For example, Business for Social Responsibility, an organization founded in 1992, currently has over 1,400 corporate members with aggregate annual revenues exceeding $1 trillion and total employees of nearly 5 million. It features household corporate names such as AT&T, Coke, DuPont, Federal Express, Home Depot, Motorola, and Polaroid. Significant numbers of mutual funds and other institutional investors also have committed to investing only in socially responsible enterprises. Some investors claim that investing this way maximizes shareholder wealth.

Many corporations have followed suit and now emphasize their social responsibility. There are well-known exemplars of the traditional left such as Body Shop and Ben & Jerry's (taken over by Unilever in early 2000 with promises to expand the social responsibility commitments of the global consumer products giant). There are also some surprising followers, such as Philips-Van Heusen Corporation, which is headed by CEO Bruce Klatsky, an adviser on U.S. trade policy to the Bush and Reagan administrations. Hasbro, Reebok, and Wal-Mart also are following this trend. This social emphasis is entirely consistent with state laws, which mandate that directors act in the best interests of the shareholders and the corporation as a whole.

German law takes more seriously the idea that the beneficiaries of directors' duties include corporate constituents other than shareholders, yet Germany also forbids directors from acting contrary to shareholder interests and indeed often requires them to act in the "aggregated shareholder interest." German corporate law—which is fairly representative of European countries on these points—and U.S. law therefore contemplate the protection of all corporate constituencies. Both prescribe this protection by imposing on management the fiduciary duties care and loyalty.

The duty of care requires the exercise of an informed business judgment, which is taken to mean that directors must gather all the material information that is reasonably available to them. Informed directors then must act prudently and reasonably in the discharge of their duties. The liability of directors for breach of the duty of care in most circumstances requires a finding by a court that the directors were grossly negligent—quite a high standard that is akin to driving while intoxicated. The duty of loyalty requires directors to subordinate their personal interests to those of the corporation if a conflict exists. Specific applications of this general duty vary among economically-developed countries, but the variation is not much more pronounced than are the nuanced differences between states within the United States.

The differences are thus more subtle between U.S./U.K. and Continental Europe director duties than is often recognized. The varying prescriptions address the content of those duties rather than their discrete beneficiaries. They are "vertical," intended to preserve and expand the size of the corporate pie rather than address how it is sliced or allocated.

When the question is pie size, the interests of managers are pitted against the interests of all the other constituencies, and so it is not surprising that these vertical mechanisms differ little across the borders of economically advanced countries. What is surprising is that they also extend to situations where allocation is at stake, a "horizontal" question that manifests itself most acutely when threats to corporate control arise.

Most U.S. state laws impose either a heightened standard of duty on directors facing hostile takeovers or a heightened standard of judicial review of director conduct. The issue in either instance is whether the directors have acted in the best interest of shareholders. While these heightened standards do not exist in German law, which only requires directors not to act contrary to the stockholders' interest and to show regard for the common interest, this does not mean that the heightened U.S. standard separates the American model from the Continental model.

Many states empower directors to consider the interests of non-shareholder constituencies in numerous circumstances. For example, although U.S. judges often remark that "shareholders come first," they simultaneously let directors consider the impact of corporate decisions on constituencies other than shareholders, including creditors, customers, employees, and sometimes as broad a group as the general community.

Judges sometimes mesh mandatory rhetoric with discretionary

reality even in extreme circumstances such as where managers fight against a hostile takeover—one of the devices on the horizon in the late 1960s that Ben Graham thought might operate as a disciplining force on underperforming managers.[5] For example, in the mid-1990s the Delaware Supreme Court accepted the arguments of Time Inc.'s directors, who resisted an unwanted takeover by Paramount, in part on the ground that doing so was necessary to preserve the company's culture of journalistic integrity. Thus, despite even the most rigorous judicial review of board actions, in takeover contexts, directors have a great deal of latitude.

Takeover laws do not require any particular action, such as an auction, or impose on directors any duty to ensure that shareholders get the highest price. The unifying inquiry in virtually all these cases is whether a threat to the corporation exists, not solely or even necessarily whether the shareholders' interests are in jeopardy.

For a dramatic example of what occurs under laws that look beyond shareholder interests, consider the fight for corporate control between AlliedSignal and AMP.[6] AlliedSignal offered a 55% premium over the market price of AMP, a company whose profitability had seriously dropped. AMP shareholders overwhelmingly supported AlliedSignal, and within a month of the offer 72% of AMP's outstanding shares were tendered into it. Shareholder supporters included the family of the company's founder, Robert Hixon, and many institutional shareholders, which owned approximately 80% of the stock, including the Teachers Insurance and Annuity Association–College Retirement Equities Fund (TIAA-CREF).

Indeed, TIAA-CREF joined a shareholder group that sued AMP's board. That group took the extraordinary step of separately filing a "friend-of-the-court" brief supporting AlliedSignal in direct litigation between AlliedSignal and AMP. TIAA-CREF argued that AMP had trampled on basic "principles of shareholder democracy."

Despite this overwhelming shareholder support for AlliedSignal, AMP's management successfully erected a series of defensive barriers to the bid. Management took advantage of Pennsylvania laws requiring directors to act in the best interests not of the shareholders, but of the corporation and permitting boards to act in what they perceive to be the best interests of employees, lenders, communities, and others. One extraordinary barrier AMP's management raised changed the terms of its "poison pill" so that it could not be eliminated even by directors who held office before any of AlliedSignal's directors had joined.

AMP sought and won an injunction prohibiting AlliedSignal's consent solicitation unless and until each proposed director-candidate affirmed that if elected, he or she was duty-bound under Pennsylvania law to act in the best interests of the corporation as a whole, not merely in the shareholders' interest.

The court upheld AMP's extraordinary actions against Allied-Signal's claim that AMP's board had breached its fiduciary duties in response to the AlliedSignal bid. In its opinion, the court repeatedly emphasized a "stakeholder" standard, which appears to be at the heart of Pennsylvania law, and used the following unequivocal terms: "Directors may weigh the interests of the shareholders against the interests of other constituencies." They "may consider the effects upon all groups affected, including shareholders, employees, suppliers, customers and creditors." They "shall not be required to regard any corporate interest or group as dominant or controlling."

These statements do not suggest a shareholder-primacy norm. A less obvious point but one that is equally true is that these Pennsylvania standards are not all that different in practice from those of other U.S. states. They are also not all that different from German law and may even capture the German sense of the common interest.

Consider both German-based Mannesmann's battle against the United Kingdom's Vodaphone and the merger of Germany's Daimler Benz with the United States's Chrysler. Although German law permits directors to evaluate the interests of workers and lenders and the so-called common interest, the law also required that the board not act contrary to the best interests of shareholders—and both boards did so, Mannesmann's with a vengeance.

That kind of deference to shareholders may not illustrate shareholder primacy, nor it it consistent with the usual rhetoric of the bank/labor model. Accordingly, U.S. practice more closely resembles European practice than it does U.S. rhetoric, and European practice more closely resembles U.S. practice than it does European rhetoric; managers in neither place are obligated to hold a thoroughgoing owner orientation.

ONE WORLD TO COME

Trends in corporate practice worldwide suggest further harmonization, and it is a mistake for investors to overlook them. These trends spell the continued erasure of differences and a tendency to make owner orientation even less compulsory. If this is the case, the already small population of true owner-orientated U.S. managers will shrink further. On the other hand, the number abroad may grow larger.

Financial markets increasingly compete internationally, just as product markets have done for decades. Investors (suppliers of capital) now look across borders for additional investment opportunities, while corporations and other organizations seek the lowest-cost capital from any market in the world. The isolation of capital markets is disappearing, and head-to-head competition among financial markets has ensued.

The EU integrates corporate finance and governance in many respects. Most significantly, the adoption of a single currency will harmonize competition through the sharing of productivity differentials—the fruits of technological advancement and higher investment. Business expense differentials, particularly wages, should evaporate. The process is just beginning as countries adopt the euro and ultimately abandon their local currencies.

Nearly as profound, new EU innovations are greatly diminishing barriers to cross-border capital flows. A series of EU directives compeled the abolition of foreign investment controls. Member states enthusiastically responded to this call by relaxing their controls. The remaining restrictions generally are limited to notification requirements or to specified sectors that pose national security or public health, safety, and welfare concerns. Many European countries simply retained the authority to implement such controls if necessary.

ACCOUNTING

A series of fundamental principles has harmonized accounting rules within Europe. These principles include (1) a requirement of uniform formats for financial statements, (2) common valuation principles, including historical cost, accrual accounting, and the principle of conservatism called prudence, (3) a general mandate that financial statements show true and fair value, (4) an annual audit, (5) public filings, and (6) consolidation principles. A trend toward unified accounting reinforces the harmonization trends in finance and governance.

Similar moves have occurred in Japan. Japanese accounting rules now require consolidation of all the accounts of a company's controlled affiliates. In the past, the absence of such a rule enabled companies to allocate the bad accounting news to affiliates, making the parent company's books look much better. New Japanese rules also require listing real estate held for sale at its current market value if that value has fallen more than 50% from the original cost. The absence of this new rule fueled the Japanese speculative bubble of the 1980s that cratered gradually throughout the 1990s (described in Chapter 5).

Around the world, increasing numbers of non-U.S. and non-English-language corporations are ahead of schedule in adopting international accounting principles and reporting their results in the English language. Nissan, for example, adopted consolidation accounting principles in late 1999, six months ahead of schedule, and issued related press releases about that period's results in English, an unimaginable act for a Japanese corporation just a decade ago (even one that is partly French-owned).

When Nissan reported its annual financial results in mid-2000, using international accounting principles, they showed staggering losses of $6.3 billion. Contributing to those losses were recognition of pension liabilities and the costs of plant closings and the assignment of more realistic values to real estate and securities holdings. Although a number of other substantive factors contributed to these results, investors considering investment in non-U.S. companies must understand that accounting principles elsewhere are not always what they seem.

The United States is harmonizing its accounting principles with those prevalent worldwide. In October 1996, Congress passed the National Securities Markets Improvement Act of 1996, which requires the SEC to report to Congress on progress in developing international accounting standards. The SEC has worked with the International Accounting Standards Committee (IASC) for nearly a decade to promulgate a core set of accounting pronouncements. In October 1997 the SEC published a report to Congress on the progress of the IASC, and it joined organizations throughout the world in supporting the IASC's initiatives.

The finance ministers and central bank governors of the G7 countries proclaimed support for the IASC and encouraged it to complete a proposed set of core principles promptly. Additionally, the World Bank requested the world's "Big Five" international auditing firms to insist that companies prepare their financial statements in accordance with international accounting standards. Leading voices from around the world, including Tony Blair, the United

Kingdom's prime minister, and Robert E. Rubin, then U.S. treasury secretary, intoned that developing and implementing international accounting standards is a key part of the emerging global financial system.

The SEC argues that international accounting standards must be comprehensive, produce comparability and transparency, provide for full disclosure, and be amenable to rigorous interpretation and application. Indeed, many view SEC Chairman Levitt's broad-based initiative to crack down on earnings abuses by management in U.S. corporations as a response to the increasing attractiveness of international harmonization of accounting standards, which the SEC wants the United States to lead rather than follow.

The future state of accounting is crucial to investors. As pliable as accounting rules are in the United States, they remain a functional way to measure business reality. Coupled with an auditing culture that insists on the integrity of financial reporting, this system adds unparalleled value to the investing enterprise. Investors looking abroad should be aware of the differences and monitor improvements worldwide as they pose both pitfalls and opportunities.

GOVERNANCE

In Europe, periodic resistance flares up against unification efforts. For example, 13 EU directives dealing with European company law, as well as a proposal to create a European Corporation (*Societas Europaea*) that would supplement but not substitute for the national corporate form in individual states, were intended to promote regional (if not global) harmonization. However, none of these measures is currently among the EU's highest priorities.

On a few occasions, particularly during early EU convergence efforts, proposals for employee board representation derailed the adoption of some integrated governance proposals. Much of this resistance originated in the United Kingdom, which has for decades debated whether its future will be served better by a U.S./U.K. alliance or a Continental European EU alliance. Despite the obstacles this uncertainty poses for EU harmony, the United Kingdom produced domestic convergence by drawing on both models.

U.S. corporate governance originally drew upon and refined U.K. traditions. Now the United Kingdom has in turn imported those principles as refined. Its 1992 Cadbury Report on corporate governance (renamed the Hampel Report in the final 1998 version) seeks to identify the "best practices" of global corporations. They tend to borrow on U.S. technical innovations in corporate governance, including some discussed in the next chapter.

The United Kingdom's substantial role in Europe, coupled with its link to U.S. corporate governance, moved the Continental models closer to the market model. The French experience provides a provocative example. The stakeholder model and financial intermediation historically characterized French corporate governance. At the same time, a state-dominated industrial policy defined French capitalism, producing firms of a smaller average size than those in other capitalist countries and an industrial elite recruited not from within industry but from outside it. This environment limits capital market depth and monitoring capabilities.

Now the French model is following the trend toward globalization and liberalism. The revisions make the French model more closely resemble a market model, beginning with a loosening of the state's grip on industry through privatization efforts. Additionally, the number of small shareholders is rapidly growing, and, following the United Kingdom, technical governance reforms based on U.S. models have been instituted widely. Moreover, audit and compensation committees are forming in French corporate boards, minority shareholders are taking on increasingly important roles, and information superior in both quantity and quality is enhancing economic transparency.

Japan is similarly racing toward a shareholder-market model and away from long-term employment commitments and horizontal coordination. Increasingly, Japan has recognized that profit-maximizing strategies actually are consistent with the protections its traditional devices provide. More and more Japanese workers—particularly younger workers—indicate that they do not intend to stay with one employer for more than a few years at a time, let alone maintain lifetime employment with a single firm.

U.S. corporate governance remains imperfect, as we'll see in the next few chapters. The principles on which it is based are sound, but a lot can be learned from studying governance in other countries, particularly as investors increasingly set their sites on companies organized abroad and competing worldwide.

MERGERS AND ACQUISITIONS

The Vodafone-Mannesmann fight rode a wave of American-style European merger activity that erupted in early 1999 with major hostile takeover battles. In France, Banque Nationale de Paris launched a $38 billion hostile bid to take over its two major French banking rivals, Société Générale and Paribas, after they had recently announced their own plan to merge with each other. In Italy, Olivetti launched a $60 billion hostile bid to acquire its major rival, Telecom Italia, which in turn erected a series of substantial defensive tactics designed to thwart the overture, including a white-knight alliance with Germany's Deutsche-Telecom.

In another cross-border battle, France's LVMH Moët Hennessy Louis Vuitton waged a protracted and intense battle to obtain control of Gucci, an Italy-based but Netherlands-incorporated company which also strenuously resisted the unwelcome overture. TOTAL-FINA made a hostile bid for Elf Aquitaine in mid-1999, shaking up the French industrial and governmental establishment. These kinds of deals—in both their offensive and defensive modes—are reminiscent of U.S.-style merger activity, which had been unprecedented in Europe.

Scores of friendly global alliances have reinforced the spread of market model behavior in Europe and Japan. Led by the merger of Daimler and Chrysler, the worldwide auto industry consolidated through cross-border deals once considered too intractable to achieve. Industry capacity ranges up to approximately 70 million vehicles annually while average annual demand generally peaks at 50 million, and only about 10 of the world's 40 auto manufacturers are profitable. Some results: Ford bought control of Mazda, Volkswagen acquired the United Kingdom's Rolls Royce, Renault bought Samsung (Korea) and a third of Nissan, and Daimler-Chrysler bought a third of Mitsubishi.

Many other industries stand on the brink of similar global consolidation. In the publishing industry, Germany's Bertelsmann pursued an acquiring and joint-venturing spree with other European and U.S. counterparts; in apparel, after surviving its own battle to resist a takeover by LVMH, Gucci took over France's Yves Saint Laurent; in finance, Deutsche Bank bought Bankers Trust, UBS bought Paine Webber, Credit Suisse bought Donaldson Lufkin Jenrette, Dresdner bought Wasserstein Parella; British Petroleum bought Amoco; and Nabisco and a U.S. buyout firm sought to buy Britain's United Biscuits only to be outflanked by a consortium of French, German, and British buyers. These and scores of other proposals on the docket of the EU merger panel have created unmatched uniformity of practices and expectations in the corporate world.

There are few ways in which a corporate board can destroy shareholder value as dramatically as through mergers and acquisitions. As globalization advances, more opportunities for deals arise. Some will be desirable; many will not. Paying close attention to the activity in this field is of great importance to investors and is addressed again later in this part.

Capital Markets

The aggregate stock market capitalization of Europe is larger than that of Nasdaq and over half that of the New York Stock Exchange. (Given Mr. Market, the aggregate market capitalizations can change dramatically in short time periods, but as of early 2000, the amounts were about $7 trillion, $4 trillion, and $11 trillion, respectively.)

The Frankfurt and London stock exchanges announced in July 1998 a plan to integrate their facilities and permit the trading of each other's listed securities on both exchanges. France, unhappy with its exclusion, quickly gained admission to the Frankfurt-London alliance (although as a 20% player, compared with 40% for each of the founding exchanges). Soon after France announced its inclusion in the emerging pan-European exchange, exchange officials in Milan, Madrid, Amsterdam, and Brussels echoed a similar eagerness to participate in the venture.

Although the European alliance had difficulty agreeing on a common trading system, the group quickly elected to permit stock trading between the various exchanges. While negotiators struggled, the once-snubbed French Bourse took advantage of the delays by signing itself up with exchange partners from Amsterdam and Brussels. This troika's single market—a full integration of these three exchanges called Euronext—boasts listings with a combined market capitalization equal to over a quarter of that of Europe as a whole.

As the Euronext group forged this deal, the London and Frankfurt exchanges agreed on a merger. The two formed iX, standing for International Exchanges, a market poised to integrate blue chips and tech stocks from the two dominant European capitals and boasting a total capitalization of over half of that of Europe as a whole. That deal was interrupted when OM Gruppen, operator of the Stockholm (Sweden) stock exchange, made a hostile bid to buy the London Exchange. However the dust settles on this array of parties, these historical deals will not end capital market integration in Europe, the pace of which races on despite the presence of a dozen or more unintegrated exchanges on the continent.

The U.S. National Association of Securities Dealers (NASD) launched its own Nasdaq Europe stock market, one that will have strong links to the emerging continental hybrids. This signifies a major step toward creating a 24-hour-a-day global stock market that began with the NASD's similar venture in creating Nasdaq Japan, a joint effort with the Softbank Corporation of Japan that is linked to the Osaka Securities Exchange. All this will compel the convergence of these markets in awesome ways, impacting finance, accounting, disclosure, takeovers, governance, and ultimately what investors expect and what managers deliver.

Evidence of integration is pervasive in securities listing and trading. Foreign firms for years have pushed for global listing, most famously achieved by Daimler-Benz's listing on the NYSE beginning in 1993. These crusades continue, with rising success. After the repeal of Glass-Steagall, the Swiss bank UBS filed with the SEC to seek an NYSE listing, chiefly to give it a U.S.-listed stock to pay for new acquisitions of U.S. financial services firms. This started with its acquisition, a couple of months later, of PaineWebber.

SAP, a 25-year-old German software firm, was listed on the NYSE in early August 1998, ten years to the day after its initial public offering on the Frankfurt stock exchange. SAP is famous for generating "U.S.-style growth" and "U.S.-style rewards." SAP executives characterized its listing on the NYSE as evidence that SAP had "outgrown" the Frankfurt stock market and evolved into a transnational company combining features of a variety of governance models.

Clear-cut signs of the conglomeration of international securities trading include the creation of the International Securities Exchange (ISE) for options trading. An on-line brokerage firm, E*Trade, and a group of broker-dealers led by Adirondack Trading Partners invested nearly $80 million to establish this all-electronic options exchange. The founders touted their ability to slash transaction costs while simultaneously conducting staggering sums of electronic trades which transcend geographic boundaries.

Investors should not ignore the shape of capital markets. How trades are made, by whom, at what cost, and over what time periods significantly affect price volatility and have an impact on market efficiency. Equally important, exchange rules often dictate accounting requirements, and so the ease of international listings can impair the integrity of financial reporting.

The Last Frontier: Information

A practical barrier to cross-border deals has been yielding. It concerns the nature and amount of available information regarding a counterparty. In market model countries such as the United States and the United Kingdom, a wealth of information is available concerning the targets organized therein. These countries tend to operate systems of public recordation for real as well as intellectual property. Well-developed securities and mergers and acquisitions (M&A) industries strengthen such an information culture.

Buyers and sellers in M&A transactions understand the need for information to allow proper valuations and the need for contractual protection to preserve confidentiality. Sellers customarily meet these needs by executing confidentiality agreements early in the exploration process and providing the buyer with substantial proprietary data before discussing agreements any further.

The culture in European and Asian countries contrasts remarkably with that of the U.S./U.K. market model. Access to property records is limited, and information is more jealously guarded. Sellers are reluctant to share information with a potential buyer who can walk away from a deal if she doesn't like what she sees; confidentiality agreements that protect such a seller in the United States and the United Kingdom simply don't do the trick. That may be sensible, since a less well-developed system of legal enforcement for such agreements justifies a seller's apprehension about a buyer's confidentiality.

Cultural disparities became acute in the Vodafone-Mannesmann battle. Mannesmann sued Vodaphone's adviser, Goldman Sachs, in a U.K. court, trying to prevent it from advising Vodaphone on the grounds that Goldman had previously represented Mannesmann and possessed confidential information about it. The British court dismissed the lawsuit after a brief hearing and in a short time, basically telling Mannesmann that its claim was frivolous.

Substantively, the type of information understood as relevant also varies between the models. In the market model and especially in the United States, disclosing potential environmental or retiree liabilities is a time-honored practice. Other countries have only recently developed environmental regulation. Also, other countries traditionally rely more heavily on public social security systems, removing private plans from center stage (even in countries such as Germany, where such liabilities are often substantial and unfunded).

For investors, U.S. corporations disclose far more than do those in Europe or Japan. U.S. federal and state law, as well as stock exchange rules and general market pressures and expectations in the United States, result in corporations disclosing extraordinary amounts and types of information. Other countries impose more limited and far less effective disclosure requirements.

As global corporations as diverse as DaimlerChrysler and SAP increasingly list shares on U.S. stock exchanges and stock exchanges around the world, they will find themselves subject to U.S.-style disclosure requirements as a matter of both regulatory mandate and market expectations and demand. As the same group consummates cross-border transactions requiring the disclosure and evaluation of information, pressures toward uniform disclosure requirements will emerge in a wide variety of settings. In fact, participants find that U.S./U.K.-style information disclosure is consistent with existing corporate traditions in most countries, most notably Germany. Accordingly, broadening global corporate laws to require such disclosure seems quite possible.

Public regulators have undertaken just such an effort. The SEC is working with the International Organization of Securities Commissions (IOSCO) to develop a set of international standards for nonfinancial statement disclosure. These efforts are intended to facilitate cross-border financing and listing by transnational companies while holding them to a single global standard of disclosure. The IOSCO issued new rules about certain kinds of cash transactions and offerings and listings of common equity securities and is working to extend them to tender and exchange offers, business combinations, privatizations, and other affiliated deals.

High-quality information is essential for intelligent investing in the modern global marketplace. Ignoring the garbage and disinformation piling up on the Internet is becoming increasingly difficult as more countries develop information-based corporate and investing cultures and as more citizens of those countries learn the ropes of the systems.

TWO-WAY STREET

Not all these trends run one way, for the idea of shareholder primacy in the United States was gradually but substantially eroded by the dramatic reallocation of corporate value from shareholders to workers throughout the latter half of the twentieth century. In the past, workers had no interest in a corporation other than a paycheck and the right to quit (and be fired). Today corporations whose workers have no interest except a paycheck are rare.

Workers have claims against their corporate employers ranging from vacation and sick pay to paternity or maternity leave, safety and antidiscrimination rights, health plans, severance claims, and retiree benefits and pensions. All these claims cost substantial amounts of money, value that in the old days was owned by the shareholders. On top of all that, somewhat paradoxically, employees have become shareholders of these corporations and, counter to the Japanese trend, are actually staying with the same employer for longer periods and expressing greater loyalty to their employers than they did in the past.

U.S. regulators are taking pages from abroad in a bolder way. A major example is the elimination of boundaries between investment and commercial banking. These boundaries were relaxed in December 1996, when the Federal Reserve Board increased the amount of investment banking income a commercial bank can earn from investment banking subsidiaries from 10% to 25%. The so-called Section 20 subs ushered in this regulatory change, which contributed substantially to the ensuing wave of commercial and investment bank mergers and reversed a historical cause of ownership fragmentation. The repeal of the Glass-Steagall Act in November 1999 has further fueled such financial reunions.

The U.S. litigation system is not the envy of the world, and it encourages large volumes of shareholder class action and derivative lawsuits against management. In contrast, most legal systems put substantial restrictions on such suits. Although it does not appear that litigation will decline substantially in the United States, it is clear that lawmakers want to curb litigation abuse. For example, the Private Securities Litigation Reform Act of 1995 substantially revised the securities laws in an effort to distinguish frivolous claims from meritorious ones.

This analysis forecasts the hybridization of corporate governance models in terms of both constituency and finance characteristics. No owner orientation is required by these models. Forces appear to be pushing for convergence, and the emerging model will not require an owner orientation either. Indeed, to the extent that there is anything real to the European corporate governance rhetoric, convergence will dilute rather than enhance any managerial mandate to run U.S. corporations mainly for the benefit of shareholders. Detecting an owner orientation in this global marketplace thus becomes more important than ever.

Buffett tells us that the most valuable lesson he learned in investing was realizing the importance of owner-oriented managers. The value of this timeless lesson will increase geometrically in a globalized world. Of course, Buffett emphasizes that while management quality can dramatically affect returns on equity, it is never a substitute for a good business within one's circle of competence, saying that "a good managerial record (measured by economic returns) is far more a function of what business boat you get into than it is of how effectively you row (though intelligence and effort help considerably, of course, in any business, good or bad)."[7] The remaining chapters focus on identifying winning managers.

CHAPTER 12

RULES AND TRUST

An investor is going to entrust her wealth to someone else. Shouldn't the investor have a high degree of confidence in that person's ability and integrity? Of course. It is simple common sense, but how to assess ability and integrity is a bit trickier.

Graham used the quantitative analysis of the sort described in Part II as a proxy. If the numbers look good year after year and provide a basis for thinking that they will continue to do so, that may suggest that management is able.

Many other investors, including Warren Buffett in his early days, learned hard lessons from paying too little attention to management integrity. True, if a company's numbers look good and are accurate, its managers are probably able and trustworthy. If the numbers look good but are misleading, management may be neither. As Buffett reminds us, "In the long run, managements stressing accounting appearances over economic substance usually achieve little of either."[1]

Therefore, integrity is an additional independent factor in investment selection. Is there a sensible way to think about managerial integrity? Buffett says the key is to invest with managers you "like, trust, and admire." His test for whether an investment meets this requirement is whether the managers are "men you would be pleased to see your daughter marry."[2]

Does this "son-in-law" standard help? It may only suggest avoiding managers you would not be pleased to invite over for a Super Bowl party, but this is a great deal more meaningful than it sounds.

THE FAMILY MANAGER

All business transactions depend on trust and always have. Contracts help define and protect rights, but entering into one calls for some expectation that the other party will do what he says he will do.

Contracts also reduce the costs of doing business and investing by enabling people to trade off future risks, but that works only if the other person can be expected to live up to the deal.

Trust in business is deeply rooted in kinship, and so it is no wonder that the son-in-law test makes sense. The link between the son-in-law test for managers and business itself comports with the broad history of business development. Most businesses start out as family enterprises and then grow in size over decades or generations, adding relatives to the management ranks (often even including sons-in-law, as at Anheuser-Busch, the Washington Post Company, and Mead, for example). In many cases, such growth leads families to give up control and the business evolves into a modern corporation, as occurred at Brown-Forman, DuPont, Eli Lilly, McGraw-Hill, Nordstroms, and countless others.

The erstwhile family business as modern corporation no longer has Dad or Granddad or Daughter at the helm but instead has a cadre of professional managers, a diffusion of control, an institutionalized organizational structure, and lines of reporting authority. The upshot is a corporation characterized by a separation of ownership from control—shareholders watching managers run the business. Trust in the modern corporation should resonate with norms and values associated with that family business.

It is rarely feasible for an individual investor to sit down and get acquainted with the chief executive officers of most major corporations, but all these chiefs write annual letters to shareholders and author other addresses periodically as well. These communications contain remarkable clues about trustworthiness. The manager's own words often reveal her character. (Chapter 14 pursues this point.)

What is it that you trust a manager to do? The answer to that question comes from thinking of him as *your* manager, something that is hardly ever done. People always speak of *their* broker, *their* accountant, *their* lawyer, but they hardly ever speak of *their* manager. Yet a corporate manager does just as much for your wealth as these sidekicks do, or more.

What should your manager do? Run the business for your benefit, as a shareholder, against the numerous and often conflicting interests of other constituencies of the business. Here is another key point that is often overlooked: The perspectives of investors and managers often diverge. When they do, investor interests can be disserved.

Managers raise funds for corporate enterprise from the investing public in the form of equity capital or stocks. Investors are regarded by managers either as partners in the enterprise or merely as consumers.

When seen as consumers, investors are deemed to have tastes and preferences that are reflected in the prices at which managers can sell them stocks and other securities. Most of these investors have little or no say in how a business is operated or even who the managers will be (other than through annual elections of directors).

Instead they are strangers to the corporation, strangers whose interests are subordinated to those of the corporation as a whole. In this type of corporation, for example, managers tend to consider the tax effects of declaring a dividend or structuring an acquisition deal on the corporation as a whole but not on the individual shareholders.

In contrast, the voices of individual investors matter more to owner-oriented managers. Seeing them as partners in the business, these managers treat investors as members of the enterprise rather than as strangers to it. Electing directors remains the formal vehicle for this voice, but a more solicitous view of owner interests is taken. For example, these managers consider the tax effects of corporate decisions such as dividends and deals on the investor rather than on, or at least separately from, the corporation.

It is far easier for managers of family and other small and privately held corporations to adopt this owner orientation. It is far easier for managers of large publicly held corporations to adopt the opposite view. The managers with whom intelligent investors should entrust their wealth are those who adopt the investor's perspective no matter how large the corporation or how many shareholders it has.

LOCAL GOVERNANCE

The reality of global corporate management means that boards and managers can run a business for the benefit of many constituencies, not solely shareholders. Laws permit managers to operate pretty much wherever they want along the spectrum from a shareholder orientation to a constituency orientation. One part of business analysis is evaluating the degree to which management has an owner orientation.

Sources for determining that orientation abound, probably more so in the United States but increasingly throughout the developed world. In the United States, corporations disclose volumes of information to shareholders and other interested people. Many corporations go beyond legal requirements, producing substantial information on their Web sites and Webcasting archives and you can get plenty of high-quality and reliable information from publications by reputable industry analysts such as Standard & Poor's, Dun & Bradstreet, and Robert Morris Associates as well as government agencies such as the Federal Trade Commission. Use your imagination.

Sift through these materials in looking for managers who act like stewards of shareholder capital. Use it to find the best managers, those who think like owners in making business decisions and who adopt an attitude of partnership, embracing shareholders as members of the enterprise rather than as strangers to it, those you would be happy to invite over for a Super Bowl party.

However, even owner-oriented managers sometimes have interests that conflict with those of shareholders. Work to identify and invest with those who make a habit of easing those conflicts and nurturing managerial stewardship of owner funds, those who exhibit Aristotelian ethical virtue.

It is not easy to detect governance indicators of an owner orientation in place at a corporation any more than it is to detect the financial or managerial performance or even value of a corporation from its financial statements. However, as with that effort, it is worth the work.

The difficulty and the possibility exist because the law requires very little of corporate governance. Yes, federal securities laws impose extensive disclosure obligations, though most of what they call for probably would be produced voluntarily by good companies participating in a vibrant market economy anyway. Yes, state laws impose duties on directors and managers, but those duties are loose and general. Some statutory rules or limits are imposed, but they are either highly formal and therefore malleable or pretty meaningless as a practical matter and can be altered in corporate by-laws or charter documents.

Corporate governance as such is not necessary. Many advocates of corporate governance argue for reforms directed toward compelling an owner orientation, usually described as aligning management and shareholder interests or enhancing board oversight of CEO performance. If a company needs these mechanisms to create an owner orientation, however, its valuation should be discounted proportionally.

Most corporate governance reforms fail to solve governance problems, and some exacerbate them. Nevertheless, institutional investors and other shareholder advocates have promulgated a variety of policies about corporate governance, most of which are designed to promote an owner orientation. But just as fads infect finance, they gum up governance too.

Perhaps the most popular governance idea in the past couple of decades has been the call for independent boards of directors. The National Association of Corporate Directors (NACD) and many institutional investors including CalPers and TIAA-CREF, urged that corporate boards be composed of at least a majority of outside directors, those without employment or other affiliation with the corporation. The idea was that this would strengthen directorial spines to keep management in check. Nearly all major companies fell into line, with 90% of Fortune 1000 companies having a majority of independent directors.

These arguments were made on the basis of intuition, however, rather than analysis. It was as if there were little or no doubt that managers needed to be kept in line and that director watchdogs could do the trick. This premise has been exploded by several studies showing that far from independent boards enhancing economic performance, there is actually a negative correlation between the degree of independence and financial results.[3]

This is not to say that having some or many independent directors is never desirable (Buffett, for example, believes that most directors should be outsiders),[4] but there is no reason to give credit ipso facto to a company just because it does this. The unanswered commonsense questions are: (1) Who are these independent directors? and (2) What value do they add to the boardroom? Independent directors famous for international diplomacy or senatorial jobbery may be far worse to have at the table than a chief financial officer with extensive industry and managerial experience. A template that calls for independence is not a virtue but a mirage.

The key is to choose directors for their business savvy, interest in the job, and owner orientation. To be avoided are celebrity directors and others who are chosen for nonfundamental reasons, such as adding diversity or prominence to a board.

Another popular move some companies fell for was the push to split the functions of the company's CEO from those of its board

chairman. This manifested the same rationale of independence prescriptions, a need to check the boardroom power of the CEO. Only
about 5% of Fortune 1000 companies succumbed to this formula,
probably with good reason.

As an empirical matter, as with board independence, most evidence shows that companies that split these functions do not perform better than those which do not.[5] As an abstract matter, it is
hard to justify giving a company governance credit for this separation
of function, for putting a watchdog on the CEO suggests as many reasons to be suspicious of the CEO as reasons to trust him. For a company whose CEO is not to be trusted, this may be a good step, but
it sounds more like probation than probity and is a strong warning
signal for investors to run from rather than embrace the business.
Only a fool, after all, thinks trust can be purchased or structured.

One aspect of this reform makes sense, however, and many companies adopted a version of it by providing for a nonexecutive board
chair for critical functions such as CEO, board, and director evaluations. After all, letting the CEO grade herself and her board does
pose a risk of self-delusion. An independent grader is in a better
position to evaluate performance objectively, and so some governance credit is justified for a company that takes this step.

Director independence is frequently encouraged for some committees and often required for audit committees. Audit committee
independence is consistent with the structure of U.S. audit practice
that requires an auditing firm to be independent of the company and
its management. Independence on compensation committees reflects the logic of a nonexecutive overseer for key functions such as
CEO and board performance review.

However, the argument for requiring independence on other
committees, such as nominating, ethics, and governance, is the same
as that for independence overall. If a corporation needs those kinds
of things, it has problems anyway. The mere fact that a corporation
has various independent board committees does not guarantee that
problems arising from collusion or delusion will be absent or disappear.

Periodic and formal evaluations of the CEO and other directors
are often recommended and do seem sensible and worthy of praise.
To deserve credit, however, the CEO reviews should be conducted
outside the presence of the CEO, something that is not easily or
commonly done. A more general way to implement this practice is
to supplement such periodic reviews with regular director meetings

outside the CEO's presence, a practice Buffett in particular champions. This is creditworthy not so much under the logic of suspicion of the CEO but as an independent check on the CEO's judgment.

Some gobbledygook about improved board processes is commonly bandied about. This is usually sheer nonsense or gloss. Requirements such as swift flows of quality information, statements of governance principles, and procedures for full and effective participation of all directors seem like mere bafflegab. These practices should simply be part of the normal operation of a well-governed corporation. Giving credit for the articulation of these practices is superfluous—like giving umpires extra credit for knowing the rules of baseball.

Other common and strange prescriptions take pages from the equally silly playbook of American politics. Term limits for directors? Why should a good director be forbidden from continuing in his job just because he's done it for a specified period of time? Age limits? Nearly 40% of Fortune 1000 companies adopted age limits in response to urgings from governance poobahs such as CalPers.

But a company that forbids persons older than, say, 65 or 70 is ordaining the exclusion of talent from its reach. One can applaud Jack Bogle for stepping down as Vanguard's chairman at the fund's mandated retirement age of 70, but is Vanguard really better off without Jack or any other (old!) sagacious person with integrity? And what should it matter—on its own terms—that 5 of the 18 members of Disney's board are in their seventies, if those people are savvy business leaders who seek to promote the interests of Disney's owners?

At the other end of the politically correct scale of corporate governance is the goal of trying to add diversity of gender or race to the board. Diversity itself is not a laudable business goal and is nothing for which credit should be given to the leaders of a business organization. It is just as out of place, silly, and off the mark as deliberately creating and maintaining a diversified portfolio of stocks. It may turn out to be fine and dandy, but if so, that is a consequence and not a cause of a more prudent disposition that focuses on fundamentals rather than frames. It does not matter one way or the other that GE's board has two women and one black person on it though it does matter that those people and GE's other directors are outstanding business thinkers with a strong owner orientation.

The problem with all these sorts of proposals is their universality. What is good for GM may not be good for GE, and what is good for either of them may not be good for Procter & Gamble or eBay, Wrigley, or Hershey. Each corporate situation justifies and calls for its own governance structure and analysis. Broad credit can be given only for governance moves that have some inherently defensible logic, such as having the board review the CEO's performance without her being present and having independence on the audit committee.

Beyond that, these general principles are of little use. Indeed, too much emphasis on them can be affirmatively misleading. You can put all the governance bells and whistles you want on a board, but if its CEO or other strong leaders lack integrity, you can be sure they will neither ring nor blow.

GENERAL GOVERNANCE

While one-size-fits-all recipes of corporate governance are inapt, a few areas justify generalizations. The most important is that active boards engaged with the companies they serve boost corporate performance. That is plain common sense, though empirical studies confirm the intuition.[6]

A key problem in all governance structures is the size of the board. You do need a minimum number of directors to generate the kind of thoughtful deliberateness that characterizes any effective group of people. But above that number—which is probably as low as six—the larger the board is, the less manageable it is. Lean is mean in business, and there is no question that ideas and energy move more quickly through leaner managerial structures, as Wal-Mart proved to Sears and GE proved to Westinghouse. Smaller boards often translate into leaner management teams down the ranks.

A similar problem is the number of other boards on which individual directors serve. The more duties a given director undertakes in various companies, the less effective she is likely to be on each one. A director's concurrent experience on two boards may add value to both. Former U.S. Senator Sam Nunn serves on the boards of a half dozen public companies (including GE, Coke, and Texaco), for example, and his work on one may benefit the needs of the others. But how effective is a director who serves on a dozen boards at once? Vernon Jordan serves on nearly that many and has been criticized for doing so. It would be a rare person whose prominence and trustworthiness, not to mention access to the corridors of power, could remain valuable to a company that shares her service with so many others.

A final point all corporations should worry about is who is next in line for the top spot. It may not be necessary for a company to have a formal succession plan for its CEO, but it is important for the board to give it some thought. The trouble is that even the best laid plan can go awry and sometimes the most surprising and unplanned succession can have terrific benefits. Succession is a matter of judgment, and just because a board has thought hard about it, that doesn't mean its plan will work (more on this in the next chapter).

All these details of corporate governance provide clues about managerial trustworthiness. A board filled with close personal friends of the CEO who lack solid business backgrounds is a red flag of caution. A board that fails to review the chief's performance regularly may not be trustworthy either. Take another area of corporate life: charitable giving. If most of the corporation's charitable contributions go to pet causes of the CEO, maybe you should wonder whether he treats the corporation more as his than as yours. Unique among major American corporations, Berkshire Hathaway rejects managerial direction of discretionary charitable giving, putting this power directly in the hands of shareholders.[7]

If these factors indicate high trustworthiness, lower your discount rate on a good business; if they suggest moderate trustworthiness, raise it upward. (If they suggest an antiowner orientation, simply stay away.)

Amid the intense interest in corporate governance there generally emerges the subtopic of corporate governance for Internet companies. Some argue that the traditional templates of corporate governance simply do not apply to new economy companies. It is hard to see exactly why, but the argument seems to be that the speed of industry change, the intensity of competition, the shortage of technology-savvy managers, and the importance of stock options in compensation packages mean that the new economy cannot abide the old rules and ways.[8]

These arguments are silly. On their face, they state very little difference in the problems of governing a new economy company versus an old economy company. Change, competition, managerial savvy, and incentive compensation matter in all businesses. A better argument would relate these different sorts of companies to their respective average sizes. Smaller companies may need or warrant less in the way of formal governance (such as board review of director performance) than do larger companies. But that argument relates to the dot-com governance debate only to the extent that dot-coms are on average smaller than non-dot-coms, something that may or may not be true and so is ultimately irrelevant.

The key issue for any kind of business also remains the same, whether new economy, old economy, future economy, or whatever. It is what constitutes good governance, and the answer varies with company specifics, including potentially to which category a company belongs. Just as a one-size-fits-all governance template is inappropriate for the run of non-dot-com companies, it is inappropriate for dot-coms.

In fairness to the advocates of new governance rules for new economy companies, they were forced into this strange stance (that dot-coms as a group were both alike and special) because governance gurus had so whipsawed old economy companies into governance uniformity that prevailing governance practices did not make sense for many dot-coms (for the same reasons they never made sense for many old economy companies).

It is therefore a colossal waste of time even to discuss whether governance principles should be different. Of course they should, but not because of anything special about dot-coms as such but instead because every business organization is special.

YOUR VOICE AT THE TABLE

Persuading boards to listen to shareholders is an ideal corporate governance method, but legal and practical limits frustrate this simple vehicle. Apathy and collective action problems limit the shareholders' voice, but this explains only part of the problem.

Most state laws authorize corporations to establish procedures governing shareholder proposals at annual or special meetings. The SEC imposes additional rules.[9] As a matter of practice, management on average strongly prefers rules that enable it to omit shareholder proposals from proxy statements.

Using the "shareholder proposal rule" has led to substantial policy changes at many major corporations. For example, beginning in the 1930s, this rule was used to enhance shareholder rights in areas such as cumulative voting and dissemination of postmeeting reports.

Virtually anyone can satisfy the eligibility requirements for compelling a corporation to include a shareholder proposal in the corporation's annual proxy statement. By law it is enough to own 1% or $1,000 in market value of the corporation's equity for one year, and the costs of making proposals are borne by the company.

Shareholder proposals are often made by only nominal shareholders, spearheaded by nonshareholder constituencies that harness the shareholder proposal rule to effect social change. (This use exploded in the 1970s, with the famous Campaign GM that led to the integration of GM's board of directors.) Social policy advocates use it to promote things such as reporting requirements concerning the environmental impact of corporate actions, race and sex discrimination, and human rights activities. Sometimes these are in the interests of shareholders, and sometimes they are not.

In the last few decades shareholders and other constituencies have employed this device innumerable times. Although most campaigns do not carry a majority vote, increasing numbers of proposals win. But because everyone knows nominal shareholders can make proposals, management can take lightly even proposals that win the support of a majority of shareholders. Thus management often opts not to implement a winning proposal. After all, if management believes in the proposal, it will adopt it without waiting for a constituency initiative or vote.

More important than the shareholder proposal rule is the possibility of a corporate takeover. This can be effected either by proxy contest or by tender offer. In a proxy contest, the more traditional method of corporate takeover, a shareholder or group of shareholders appeals to other shareholders to change control of the company by electing new directors to the board. They argue their case in a proxy statement delivered to all shareholders, and the incumbent group presents its case in its own proxy statement. The shareholders vote, and their voice is heard.

Before the late 1960s and early 1970s, Ben Graham lamented the difficulty shareholders faced in changing poor management in this way. (Graham knew firsthand about those difficulties, for he waged a proxy contest to wrest control of a company earlier in his career.)[10] But proxy contests became far easier to wage and more effective in that time, signaling the dawn of the corporate governance movement that took firm hold in the 1980s. As a consequence of the rise in proxy contests in the late 1960s and early 1970s, Graham said that "boards of directors have probably become more alive than previously to their fundamental duty to see that their company has a satisfactory top management."

The 1980s brought more sophisticated and better-funded takeover tactics to corporate America, chiefly the tender offer, by which shareholders simply exit a company with unsatisfactory management and performance. The result has been the creation of a market for control of corporations, a way to give real meaning to the shareholders' voice. Thus, Graham's plea made at the dawn of the corporate governance era assumes greater value now: "that stockholders consider with an open mind and with careful attention any proxy material sent them by fellow stockholders who want to remedy an obviously unsatisfactory management situation in the company."[11]

DIRECTORS AT WORK

An increasingly common lament sung across corporate America is that directors are overworked. They are asked to do too much, must satisfy too many competing interests, and so on. There is a simple and sufficient solution to this condition. Directors should be asked to do a short list of five things and do them well. The key jobs entrusted to any board of directors are as follows:

- Selecting an effective chief executive
- Setting executive compensation
- Evaluating takeovers
- Allocating capital
- Promoting integrity in financial reporting

Effective performance of these jobs ultimately depends not so much on governance mechanisms as on board trustworthiness. An investor should pay attention to how well directors perform these tasks as a way to gauge where along the continuum from owner orientation to manager orientation they sit. A management-oriented position is suggested by fat executive paychecks for a dismal performance. A stakeholder-oriented position reveals itself in poor returns on invested capital that keep unproductive plants operating in a bow to labor pressure. An owner orientation is reflected by good performance, reasonable executive pay, and the cultivation of productive workers in productive jobs.

As a management orientation example, ask yourself whose interests were really going to be served by AMP's resistance to Allied-Signal's bid discussed in Chapter 11? AMP's shareholders objected, and so they obviously thought their interests were being disserved, and AMP's plan to boost the company's profitability included cutting the work force by about 9%, or 4200 jobs, and closing ten factories.[1] AMP's board ultimately may have served the corporation's interests in concluding a deal with a friendly partner, but AMP's CEO and management undoubtedly pressured the board to resist what by all accounts looked good for shareholders in favor of something that looked bad for the workers.

The best way to tell where a company sits is to investigate the way its directors tackle their key jobs. Focus on those jobs and decide which boards do them well.

HAIL TO THE CHIEF

The CEO sets the tone at the top. The CEO's historical performance on matters such as compensation, acquisitions, and capital allocation generally is the key question an investor should ask when judging a CEO and deciding whether to entrust wealth to his or her management. Special attention must be paid to selecting a CEO because of his or her unique role in the organization.

Warren Buffett notes that standards for measuring a CEO's performance are either inadequate or easy to manipulate, and so a CEO's performance is harder to measure than that of most workers. The CEO has no senior other than in theory the company's board of directors. That board is often handicapped in its performance review, however, because of a lack of measurement standards and because as meetings come and go, the relationship between the CEO and the directors increasingly becomes congenial rather than supervisory.

Maintaining that supervisory attitude is critical. The board's role in reviewing the CEO's performance is most acute precisely where it can be most easily impaired: dealing with a mediocre manager. It is easy for a board to get rid of a terrible manager; the hard case is a so-so one. Recruiting the top talent and a roster of succession candidates is a critical board function. Too often the importance of this role is overlooked, as occurs when a board simply replaces an outgoing CEO with the number two fellow at the company (which happens about two-thirds of the time). This means that many boards fail to evaluate changing organizational needs and variations in the personal talents of the two at the top.[2]

Abdication of a board's responsibility for CEO selection is most clear when a board simply allows an incumbent CEO to handpick the successor. There is little reason to believe that even the most outstanding CEO is as good as a top board at picking a new CEO. The result is too often the need to oust the new CEO pretty early in his or her tenure.

Still, boards must evaluate a CEO's performance regularly and out of the CEO's presence, and evaluating that performance is harder than it seems. Both short-term results and potential long-term results must be assessed. If only short-term results mattered, many managerial decisions would be much easier, particularly those relating to businesses whose economic characteristics have eroded.

Recall again Al Dunlap's aggressive and doomed plan to turn around the ailing Sunbeam. The huge accounting scandal that followed in its wake also suggests its inherent stupidity. Once it was clear that Dunlap was a terrible manager, it was easy for the Sunbeam board to throw him out, but before the fallout he looked at worst mediocre and therefore harder to disagree with.

PAY

Plenty of evidence shows that the total level of executive compensation in the United States is positively correlated with the level of corporate performance. Some evidence even shows a positive correlation between performance and the portion of total compensation paid in stock.[3]

Even so, it is also obvious that some executives are paid substantially more than they should be in light of their performance. Accordingly, investors should pay close attention to potentially piratical executive compensation.

COMPENSATION LEVELS

This is not to say that it is desirable to have governance rules that limit top executive compensation to some ratio of the pay of the least compensated employee at a company. Indeed, Ben & Jerry's tried this during its early years of business life, capping its founder's and chief's compensation at seven times that of the lowest-paid worker. But once the company outgrew its founder's managerial skills, it was forced to go on the market to recruit top talent, and that required a pay package way higher than that cap.[4]

If the early Ben & Jerry's policy showed bad judgment, some of the pay packages seen lately show something far worse. The CEO of Network Associates (owner of the McAfee computer antivirus programs), for example, got about $7 million in shares of McAfee.com just ahead of its IPO even though the business of Network Associates performed poorly and McAfee itself was losing money.[5]

A key issue in the merger between Chrysler and Daimler-Benz was the enormous difference between the two companies both in the level of executive compensation and in the compensation ratios of the highest-paid and lowest-paid employees. In 1997, for example, Robert Eaton, Chrysler's chairman of the board, received total compensation of about $10 million, over 200 times the average worker's pay and nearly as much as the total compensation paid to all ten members of Daimler-Benz's management board combined. Daimler-Benz's chairman, Jurgen Schrempp, was paid about one-tenth as much as Eaton, making his compensation approximately twenty times that of the average Daimler-Benz worker.

Thus, a major question in the merger was the form that the combined entity's compensation structure should take. Schrempp pointed out that the existing pay differences reflected cultural differences, particularly the somewhat more egalitarian corporate culture in Germany, as demonstrated by labor representation on supervisory boards. He also predicted that the U.S. model would prove to be the proper form for DaimlerChrysler and other transnational companies, except that "the only way to make big pay packets socially acceptable is by linking them closely to performance."[6]

Schrempp's statement mirrors the rhetoric of corporate America. Given that the other differences in corporate governance between Germany and the United States are more nuanced and subtle than is generally understood, you have to wonder if this was Schrempp's main point when he said that DaimlerChrysler created "the first German company with a North American culture." Any doubt was cleared up when Schrempp subsequently proselytized for American-style executive options at DaimlerChrysler's April 2000 shareholder meeting, something his German shareholders sensibly resisted.

STOCK OPTIONS

A decade ago corporate governance mavens urged boards to pay managers more in stock than in cash to promote an alignment of interests between managers and shareholders. The response was tremendous, a bit like the apocryphal story of Lady Astor's famous quip on the Titanic: "I asked for ice, but this is ridiculous."

What the governance gurus got was a proliferation of payment not in stock that was the functional equivalent of the forgone cash but instead stock options with a value vastly exceeding what the cash payment could reasonably have been. The explosion of option-based compensation remains one of the most controversial subjects in corporate governance history.

Some say that the widespread use of stock options in the United States simply reflects the priority given to this alignment goal in the United States and that its relative infrequency in Europe and elsewhere reflects the absence or irrelevance of this goal. However, the talk of alignment is more myth than truth and too often represents an attempt to sanitize management compensation packages that conflict with shareholder interests (not to mention labor interests).

STOCK OPTION MYTHS

No evidence indicates that the prevailing structure of executive compensation in the United States comes anywhere close to aligning manager and shareholder interests. On the contrary, a great deal of evidence demonstrates that the compensation structure is random.

Many corporations give their managers stock options which increase in value simply through earnings retention, rather than because of improved performance resulting from superior deployment of capital. By retaining and reinvesting net income, managers can report annual earnings increases without doing anything to improve real returns on capital.

Buffett makes the point: "You can get the same result personally while operating from your rocking chair. Just quadruple the capital you commit to a savings account and you will quadruple your earnings. You would hardly expect hosannas for that particular accomplishment."[7]

When that happens, stock options rob the corporation and its shareholders of wealth and allocate the booty to the optionees. Indeed, once granted, stock options are often irrevocable and unconditional and benefit the grantees without regard to individual performance—a form of instant robbery.

Even if stock options encourage optionees to think as shareholders would, optionees are not exposed to the same downside risks as shareholders are. If economic performance improves and the stock price rises above the exercise price, the optionees will exercise the option and share in the increase with shareholders. But if economic performance is unfavorable and the stock price remains below the exercise price, optionees simply will not exercise the option. Shareholders suffer from the corporation's unfavorable performance, but an option holder does not.

These awards also exacerbate the misalignment of interests between corporate option holders (usually senior executives) and other workers. The awards dramatically increase the compensation differential between highly paid executives and ordinary laborers, a ratio which is significantly higher in the United States than it is in Europe and elsewhere. Accordingly, when stock options are used, they should be spread throughout the employee base—as GE has done—rather than limited to the top dogs.

STOCK OPTION COSTS

The direct cost to shareholders of stock option compensation is the dilution of their ownership interest. A common managerial response to the dilution is to buy back outstanding shares. The trouble with that solution is that it devours corporate funds that might be more profitably deployed.

Shocking indirect costs are accounting rules that fail to require employee stock options to be recorded as an expense on the income statement.[8] This translates into earnings per share figures that overstate actual earnings for companies with executive stock options outstanding. Even the diluted earnings per share figure does not reflect these costs.

Accordingly, you must adjust earnings figures for the cost of options. Doing this is not easy, however, for not all information is necessarily found in the financial statements. You need to examine the footnotes for something called overhang, which is the percentage of the company that outstanding stock options would represent if they were exercised. The average percentage has mushroomed from under 10% a few years ago to nearly 15% now.

Still, the actual cost of options is not presented directly, though there is some footnote disclosure about this. The real cost equals the price at the time of exercise minus the amount the executive pays (the exercise price). This is the truest measure of cost because the company could have generated that much by selling the optioned shares to others at the prevalent price instead of at the option price.

The cost of executive stock options is substantial, averaging about 5% of annual earnings among S&P 500 companies and in some cases amounting to half of reported earnings, including at Yahoo!, Polaroid, and Palm.[9] In less dramatic but still striking examples, if stock options were recorded as a cost, the 1999 earnings of some major companies would be slashed: Cisco, 24%; Microsoft, 12%; IBM, 8%; and Oracle, 16%.[10]

These cost effects extend for many years, depending on the life of the options. At many companies, options have a life of five years. Increasingly, companies extend their lives to as long as 10 and 15 years.

Accountability

Legal rules are ill equipped to police executive compensation. The general stance of U.S. courts is to evaluate compensation issues, if at all, under a waste standard. This standard rarely upsets corporate decisions. Waste requires pretty much the irrational trashing of corporate assets in ways akin to dumping truckloads of cash into the Hudson River. In the case of executive compensation, U.S. courts are quite deferential to management indeed.

As for securities disclosure laws, the SEC requires substantial and focused disclosure of top executive compensation in comparative performance charts. Nevertheless, corporations continue to structure executive compensation packages so that they don't show up in the bottom-line numbers. For example, after accounting standard setters ruled that a reduction in the exercise price of a previously issued option had to be recorded as an expense on the income statement, many companies chose instead to extend the life of the option.

Without effective legal or accounting regulations, the chief job of policing executive compensation lies with the corporate board. Board members must insist that executive compensation peg individual contributions to corporate performance. Measuring executive performance by business profitability is the most definitive yardstick with regard to shareholder as well as labor interests. When measuring performance, companies should reduce earnings by the capital employed in the relevant business or by the earnings the firm retains.

Caveat

While Warren Buffett tends to share these criticisms of stock option compensation packages, he is careful to record the following caveat:

Some managers whom I admire enormously—and whose operating records are far better than mine—disagree with me regarding fixed-price options. They have built corporate cultures
that work, and fixed-price options have been a tool that helped
them. By their leadership and example, and by the use of options
as incentives, these managers have taught their colleagues to
think like owners. Such a culture is rare and when it exists
should perhaps be left intact—despite inefficiencies and ineq-
uities that may infest the option program.[11]

Investors should look for boards that take the lead in policing
stock option compensation, but beware—they are scarce.

DEALS

Just as the disease of random executive compensation must be
avoided by intelligent investors and trustworthy boards, so must the
costs of imprudent acquisition policies and defensive tactics.

OFFENSIVE

Offensive acquisition strategies require careful board attention because of the strong possibility that even outstanding senior managers
possess individual interests that conflict with owner interests. Acquisitions give CEOs enormous psychological benefits by expanding
their dominion and generating more action. Acquisitions driven by
these sorts of impulses come at shareholder expense.

Most acquisitions do not achieve gains in business value. A 1999
study by the global accounting firm KPMG concluded that "83% of
mergers [during the period 1996–1998, when trillions had been paid
in merger deals] failed to produce any benefits for shareholders and,
even more alarming, over half actually destroyed value." That study
also found, based on interviews with managers involved in mergers,
that less than half did any postdeal review to test whether value was
added or subtracted![12]

A governance problem exists because most acquisition attempts
do not come to the board for discussion until the process is substantially under way and until after the CEO has invested substantial
personal capital in them. Rejecting an acquisition proposal after the
CEO invests substantial personal capital is often considered a rejection of the CEO who presented the proposal to the board. This problem is especially acute among CEOs who resent hearing bad news.

Cascades of stupid acquisitions come pouring in, often drowning the board's better judgment.

These timing problems make it difficult to design a governance mechanism that would alleviate this pressure on the board. The ego problems are just as intractable, as another Buffettism suggests: "While deals often fail in practice, they never fail in projections—if the CEO is visibly panting over a prospective acquisition, subordinates and consultants will supply the requisite projections to rationalize any price."[13]

Mattel, for example, is a worldwide leader in the design, manufacture, and distribution of toys. In May 1999 it bought the Learning Company, a producer of educational software for personal computers. Mattel paid for the $3.8 billion purchase by using Mattel stock at a time when the stock was trading at about $26 a share (down already from an average trading price over the prior year of around $40). Mattel's chair, Jill Barad, announced in July 1999 that the Learning Company was contributing to Mattel's overall operations with "exceptionally strong growth" in revenues and margins and said this "was one of the reasons this merger made so much sense for Mattel."[14]

Barad did not say how the computer software business related to Mattel's traditional products, such as Barbie dolls, Fisher-Price toys, and Hot Wheels. But just three months later, in October 1999, Mattel announced that the Learning Company division's revenues had declined and it had lost money because of, among other things, higher than expected product returns from customers and write-offs of bad debts.[15] Instead of earning $50 million that quarter as Barad estimated, it lost over $100 million, and Mattel's stock plummeted to about $11 a share. Many analysts, at least in hindsight, reported that these problems at the Learning Company were not new and should have been uncovered and discounted before Mattel bought it.

These analysts also thought that Mattel fit the description of a company about to make a bad acquisition. If sales growth in your core business is declining and you can't seem to do anything about it through product, marketing, or distribution improvements, one impulse is to buy yourself some growth through an acquisition. Mattel's sales growth, incidentally, was declining in its core products right before the Learning Company acquisition. So too, for that matter, was the Learning Company's. (Mattel's board ousted Barad in early 2000, awarding her an exorbitant severance package, and replaced her with Kraft Foods CEO Robert Eckert.)

Contrast Mattel's story with the policies of Disney. Disney's philosophy is to make only acquisitions that are in a related or complementary field that current management understands fully, and at a fair price. In its most important acquisition, Capital Cities ABC fit the bill. Disney's long-time chairman, Michael Eisner, had worked at ABC from 1966 through 1976 and had seen it grow from a network critics called the "fourth of three" to first place in every category.

After Capital Cities bought ABC in 1986, Tom Murphy and Dan Burke catapulted it to yet new heights, and the combination with Disney made sense. Walt Disney himself liked ABC as well. After all, ABC helped finance Disneyland in 1955, and Walt brought ABC to Hollywood when he began what is now *The Wonderful World of Disney*. Disney's Internet business benefited enormously from the addition of ABC.com, ESPN.com, and a host of cable assets that enable important growth opportunities.

DEFENSIVE

Takeover defenses are the flip side of offensive acquisition strategies. Antitakeover devices such as the poison pill protect management's decision making by discouraging attempts to acquire the corporation or remove incumbent directors (as AMP's defense against Allied-Signal attests). If some or a majority of stockholders deem a takeover attempt to be in the corporation's and their best interest and the potential acquirer is willing to pay a premium over the prevailing market price or intrinsic value of the corporation's common stock, antitakeover devices work against shareholders.

Disney's acquisition philosophy is also illustrative on this side of the table. Corporate raiders of the early 1980s sought to acquire Disney and bust it up but Roy Disney would not let that happen. He preserved Disney as a great American institution and facilitated a recommitment to the fundamental businesses that had made it great. Disney animation, for example, with Roy at the helm, reinvented itself and surged with a long series of critically and popularly acclaimed films. In doing so, Disney adopted the best takeover defense strategy there is: an extraordinary business. (More on Disney in the next chapter.)

To be sure, situations exist in which hostile offers are inadequate and not in the interests of the corporation or any of its constituents. Yet incumbent managers facing unwanted takeover talks naturally will resist the efforts of the acquiring firm whether or not their resistance best serves the corporation. After all, in most cases their jobs are at risk.

Within U.S. corporations—and probably increasingly within corporations organized elsewhere—takeovers put unmatured stock options at risk. Faced with this prospect, managers may employ mechanisms designed to resist inferior bids in an effort to resist superior bids. They thus may use a poison pill against a bid that is great for shareholders when it should be used only to deter bids that are bad for shareholders.

In these situations, boards must recognize that CEOs and their troops are under fire, just as they are when a board challenges one of their proposed offensive acquisitions.

In both situations boards should expect managers to adopt a siege mentality which obscures honest thinking about what is in the owners' interests. In both offensive and defensive situations there is no clear mechanism that can assure that boards will respond properly, but boards must at least recognize what is happening psychologically in these situations if they hope to respond effectively at all. For investors, identifying directors with that capacity is key.

CAPITAL

A company generating substantial amounts of excess cash can deploy it in one of four ways. It can reinvest in the business, repurchase its own shares, distribute the cash in dividends to shareholders, and, as was just noted, make acquisitions.

Aside from a few formal and manipulable limits, U.S. law gives boards of directors unbridled discretion in the choice of these uses, including declaring and paying dividends and making or not making repurchases. Corporate charters rarely restrict dividend policies, although a corporation's loan and credit agreements sometimes do.

The policy of most U.S. boards is to pay regular quarterly cash dividends at a stable or steadily increasing dollar amount. This pattern is inconsistent with the reality that underlying business performance is hardly ever that smooth. Earnings are almost always bumpy (even if less bumpy than average stock prices).

Dividends tend to be way higher than they should be. Given the importance of dividend policy in capital allocation decisions, certain common reasons that boards use to justify their policies, such as signaling confidence and giving the appearance of reliability, are either strange or disingenuous.

We should give credit to boards that use a more rigorous approach for setting dividend policy, an ideal set forth by Warren Buffett. The test distinguishes between restricted earnings, those which must be reinvested in a business just to maintain its competitive position, and unrestricted earnings, which should be retained only when there is a reasonable prospect that for every dollar retained, at least one dollar of market value will be created for shareholders; otherwise, the dollar of earnings should be paid out.[16] Microsoft follows this policy pretty well, never having paid a dividend and generating great returns on the reinvested capital.

Boards can justify retaining earnings under this test only if the capital retained produces incremental earnings at least equal to the return generally available to the shareholders. For companies that can reinvest earnings in this manner, dividends should not be paid and boards should ignore any negative signals this policy sends, such as lack of confidence or unreliability (though they should pay attention to the resulting tax advantages to shareholders).

The smartest thing a company can do with undervalued stock is to buy it back. Obviously, if a stock is selling in the market at half its intrinsic value, the company can buy $2 in value by paying $1 in cash. You rarely find better uses of capital than that. Stock repurchases usually give a stockholder a slight tax advantage. Dividends on common stock are taxed as ordinary income at rates as high as 39.6%, whereas income generated by the repurchase of stock held longer than a year is treated as capital gains at rates no higher than 20%.

Stock buybacks are not always what they seem. They reduce the number of a company's shares outstanding, thus increasing earnings per share. The typical result is that investors buy more of that stock and thus bid the price up, mistakenly believing that the repurchases are a managerial signal that the company's stock is underpriced. Often, however, the repurchase program is a cognate of a stock issuance program to offset shares issued upon the exercise of stock options. The increased stock price, after all, means increasing the value of stock options on that stock. When a repurchase program and an issuance program are run simultaneously, you should be more discriminating in your judgment of what management is doing.

It is possible that this effect could lead management (with many stock options at its feet) to prefer buybacks even if that were not the smartest way to allocate the company's capital. Indeed, options create incentives to borrow money for stock repurchases that boost earnings per share and return on equity. That poses a major risk, as a smaller equity base in a crisis can push a company closer to bankruptcy, severely damaging shareholder interests (as well as the interests of others).

In contrast to the occasional wisdom of stock repurchases is the universal folly of stock splits. Stock splits have three consequences, none of them beneficial to the stockholders. They increase transaction costs by promoting high share turnover; they attract shareholders with short-term, market-oriented views who unduly focus on stock market prices; and, as a result of both of those effects, they lead to prices that depart materially from intrinsic business value.

With no offsetting benefits, splitting a stock is nonsense. Nevertheless, most companies do it, including GE, Microsoft, and Amazon.com. Berkshire Hathaway is one of the handful that don't. After going public in mid-1997, Amazon.com split its stock three times from June 1998 to September 1999! GE split its stock only nine times in its hundred-plus-year history, though three of those splits occurred in the last six years of the 1990s.

The only meritorious argument favoring stock splits is that they reduce the per share price of stock and thus enable a wider investor group to participate. If no U.S. company in history had ever split its stock, the per share price of some of the best companies would be in the tens of thousands of dollars (as is the case at Berkshire Hathaway, for example). That price level is prohibitive for many investors. This argument does not justify the high frequency of stock splits, however, which are used to keep prices below a couple of hundred dollars—an amount that is affordable by all investors.

CHECKING UP

As Chapter 10 showed, for accounting information to be valuable, users must have justifiable confidence in its integrity. Forces that jeopardize integrity are often intractable: Business innovation, evolution, and complexity, coupled with the formal nature of accounting rules inevitably create a substantial zone of managerial discretion in financial reporting.

Integrity in financial reporting is promoted through internal control systems and by external auditor certifications, both of which can constrain managerial discretion somewhat. For these mechanisms to be effective, however, the board of directors must assure that both internal controls and external audits do this.

Internal financial reporting controls are designed to assure that transactions are executed in accordance with management policy and are recorded properly in the accounting records (and to assure that assets are deployed only in accordance with management policy). They range from daily journal entries that are reviewed regularly by others, to periodic taking of inventory, to procedures for review of judgments concerning depreciation, to the articulation and review of risk management policies. Some of these tools are required by federal securities laws.

Within a corporation, both the board of directors and the managers play a role in defining, implementing, and evaluating internal controls. In principle, however, the chief and ultimate responsibility for internal controls rests with the board of directors, both as a matter of common sense and as a matter of policy. Boards have a comparative informational advantage and greater motivation to police managerial opportunism than managers do. This obligation entails supervising the design of internal control systems and supporting their administration.

The critical importance of internal controls to the integrity of financial reporting is evidenced by the requirement that outside auditors review them in connection with annual audits of a company's financial statements. This audit is intended to obtain objective assurance that the financial statements are relevant and reliable, based on a general review of the financial statements and the underlying day-to-day records and periodic summaries on which they are based.

The audit is a monitoring mechanism that lends credibility to the financial statements. For that credibility to be meaningful, however, the auditor must work closely with members of the board of directors, and both the auditor and those directors must act with diligence, independence, and awareness. Several challenges are posed for a board and its audit committee.

First, an audit conducted by an independent firm does not change the fact that a company's management prepares the financial statements and is responsible for them. The audit is a review of those statements. The audit does not entail a review of every financial transaction in which the company engaged during the period covered by the financial statements. That is a practical impossibility for any auditor and even more so for any audit committee. Businesses engage in huge numbers of financial transactions during the course of the typical financial period, usually one year. Instead, audits are conducted on a "test basis" by reviewing a sample of the hundreds or thousands of transactions of a variety of kinds engaged in by the firm over time.

Second, with respect to the detection of fraud, neither the auditor nor the audit committee is always in a position to root it out. This is the case principally because it is impossible for the audit to include an examination of every single transaction in which a company engaged or in which management says it engaged.

Third, the auditor must be independent of the company, a requirement imposed by the canons of professional responsibility of the auditing profession; so too must the members of the audit committee, a requirement of stock exchange rules endorsed by the SEC. Audits lacking impartial and objective professional judgment fail to promote financial reporting integrity. At best, they end up functioning as merely another type of internal control.

Audits are harmful if they carry a false appearance of independent certification that induces undue reliance. Also, since effective independent audits include testing internal controls, the integrity of those systems is undermined by a nonobjective and potentially biased audit that diminishes rather than enhances overall integrity.

Audit firm independence is a hot topic. The big global auditing firms have expanded their businesses beyond the traditional audit function to include consulting and other practices that could in some circumstances compromise their ability to contribute integrity to financial reporting. These firms have merged, restructured, or been acquired by other corporations. Their clients and business are evolving into more sophisticated, technologically advanced, and transnational operations.

The SEC established the Independence Standards Board (ISB) to address auditor independence issues,[17] but it remains a principal responsibility of the board of directors and its audit committee to assure an independent financial review. Those in charge are accountable for adopting a diligent and alert mind-set that lets them rigorously assess the company's internal controls, the testing of its reported accounts, and the likelihood that what they see accountingwise is what really happened businesswise.

The audit committee is the one place where independent directors are called for, but independence is not as essential as expertise in accounting and/or auditing, as the new stock exchange rules now require. That is a crucial step (though by no means a sufficient one) in giving assurance that, in the words of the traditional SEC standard, "a reasonable investor, knowing all relevant facts and circumstances, would perceive an auditor as having neither mutual nor conflicting interests with its audit client and as exercising objective and impartial judgment on all issues brought to the auditor's attention."

Only then are financial statements worth analyzing. Auditing is an area over which the board of directors must take control and provide leadership. Boards that consistently do this deserve credit. Those which do not should be penalized—and they should be penalized long before the outside auditor gets around to blowing the whistle, as shareholders of Rite-Aid discovered to their chagrin and loss in late 1999, when its outside auditors resigned from their audit engagement on the grounds that they could no longer trust management to tell them the truth!

Important as the auditor, audit committee, and board are in their key jobs, there remains one person holding the torch for investors—the CEO. Buffett says:

> The term "earnings" has a precise ring to it. And when an earnings figure is accompanied by an unqualified auditor's certificate, a naive reader might think it comparable in certitude to π, calculated to dozens of decimal places.
>
> In reality, however, earnings can be as pliable as putty when a charlatan heads the company reporting them. Eventually truth will surface, but in the meantime a lot of money can change hands. Indeed, some important American fortunes have been created by the monetization of accounting mirages.[18]

Avoiding charlatans is even more important than identifying excellent boards, so let's move on to the corner suite.

CHAPTER 14

THE FIRESIDE CEO

The legendary investor Phil Fisher described his scuttlebutt approach to investing as requiring diligent investigation of management. He boldly interviewed a company's customers, suppliers, and employees about the managers and also spoke to management directly. The Fisher method is followed today by venture capitalists but is prohibitive for most average investors, who cannot get out and visit those folks or even talk to them.

Some reasonable substitutes are available, though. You can listen in on the investor conference calls held by most companies on a quarterly basis and chaired by the CEO (the dial-in numbers for these calls are available from the company and from most brokerage firms). You can also attend the periodic "road shows" that companies take through your locality; they are particularly worthwhile when the CEO is in tow (which isn't always the case) and you can attend annual meetings to get a bird's-eye view of the chief. These and other events are often available on the Internet as Webcasts.

You can also read the voluminous material written about the CEOs of most companies and by the CEOs themselves. At the top of the reading list for insight into the character and business orientation of a CEO is his annual letters to shareholders. Most of these are public relations documents, ghostwritten, stylized, and full of puffery. No one is fooled by messages written in the promotions department, but among the glossy, photograph-laden, chart-strewn marketing materials are a handful of letters actually written by the CEO. Those are the letters worth reading.

MASTER SERVANTS

The seven basic characteristics most widely cited by venture capitalists as important to look for in managers are integrity, achievement, energy, intelligence, knowledge, leadership, and creativity.[1] Which of these is the most important?

Obviously, you want to avoid entrusting your wealth to a brilliant crook or a trustworthy idiot. An above-average IQ and these other traits are certainly assets, but your CEO need not be in the top 10% in the world on all these scales (who is?).

You might be tempted to follow the line of Fred Schwed in *Where Are the Customers' Yachts?* who joked that he'd prefer a smart criminal to an honest bonehead because at least with a writ and a cop he'd collect from the thief whereas all he'd get from the bonehead was a pathetic apology. Don't do this.

Buffett repeatedly emphasizes that the one characteristic that belongs on a pedestal is integrity. This means a CEO who thinks of your interests first, one who has what Buffett calls an owner orientation. CEOs reveal the degree of their owner orientation in their letters, as described by the rules Warren Buffett sets for himself when he writes his annual letter to Berkshire Hathaway shareholders: "to tell you the business facts that we would want to know if our positions were reversed. We owe you no less. . . . The CEO who misleads others in public may eventually mislead himself in private."[2] Apply that standard in evaluating whether a CEO deserves your trust.

Everyone knows that Warren Buffett is an enormously successful investor, but not everyone is aware that he is also an enormously successful and owner-oriented manager. On this score, Buffett is to business management what Ted Williams was to baseball. Both are in classes by themselves, Ted constantly hitting near .400 and Warren constantly writing lucid and candid reports of his successes and failures at Berkshire Hathaway (compiled into the book *The Essays of Warren Buffett: Lessons for Corporate America*).

While Buffett is in a class by himself, there are many runners-up, and searching for them by reading CEO letters is a valuable and often entertaining investing exercise. This chapter looks at what is revealed by the letters of three leaders who display not only honesty, the key characteristic you should seek in a CEO, but also in various degrees achievement, energy, intelligence, knowledge, leadership, and creativity.

ACTION

Few CEOs have affected corporate America as GE's Jack Welch has.[3] By word and action since taking the helm at General Electric in

1979, Welch has redefined major aspects of business management. In his widely followed annual letters to GE shareholders, Welch articulates a creative set of core operating elements and explains how their practical applications produce a new kind of company that exploits the vast resources of a large organization with the passion and hunger usually associated with smaller companies, all within a corporate culture committed to cultivating the best practices.

GE is one of the largest companies in the world. Welch transformed it from a widely diverse set of 350 businesses and major product lines into what he calls an "integrated, diversified company." Welch determined that GE's strength from diversity could be real only if each business was number one or two in its particular market. Through a policy of "fixing, selling, or closing" businesses that weren't, Welch led GE to occupy a leadership position in the dozen businesses it now operates. Those businesses are integrated as an overall company through a boundaryless culture united by a shared thirst for better ideas to work faster and reach higher.

GE shareholders benefited enormously from this culture of boundaryless and integrated diversity, enjoying average annual returns on equity exceeding 24% during Welch's stewardship. Hundreds of thousands of GE employees also benefited through an enhanced system of internal rewards and recognition that encourages involvement. A large number of GE alumni moved on to lead other businesses, including Larry Bossidy, former CEO of AlliedSignal and coauthor with Welch of a number of his letters.

Ideas generated or adapted at GE were celebrated among other businesses and leaders, for the concept of boundarylessness is taken so literally at GE that it shares its ideas the world over. As Welch notes, a key GE value is to treat resource allocation as a dynamic process: "Sometimes a business benefits as a net importer of dollars, ideas and talent while at other times the same business will be called upon to be a net exporter for the benefit of the Company as a whole."

Accolades for GE flowed during Welch's stewardship. *Fortune* magazine named GE its "Most Admired Company in America" in 1998 and 1999, and *The Financial Times* named it "the World's Most Respected Company" in those two years. *Time* magazine upped the ante, calling GE "the Company of the Century," and a 1999 *Business Week* survey said that GE boasted the best board of directors. As Welch said in his 1999 letter, Thomas Edison would be pleased with the company he founded over a century ago.

Welch's letters not only contain a firsthand account of the de-

velopment of GE's unique culture but also reflect Welch's imagination, energy, and vision. They are a concrete exposition of the
values that pervade GE's culture, how those values are implemented,
their fruits, and the qualities of leadership that make it all possible—
a great resource for the sophisticated investor as well as the intelligent manager.

The Core Operating Elements

Welch envisions an organization without boundaries. Artificial walls
dividing parts of the inside of an organization are to be destroyed.
The entire enterprise is a team, and responsibility is shared. A culture without boundaries renders impossible excuses such as "not
invented here," a common way to evade responsibility. In this culture, Welch created "a vast laboratory whose principal product is new
ideas." Ideas generated in one place are transported to others.

External boundaries are also exploded in this corporate culture.
Employees engage with broader communities through volunteer
work, and the company participates in outreach programs. GE engages its various constituents as part of its daily life, learning how
better to serve customers as well as coventurers, distributors, and
others. GE is happy to learn from its own but equally happy to adapt
ideas created by others, including suppliers and competitors.

Boundaries retard development, stifle creativity, and complicate
operations. Destroying boundaries enabled GE to flourish amid
Welch's three other core operating elements: speed, stretch, and simplification.

Speed thrives on change. Teamwork enhances speed, enabling
substantial increases in measures of performance straight across a
business. For example, by diminishing the cycle from order to re-
mittance, speed enhances inventory turnover. For a company GE's
size, every single-digit improvement in its inventory turnover produces over a billion dollars in free cash for investment.

Speed's "fun and excitement" facilitates *stretch*, the idea of always setting outsized goals. The stretch philosophy says that if you
think you can increase inventory turnover by one point in the next
cycle, set your goal at increasing it by two points. A boundaryless
culture is the key to a successful stretch philosophy because it emphasizes that "the quality of effort toward achieving the 'impossible'
is the ultimate measure" of performance.

Stretch reverses much of conventional practice and incentive structures in business. At many businesses, managers set targets and are evaluated on the basis of whether they meet them. The incentive is to set modest targets. In a stretch setting managers are encouraged to set extraordinarily ambitious goals and are then evaluated according to how they did in one period compared to how they did in the prior period. In short, "performance is measured against how the world turned out to be—how well a business anticipated change and dealt with it—rather than against some 'plan' or internal number negotiated a year earlier."

Speed and stretch are complemented by the final core operating element of a boundaryless environment: *simplification.* Complexity, whether in business organization charts, communications, or goal setting, impairs speed and stretch and is foreign to a boundaryless culture. Simplicity breeds self-confidence, which is conveyed through direct plans and straightforward speech, setting "big, clear targets." The clarity arising from simplicity has another big virtue: It enhances speed. As Welch says, "simple messages travel faster, simpler designs reach the market faster, and the elimination of clutter allows faster decision making."

THE IMPLEMENTING PRACTICES

GE implements its core operating elements of speed, stretch, and simplification to realize the fruits of these elements. The key to producing those fruits is the concept of integrated diversity. It is the strength a company generates from being number one or number two in all its businesses and drawing on the resources of each business to sustain or enhance its position in others.

Two steps were necessary to achieve integrated diversity at GE. The first was to keep only the businesses that were number one or two in their particular markets. Each business needs to be strong in its own right. Then the collection of businesses produces "a critical mass of competitive advantage." To exploit that competitive advantage in turn requires delayering the management structure, which Welch achieved by dismantling the multiple layers of management that had clogged the company in the earlier era. Delayering enhanced productivity, making the aggregate of the parts far more powerful than their mere sum.

Through a strategy called "Work-Out," Welch sought and got input from everyone in the company (and some people outside it). Long before Perot and Clinton repopularized the town meeting concept in American politics, GE practiced it, getting ideas from those closest to the particular problem. This technique not only is most likely to generate the best solutions, it also builds self-confidence through participation and counters insecurity by discouraging turf battles, parochialism, and other impediments to speed and stretch.

Apart from these practices within the boundaryless culture, Welch instilled a sense of the right sorts of managers for a thriving enterprise. Four types of managers are defined. The first two are easy: Type I believes in GE's values and delivers (and sticks around), whereas type II does neither (and doesn't last long). Type III is a believer but an erratic deliverer and usually gets another chance. Type IV is the trickiest: He or she delivers short-term results but does not believe in GE's values. Instead of living and breathing boundaryless values and energizing and exciting people to new heights of creativity and productivity, this manager controls, oppresses, intimidates, and squeezes people. Welch solved the type IV case by elevating shared values above short-term results, and so these types don't last long at GE either.

GE's system of rewards and recognition glues these managerial qualities to GE's values by reinforcing its boundaryless and speed/ stretch culture. Under Welch's stewardship at GE, the number of employees eligible for stock options soared from 400 to nearly 30,000. Speakers at big company meetings are selected not by their title or rank but on the basis of "what people know that can be shared, borrowed, and expanded on."

Finally, GE's "360 degree" management appraisal calls for managers to be evaluated not only by their superiors but also by the people who work under and alongside them. This evaluation focuses GE's leaders "on finding and rewarding people who demonstrated an ability to get every mind in the organization into the relentless search for ideas."

FRUITS OF THE CULTURE

Concrete results of the core operating elements implemented through a strategy of integrated diversity and Work-Out include those generated at GE's Crotonville Institute management school and those originating on shop floors throughout the company. Best practices has become a model emulated throughout the world and is a hallmark of Welch's GE. Crotonville is a wellspring of thought on management and business, producing great ideas for decades and sharing them not only with GE businesses but with businesspeople the world over.

Welch notes that "the intellectual underpinning of Work-Out consists of ideas like worker involvement, trust and empowerment—shopworn and even platitudinous concepts." Yet he goes on to say that at GE, "the difference is that our whole organization is, in fact, living them, every day." GE wields these "soft concepts" as real competitive weapons in victorious battles, not merely "inscribing them on coffee mugs and T-shirts."

Crotonville, as Welch describes it, combines the "thirst for learning of academia with an action environment usually seen only in small, hungry companies." Animating GE's culture of ideas is a mode of thought linked to the core operating elements of speed and stretch called *bullet-train thinking*. Originated by the CEO of Yokogawa, this metaphor signifies that if you want to increase a train's speed by 10 mph, tinker with its horsepower; if you want to double it, break out of conventional thinking and goal setting.

The fruits of the *learning culture* reinforce the core operating elements by producing additional mechanisms. Consider two big ideas embraced at GE that also exhibit the speed and stretch philosophy. *Co-location*, Welch says, is the "ultimate boundaryless behavior." As "unsophisticated as can be," it means conducting all the functions for a product in one room without walls. All project participants are simultaneously involved, including at the design stages people from manufacturing and marketing as well as suppliers and customers. *Quick response* is a cycle-time reduction technique that similarly erases barriers between functions for a product. With co-location, it vastly reduces average inventory and proportionately bolsters inventory turnover.

Other fruits of this learning culture taken from outside GE help implement the core operating elements. *Demand Flow Technology* was borrowed from the GE customer American Standard to multiply inventory turnover and move toward GE's goal noted in an earlier chapter of zero working capital. *Quick Market Intelligence* (QMI), a strategy adapted from Wal-Mart to get direct customer feedback weekly, "employs out-of-the-box thinking and cross-functional teams dedicated to removing obstacles to cost reduction." The Toshiba-originated idea of *Half Movement*, another variation on the speed-stretch operating elements, envisions each product being produced with half the parts and half the weight in half the time.

Six Sigma quality is perhaps the most famous concept Welch pioneered at GE. It means "the virtual elimination of defects from every product, process and transaction [GE] engages in every day around the globe." It is not just a slogan but a measurement: It means "fewer than 3.4 defects per million operations in a manufacturing or service process." That is nearly perfect quality when you consider that average sigma quality in corporate America is around 3 or 4, at a cost of about 10 to 15% of corporate revenues, Welch reports.

Led by experts on quality who, depending on their skill level in Six Sigma thinking, are creatively called Master Black Belts, Black Belts or Green Belts, the activity dissects every process to improve key business concerns such as enhancing customer productivity and reducing customer capital outlays while increasing the "quality, speed and efficiency" of all GE operations.

Launched in 1995, Six Sigma quality spread "like wildfire" throughout GE to generate substantial returns on the billion-plus dollars invested in it. For example, Six Sigma contributed over $300 million to GE's operating income in 1997, $750 million in 1998, and about $2 billion in 1999, and the impact continues. Profit margins at GE historically ran around 10%, but with Six Sigma they were boosted to 15% to 17% and higher.

All this leads to what Welch hoped for all along: a new kind of company that is a hybrid of typical large companies with vast resources and typical small companies with insatiable appetites. Welch denies that GE is a conglomerate in the usual sense of the word. Welch's model is very different. It calls for GE to reign only over businesses where it is number one or number two, generate ideas from those businesses, and spread them to the others, all in a culture of energy, excitement, and creativity.

The learning culture created by Work-Out and boundarylessness that fueled Six Sigma gains enabled GE to get into e-business far more rapidly and with greater depth and breadth than pretty much any company close to its size. GE generates billions in revenue from its e-business, but Welch notes that the transformation it has brought is more pervasive.

Tackling the question of why the Internet revolution began at small start-ups rather than big resourceful companies such as GE, Welch speculated that it was a mystery of the unknown. At GE, however, it did not take long for people to overcome that e-fear and digitize the entire company, a task Welch says was way easier than anyone at the company had ever imagined. E-business was made for GE, he says, telling us that the "E" in GE assumes a whole new meaning in this learning culture that rides out all great new ideas.

LEADERSHIP

Creating, implementing, and harvesting best practices from a boundaryless culture built on speed, stretch, and simplification require leadership. The cornerstone of successful leadership is recognizing that people matter most in any organization. Welch repeatedly emphasizes this characteristic, which is the essence of Work-Out, the bedrock of best practices, and the sine qua non of superior management teams.

Leaders must constantly be on guard. They must take reality checks and face the results. They must avoid the pervasive temptation to wish, hope, and temporize. Equally important, leaders must encourage their troops to do the same. To ignite a mammoth company like GE with the energy of a small company requires "passion, hunger, appetite for change, customer focus, and, above all, the speed to see reality more clearly and to act on it faster." Doing all this, Welch concludes, requires leaders to foster a culture in which everything "comes back to people—their ideas, their motivation, their passion to win."

Effective leaders share the same values as their troops. GE's enormous size and diversity are bound together through common values. These valves include excellence measured in terms of customer satisfaction, acceptance of change as a constant force, candid communication in all directions, and acceptance of the paradox of managing such an organization, which is simultaneously a single entity and a collection of many different businesses.

Driving all GE's initiatives are what Welch calls a "a unique brand of 21st century business leader—the GE 'A' player." These are leaders with "a vision and the ability to articulate that vision to the team, so vividly and powerfully that it also becomes their vision." They embody GE's "4Es" of leadership—Energy, Energize-ability, Edge, and Execution. In other words they embody enormous personal energy, the ability to energize others, "the instinct and the courage to make tough calls decisively but with fairness and absolute integrity," and "the consistent ability to turn vision into results." The best A leaders, Welch concludes, are like the best coaches: They insist on having only A players on the field.

Welch developed a culture of creativity—one without the barnacles of bureaucracy that retard progress—where it is possible to blend the virtues of both large and small organizations. Boundarylessness is a "behavior definer" that gets people together as teams with speed and drive. Work-Out epitomizes a process designed to generate and capture good ideas whatever their origin. This culture and these processes characterize the type of company GE has become: a company of action, just like its leader.

LIGHTS

The Walt Disney Company is no Mickey Mouse operation, and CEO Mike Eisner knows it.[4] Eisner has one of the most enviable jobs in the world, but he makes it look easier than it is. Since 1984 he has run Disney as if he himself were Walt Disney—the ultimate owner orientation. The animation, the characters, the films, the broadcast TV, and now publishing and bigger theme parks keep Eisner on his toes at this multi-billion-dollar entertainment company.

In his letters to shareholders, Eisner summarizes his views on management and strategies for growth through times of change and economic adversity. Direct commentary on specific aspects of Disney's entertainment business—animation, characters, television, Euro Disney, and the Internet—evinces qualities of trust as well as creativity and leadership. Eisner discusses some of the special problems a large, exquisitely public company such as Disney confronts as a business operated in the limelight of public opinion.

THE MORE THINGS CHANGE . . .

Eisner sums up his whole philosophy of business as follows: "call meetings about subjects that really matter—and show up." Paralleling the situation at Welch's GE, the big meetings at Disney are the "synergy meetings" that bring together the heads and top managers of each division to share ideas so that the best of one division can be transplanted to the others. Motivated by Disney's general devotion to synergy and all the participants' desire to impress their colleagues "with the breadth and creativity of their synergistic initiatives," participants prepare hard for these gatherings, with tremendous results.

The synergy meetings reflect an overall strategy at Disney anchored on four guiding lights. First and foremost is the goal of increasing shareholder wealth while simultaneously discharging responsibility to Disney's employees and its communities in an ethical manner. The second goal is "to increase productivity through superior work," emphasizing that setting "the highest standards drives the highest results." The third goal is to "concentrate on continuing to lead creatively," and the fourth is a "strategic direction of quality and innovation."

These anchoring qualities are necessary to exploit the opportunities and confront the challenges posed by constant change. "Change is the engine of growth and the muse of creativity," Eisner says. It's what makes things happen in life and at Disney. Eisner addresses technological change with special lucidity. Soothsayers regularly announce the edge of technology as spelling doom for certain industries, such as entertainment, in the face of advances such as 500-channel television capability.

Eisner loves it, likening such predictions to those Walt faced when TV first emerged and forecasters foretold the death of film. Far from shutting down any aspects of Disney's business, TV gave Disney a new outlet for its products. For those who are creative and driven, such technological and other changes mean opportunity, not obsolescence.

Tough times must be dealt with when they come, of course, but it is far better to deal with them before they come—in robust economic times. Eisner thinks that way, and Disney's business is organized that way. Although Eisner no longer likes the term "recession-resistant" as a description of Disney, the account he gives of its ability and strategy to make headway in tough economic times makes the label apt.

The roaring economic climate of the 1980s led many companies (and individuals) down shortsighted and treacherous paths, but not Disney. It stayed clear of overpaying for businesses; didn't acquire what it didn't need; kept its balance sheet clean, strong, and financially conservative; grew internally; preserved its franchise by nurturing its core values; and avoided teaming up with others who could detract from the Disney brand.

Opportunities present themselves, of course, and even a conservative company must be ready to exploit them. The fall of communism opened enormous new markets. Disney penetrated them through Euro Disney and through television programming in former Soviet bloc countries.

Through adversity and opportunity, Eisner recounts how the challenges he faces are not all that different from those Walt Disney faced 50 or 60 years ago. The challenges listed in Disney's annual report of 1940 were eerily similar to its list in 1990: external world crises such as war, studio expansion, film production expansion, foreign currency fluctuations, and control over the cost of creative talent. All these things remain, including, the pundits notwithstanding, the risk of war, which is hardly expected far in advance by the investing public.

Disney's recession resistance comes from a combination of a strong brand, financial conservatism, and a disciplined emphasis on growth that concentrates mainly on internal expansion supplemented with selective expansion through prudent acquisition. External expansion is prudent when it is necessary to preserve access to the means of entertainment delivery, especially to the home entertainment environment. That often entails expansion through technological advances, but Eisner cautions that he will not let Disney invest in technology for its own sake.

Disney's commitment must be to the content of the entertainment, Eisner says, not its delivery mechanisms. He regards Marshall McLuhan's claim that "the medium is the message" as anachronistic, maybe true when written but no longer the case in a world of proliferating delivery systems—numerous broadcast networks, independent television stations, and the advent and multiplication of home video, satellite, and the Internet. "What has counted from the time of Homer, Chaucer and Shakespeare to the present is the story and the skill with which it is told, whatever the medium," he observes.

Even so, Eisner aggressively led Disney to embrace the Internet. Among Disney's major assets are some of the most visited Web sites: Disney.com for entertainment, ESPN.com for sports, and ABC.com for news. By partnering first with Starwave, a leading technology company, and then with Infoseek, one of the most popular Web search engines, Disney also created the Go Network, an Internet space that collects and offers content from all Disney units.

Magic and Mice

Eisner explains that many people in the early 1980s thought animation was dead, a lost art. Roy Disney disagreed and proved that when done properly, animation was magic. And as Eisner says, "magic is the essence of Disney." Disney's success in renewing animation was the product of a two-part strategy. First, it successfully rereleased the great classics in old and new venues—in theaters and then on the Disney Channel and on home video. Second, Disney bolstered its motion picture animation organization. That effort was a splash, producing such phenomenal productions as *Who Framed Roger Rabbit?*, *The Little Mermaid*, *Beauty and the Beast*, *Aladdin*, *The Lion King*, and *Pocahantas*. These efforts continued through the 1990s with *Tarzan*, a smash hit which weighs in as the second most successful animated film Disney ever released.

These blockbusters tower alongside such brand-name Disney characters as Mickey Mouse and help define Disney as a family-oriented company. That enables it to avoid dependency on the hit-or-miss business orientation shackling many other studios. Film-making is a high-risk industry: Millions can be invested in a film with no assurance of any return. That is why most major movie studios release a dozen or more films per year, betting that the hits will offset the misses (a practice not unlike that of dot-com speculators in the late 1990s and early 2000s).

Disney's strategy for overcoming these industry conditions is to concentrate on cost control and selectivity. Two applications follow. First, Disney emphasizes its family-oriented brand identification. This creates a special niche that largely liberates Disney from the hit-or-miss strategy. Second, that emphasis also gives Disney an operating edge in the live-action film (and television) business, allowing successes such as *Father of the Bride*, *The Hand That Rocks the Cradle*, and *Sister Act* (plus scores of others too numerous to mention, but think of *Toy Story*, *Armageddon*, *The Horse Whisperer*, and *Good Will Hunting*).

The television business is even tougher than the motion picture business, but again, Disney leverages its animation strengths to overcome industry challenges. The Disney Channel is a major vehicle for animation and a major competitive advantage for Disney in the television business, with subscriber increases generally outpacing those at competitor channels. Even before it acquired ABC in 1995, Disney placed numerous successful shows with the networks, including *Home Improvement*, *Golden Girls*, and *Empty Nest*. It later scored knockout points with the ABC hit *Who Wants to Be a Millionaire?*, which Eisner says "transcended being a mere television show and has entered into the culture."

If magic is the essence of Disney, Mickey Mouse is its manifestation. Mickey's prominence leads Eisner to explore the intriguing question, "Which came first, Mickey Mouse or the Disney company?" The answer is not easy. Of course the company came first as a logical and chronological matter, but Mickey was the company's real launching pad. Eisner quotes Walt Disney as fondly repeating: "Remember, this all started with a mouse." And it continues with that mouse, as Eisner describes how Disney pulled out all the stops to stage a worldwide celebration of Mickey's sixty-fifth birthday in 1992.

Among the toughest business challenges Eisner and Disney faced in recent years was the development of Euro Disney. This ambitious theme-park undertaking was years in the making. During many of them, Eisner expressed high hopes and great optimism. Then struggles ensued, delays slowed progress, and hopes were lowered. But with tenacity bolstered by a long-term vision, Eisner and Disney pulled through and Euro Disney opened with success. Eisner's candor in admitting trouble and accounting for his own errors is a sign of trustworthiness that no investor should ignore.

Managing in the Spotlight

Euro Disney got a lot of press, but so do most activities of a company that is a piece of American cultural history. This unyielding spotlight poses special management problems that Eisner describes with great understatement and felicity. Disney takes the lumps for its mistakes but gets praise when it deserves to. Under Eisner's stewardship Disney regularly ranks among the best entertainment companies in the world, one of the best-managed companies overall, and one of the most profitable and financially stable entertainment companies. In 1991 Disney also joined the Dow, the only representative of the entertainment industry in that barometer of American (and world) financial health.

Eisner attributes these successes to his entire management team as well as all Disney employees, whom he affectionately refers to as the "cast of Disney." The spirit Eisner conveys to the cast of this family entertainment company resonates with civic virtue and public-spiritedness. From generating research funding for AIDS at the 20th Anniversary Celebration of Walt Disney World in 1991, to furnishing financial sustenance to a downtown theater in Los Angeles in 1997, to practicing sound environmental policies company-wide, Disney is long on public values. Disney is a major supporter of education through an effort that dramatizes the importance of teachers in society and responded generously to the upheaval reflected in the Los Angeles riots of 1992.

Eisner's exorbitant stock options remain controversial and a sticky issue (as was his decision to hire talent tsar Mike Ovitz, who lasted at Disney for 14 months but cost the company several hundred million dollars in severance payments). These options warrant careful scrutiny in his case, as with all managers. Eisner makes no bones about his pay level, arguing that his performance at Disney justifies it. Whether you agree is a judgment call. Some investors could reasonably adjust their valuation of Disney on the basis of both the awards and Eisner's defense of them; the question is what his account tells you about whether you want to entrust your wealth to him.

TRUST

The Coca-Cola Company remains one of the world's premier corporations.[5] Three priorities guided Coke's actions under its late CEO, Roberto C. Goizueta: creating value, strengthening the company's trademarks, and focusing on the long term. These priorities pervade and define Coke, a $150 billion operation when Goizueta died in 1997, up from a $4 billion operation when he became CEO a little more than a decade earlier. The lively pages of Goizueta's passionate and clear writings, some cowritten with his former right-hand man, Donald Keough, explain why.

Consider first a few of the benchmarks. In 1995 and 1996 Coca-Cola led *Fortune*'s ranking of wealth creators. As of year end 1995 its market cap was $93 billion, an increase in shareowner wealth of $38 billion over the prior year. As of year end 1996 that figure had increased to $131 billion, adding another $38 billion. While in 1976 Coca-Cola was the twentieth best wealth creator among publicly traded U.S.-based companies, by 1995 it was fourth and in 1996 it was first.

In 1995 and 1996 the total return on Coca-Cola stock exceeded 40%, and during the preceding 15 years it produced an average compound annual total return rate of 30% (counting reinvested dividends). From 1980 through 1995 Coca-Cola's share price grew at an average annual compound rate of 24%, creating nearly $89 billion in shareowner wealth, compared with increases of 12% in the Dow and 11% in the S&P 500. The annualized total return from 1981 through 1990, assuming reinvestment of dividends, was 37%, and from 1986 through 1990, it was 34%.

Driving these spectacular results, Goizueta repeatedly emphasized, was growth in unit case volume. From 1985 through 1995, unit case volume outside North America grew at an average annual compound rate of 8.2%, while within the United States it grew at an average annual compound rate of 4.2% (compared with 2.7% industrywide). In 1996 Coca-Cola set another record, with worldwide unit case volume up 8% and selling 13.7 billion unit cases. Sales of the Coca-Cola brand itself grew by nearly 450 million unit cases (a 6% increase over 1995), while Sprite grew by more than 138 million unit cases (up 13%, its third consecutive year of double-digit growth).

OWNER ORIENTATION AND LONG-TERM THINKING

Adding fuel to this unstoppable engine was Goizueta's business philosophy. Goizueta saw himself as the steward of shareholder capital, always tying Coke's activities to shareholder values. He said that "solid unit case volume growth is the foundation for generating economic profit, which, experience teaches us, is the key to increasing the value of [our shareowners' investment]."

Under Goizueta, Coke focused on its core businesses and adopted a long-term time horizon. Through disciplined and patient attention to building the Coke brand for the long term, Goizueta also created another trademark at Coke: a company with an unquenchable thirst for selling more product to more customers all over the world.

Goizueta believed that "the best way to generate consistently strong short-term results is to keep our attention riveted on the long-term." That long-term focus during the 1980s and 1990s meant building step by step a "global business machine capable of sustaining strong, profitable growth" over the decades to come.

BRANDING

At the foundation of that global business is the Coke brand. It "not only has universal appeal and accessibility, but also meets the fundamental, frequently recurring human need for refreshment." To get people to choose Coke to meet their daily liquid needs, building brand strength was the key. Brand strength was for Goizueta not solely about delivering value to the marketplace, marketing research results, or balance sheet impacts. Goizueta defined brand strength in terms of its "ability to command a premium price in exchange for the very real and obvious value it delivers in return."

Managing brand strength need not be tricky, although enough businesses have squeezed brand strength to the point where its price-value relationship led to its rejection by the market. Coke did not make that mistake under Goizueta's leadership. Instead, it continually sought to find ways to add brand strength by differentiating the products, "making them unique and distinctive." For many years Coke used the AAA approach to its brand strength: availability, affordability, and acceptability of its products. That strategy worked well, but Goizueta moved to the next level in 1995, to the PPP approach: pervasive penetration (rather than mere availability), price-to-value ratios for customers (rather than mere affordability), and preferred (to merely acceptable).

FINANCIAL PRUDENCE

Another foundation of Coke's enormous success was Goizueta's commitment to financial prudence, epitomized by his decision in 1994 to effect at Coke a "financial reformation." Noting that Coke's historical financial prudence had ossified by the early 1980s—"effectively trapping a live organism within the hard constrictions of its own fossil shell"—and rejuvenated in the latter 1980s, Goizueta restated that commitment.

Goizueta announced a new way of measuring Coke's performance. Economic profits (a version of what would later be called economic value added), not just growth in revenues or earnings, became the yardstick. Economic profit is "net operating profit after taxes, less a charge for the average cost of capital employed to produce that profit."

Evaluating businesses with this measure led Coke to divest some poorly performing operations and renewed the focus on the core business of soft drink concentrate (with some holdings in bottlers complemented by an economically profitable foods business).

Coke used debt sparingly to enhance shareholder returns and effected share repurchases to enhance earnings per share. It lowered its dividend payout ratio while increasing the annual dividend to free up cash for reinvestment at low cost. It reinvested those and other funds to expand its global bottling network to erect an extensive and efficient business system. All this Goizueta explained with great clarity to his fellow shareholders.

INFRASTRUCTURE FORTIFICATION

Part of that investment helped finance improvements in its bottlers' processing and distribution systems. Not only did those investments bolster current and future product sales (and strengthen the Coke-bottler partnership), Coke could subsequently sell its interest in the investment at an additional profit for its shareholders.

Goizueta called Coke's investment in and development of an extensive and efficient bottling and distribution system "infrastructure fortification." It entailed continued and deeper investments in the system that bottles and distributes Coca-Cola products. A variety of means were used to fortify the system, from encouraging bottlers to reinvest to investing equity directly and supplying managerial expertise.

Through these practices, Coke expanded around the globe to nearly two-hundred countries to create billions of new potential customers. Between 1980 and 1994 the number of potential Coke customers more than doubled. With sales volume growth as the key to sustaining value growth, this shows why Coke's average return on capital was over triple the approximate cost of that capital.

Adding strength to Coke's focus on the core brands in its global business system was geographic diversification. Coke enjoys a strong—maybe dominant—position in blue chip markets such as the United States, Germany, and Japan. It is committed to dominating new worlds of opportunity such as eastern Europe and Indonesia. Add to that the "start-up" markets of China and India and you have overall diversity through which to "use existing strengths to create future strengths." (That fortification is one of the reasons Coke prevailed against the adversity of the Asian financial crisis of 1998.)

RESOURCE ALLOCATION

In Coke's global business environment, Goizueta said, his primary challenge was to optimally allocate resources generated in developed markets to invest in less developed ones. The greatest growth potential for Coke in the world, Goizueta told a group of students in 1995, was in southern California! Coke sold more cans and bottles of Coke per capita in Hungary than in southern California, making the latter the more "emerging" of the two markets.

Financial reformation, infrastructure fortification, and geographic expansion were meant to create the "best machine possible." A complementary initiative would "equip that machine with a uniquely powerful growth engine." This was the consumer marketing effort designed to drive world demand for the brand. It called for Coke to market its products as distinctive—"different, better and special"—relentlessly deepening brand power.

Goizueta ignored the varied views from the sidelines that ranged from those who said Coke already was a premier consumer marketing outfit and could do no more to those who said there were plenty of other great companies that hold that title. Noting that the average human body needs at least 64 ounces of liquid daily to survive, Goizueta saw Coke as having a huge window of opportunity.

Goizueta sought to promote the brand everywhere in the world, driving dramatic growth in already developed markets such as the United States, Japan, and Europe. To deepen brand strength vertically—that is, in existing strong markets as compared to horizontal building in new ones—required exploiting Goizueta's commitment to product differentiation. Goizueta said that if the keys to selling real estate are location, location, location, the "keys to selling consumer products are differentiation, differentiation, differentiation." Many were astonished in 1996 when Coke did what they thought was impossible: It surpassed the combined consumption of the two leading teas in the United Kingdom and that of the leading bottled water in France!

LEARNING CULTURE

These insights guided Coke instinctively for years. Goizueta set them out in writing as part of an effort to create throughout the company a "learning culture" in which these principles were institutionalized. Like GE's Welch, he sought to learn from every participant in Coke's business: consumers, customers, partners, competitors, and even unrelated organizations. For example, another reality at Goizueta's Coke was his team's ability to find opportunities others could not see. His people search the world not to see where Coke already is but to see where it is not.

Goizueta helped create another extraordinary reality: Coca-Cola adds value "to everyone who touches it." Shareholders, bottlers, Coke's customers, and end consumers all benefit from Coke. Goizueta emphasized particularly Coke's relationships with its bottlers. Throughout the world, a once-fragmented group of bottlers increasingly consolidated on a country-by-country basis—in Japan, Germany, and elsewhere—to gain substantial competitive advantages. As for the customers, many restaurants must sell three hamburgers to make the same profit they make from selling a large Coke. Coke went out of its way to let its customers know this.

Conquering Economic Adversity

Concentrating on the long term by emphasizing short-term prudence is how Coke and Goizueta conquered the economic adversity of the early 1990s. Coke deployed its resources amid global economic malaise to cope with the slowdown through strategic pricing and cost controls. It deployed those resources to capitalize on those conditions by making flexible marketing investments. In this two-front campaign Goizueta never wavered from his conviction, shared by Keough and Coke's other top managers, that a hybrid perspective is optimal: What distinguished Coke was its simultaneous "constancy of purpose" and its "continuous discontentment with the immediate present."

That hybrid perspective was doubly valuable in facing adversity and proved the adage that tough times make the strong stronger. The aggressive investment in the long-term growth and value of the business, in good times as well as in bad, is what's behind *Fortune* magazine's regular ranking of Coke as one of the most admired companies in America, especially for its long-term investment value.

Goizueta's long-term orientation gave succor in bad times, as did his unwillingness to waste energy on forecasting the economic future. It is not possible to control external events such as "global economic trends, currency fluctuations and devaluations, natural disasters, political upheavals, social unrest, bad weather or schizophrenic stock markets," but Goizueta notes that he and every other manager has complete control over his or her own behavior.

Managers cannot allow themselves to be distracted by the external environment. What they can and should do is focus the management team on what it can control: resource deployment to build a foundation for future growth, whatever the current economic climate. The future, in those terms, is in no way preordained but in-

stead is "an infinite series of openings, of possibilities." He emphasized that what uncertainty calls for, especially in difficult economic
environments, is what the Greeks called practical intelligence. This
world view "forces adaptability and teaches constant preparedness."

PRAGMATISM

Practical intelligence also "acknowledges that nothing quite suc-
ceeds as planned" and that what is crucial is "pragmatic adaptability"
to what is new. And new always comes—change is inevitable. The
sharp business focus at Coke is what best prepared the company to
meet change. Indeed, as Goizueta suggested, few large companies
are as focused as Coke or as "tightly riveted" to a particular business
as Coke is to soft drinks.

Animating Goizueta's letters was an overarching dominant
theme: The company's shareholders own it. All other themes—building brand strength through the AAAs or PPPs, differentiating the
brand as special and better, fiscal prudence, and focus—serve the
ultimate principle that the investors are the owners.

Success at Coke, Goizueta emphasized to all the troops, was
"creating value for the people who have entrusted their assets to us."
That is the reason why the company (and any other business) exists.
All the other social benefits Coke or any other company generates
by "serving customers and consumers, creating jobs, positively impacting society, supporting communities—happen only as long as we
fulfill our mission of creating value for [shareholders]," Goizueta
said.

Shortly before his death Goizueta quoted for his management
team the words of the German poet and playwright Goethe: "Whatever you can do or dream you can, begin it. Boldness has genius,
power and magic in it. Begin it now."

Goizueta believed that boldness sustains growth. He expressed
gratitude to all the participants in the Coke venture—associates,
customers, bottling partners, board members, and most of all, he
said, his fellow shareowners—for their trust and confidence in his
team's ability to create value.

Well-earned trust indeed, and indispensable when markets, numbers, and governance tell only part of the story in business analysis.

CONCLUSION:
THE V CULTURE

Readers with an arbitrage orientation may regret that the exemplars of great modern CEOs covered in the last chapter, apart from Warren Buffett, consist of one who is dead, one who has announced his retirement, and only one who is likely to reign for the foreseeable future. Who's next, and why not name them?

If I knew, I would not say. Not so much because I want to gain a competitive edge. No, my reticence is precisely because of an insight in this book: Judgment is the key, and my judgment will invariably differ from yours. Our circles of competence are necessarily different. Our interpretation of the past differs, and our prognosis for the future must as well. It contradicts the whole point of this book for me to tell you who I believe are the up-and-coming star CEOs. My picks are irrelevant to your judgments.

Go back to the masters mentioned in Chapter 1 and you'll see that it was precisely their independence of thought, their utter and profound common sense, which led to their remarkable success. I condense these ideas and insights in the spirit of a teacher and professor, not an investment adviser. I hope you'll use these pages as a foundation for picking stocks as a savvy, sophisticated investor (or, failing that, picking advisers who share respect for the basic philosophy of outstanding investors such as Graham and Buffett).

The basic philosophy of business analysis investing integrates three branches: finance, accounting, and governance. Finance is commonly defined as "the science of management of money and other assets." So much for this definition, if you agree that finance is one part science and the other part art. Behavioral economics, a field that draws on numerous disciplines, including psychology, statistics, history, and sociology, may deserve to be called a social science. Its approach to finance is the most promising, for it recognizes the first branch of intelligent investing: Graham's foundational insight that price and value are different things.

The meaning and measure of value are the second branch, pursuits requiring a grasp of basic ideas from the world of accounting. Accounting has long been known as the language of business, and the discretion managers have in applying accounting principles requires intelligent investors to become translators of that language. When that discretion is abused, it is safer to side with those who declare accounting a state of mind rather than an art or science. Fluency in accounting gives you a huge investment edge, and even conversational accounting will put you at the top of the investing class.

Since market prices and accounting numbers are both fragile grounds for firm and final investment decisions, the third branch is managerial trustworthiness. Formal and overly general governance principles don't help very much here. What you need are people you are happy to entrust your wealth with. Identifying them is all art.

In the stock market forest, look for these three branches. They enable you to steer away from the Q culture and thrive in the V culture, a value-oriented investing culture nurtured by Graham and Buffett.

NOTES

CHAPTER 1

1. Benjamin Graham, *The Intelligent Investor* (1st ed. 1949; 4th rev. ed. Harper & Row, 1973), 108.

2. Fred Schwed, Jr., *Where Are the Customers' Yachts?* (1st ed. 1940; rev. ed. John Wiley & Sons, 1995), 6–7.

3. *The New York Stock Exchange Fact Book* (New York, 1999), http://www.nyse.com; Gretchen Morgenson, "Investing's Longtime Best Bet Is Being Trampled by the Bulls," *The New York Times*, January 15, 2000.

4. Report of the Presidential Task Force on Market Mechanisms (the Brady Report), 1988.

5. Greg Ip, "Market on a High Wire," *The Wall Street Journal*, January 18, 2000.

6. Burton G. Malkiel, *A Random Walk Down Wall Street* (1st ed. 1973; 7th rev. ed. W. W. Norton, 1999), 57–61.

7. Warren E. Buffett and Lawrence A. Cunningham, *The Essays of Warren Buffett: Lessons for Corporate America* (The Cunningham Group, 1997), 72.

8. Robert J. Shiller, *Irrational Exuberance* (Princeton University Press, 2000), 118–132, catalogs and evaluates the 25 top bursts and busts on global stock exchanges during one- and five-year periods from the 1960s through the 1990s.

9. Joseph de la Vega, *Confusión de Confusiones* (1st ed. 1688; rev. ed. John Wiley & Sons, 1996), 159–165 (the selected quotation condenses original material without indicating omissions).

10. Malkiel, *Random Walk*, 185.

11. Buffett and Cunningham, *Essays*, 63, 84. The price per share was $5.63, aggregating $100 million, compared to a value of $400 to $500 million.

12. Graham, *Intelligent Investor*, 289 (footnote omitted).

CHAPTER 2

1. For additional analysis and sources, consult Lawrence A. Cunningham, "From Random Walks to Chaotic Crashes: The Linear Genealogy of the Efficient Capital Market Hypothesis," *The George Washington University Law Review*, vol. 62 (1994), on which this chapter is based.

2. Louis Bachelier, "Theory of Speculation," reprinted in *The Random Character of Stock Market Prices*, Paul H. Cootner, ed. (rev. ed. MIT Press, 1964).

3. Eugene F. Fama, "The Behavior of Stock Market Prices," *Journal of Business*, vol. 38 (1965).

4. Sidney S. Alexander, "Price Movements in Speculative Markets: Trends or Random Walks?" *Industry Management Review*, May 1961.

5. Benjamin Graham, *The Intelligent Investor* (1st ed. 1949; 4th rev. ed. Harper & Row, 1973), 133.

6. Paul A. Samuelson, "Proof That Properly Anticipated Prices Fluctuate Randomly," *Industry Management Review*, Spring 1965.

7. Milton Friedman, "The Methodology of Positive Economics," in *Essays in Positive Economics* (University of Chicago Press, 1953).

8. Andrew Lo and A. Craig MacKinlay, *A Non-Random Walk Down Wall Street* (Princeton University Press, 1999).

9. Eugene A. Fama, "Efficient Capital Markets: II," *Journal of Finance*, vol. 46 (1991).

10. James Tobin, "On the Efficiency of the Financial System," *Lloyds Bank Review*, July 1984.

11. William F. Sharpe, *Portfolio Theory and Capital Markets* (McGraw-Hill, 1970); Kenneth J. Arrow, "Risk Perception in Psychology and Economics," *Economic Inquiry*, vol. 20 (1982).

12. Lawrence H. Summers, "Does the Stock Market Rationally Reflect Fundamental Values?" *Journal of Finance*, vol. 41 (1986).

13. Fischer Black, "Noise," *Journal of Finance*, vol. 41 (1986).

14. Andrei Shleifer, *Inefficient Markets: An Introduction to Behavioral Finance* (Oxford University Press, 2000).

15. Harry M. Markowitz, *Portfolio Diversification: Efficient Diversification of Investments* (John Wiley & Sons, 1959).

16. Sharpe, *Portfolio Theory and Capital Markets*.

17. Andrei Shleifer, "Do Demand Curves for Stocks Slope Down?" *Journal of Finance*, vol. 41 (1986).

18. Francis Fukuyama, *Trust: The Social Virtues and the Creation of Prosperity* (Free Press, 1995).

19. Graham, *Intelligent Investor*, 61, n. 2.

20. Lawrence A. Cunningham, ed., "Conversations from the Buffett Symposium," *Cardozo Law Review*, vol. 19 (Sept.–Nov. 1997), 812.

CHAPTER 3

1. For additional analysis and sources, consult Lawrence A. Cunningham, "From Random Walks to Chaotic Crashes: The Linear Genealogy of the Efficient Capital Market Hypothesis," *The George Washington University Law Review*, vol. 62 (1994), on which this chapter is based.

2. H. E. Hurst, "Long-Term Storage Capacities of Reservoirs," *Transactions of the American Society of Civil Engineers*, vol. 116 (1951).

3. Edgar E. Peters, *Chaos and Order in the Capital Markets* (John Wiley & Sons, 1991); Edgar E. Peters, *Fractal Market Analysis: Applying Chaos Theory to Investment and Economics* (John Wiley & Sons, 1994).

4. Henri Poincaré, *Science and Method* (1st ed. 1908; rev. ed. Dover Press, 1952).

5. Edward Lorenz, "Deterministic Nonperiodic Flow," *Journal of Atmospheric Sciences*, vol. 20 (1963); Edward Lorenz, *Nonlinear Dynamical Economics and Chaotic Motion* (Springer-Verlag, 1989).

6. Alan Wolf, "Chaos in the Stadium," *Algorithm*, April 1992.

7. These figures were prepared by Alan Wolf.

8. Alan Wolf, et al., "Determining Lyapunov Exponents from Time Series," *Physica*, vol. 16D (1985).

9. Benoit B. Mandelbrot, *The Fractal Geometry of Nature* (W. H. Freeman, 1988); Benoit B. Mandelbrot, ed., *Fractals and Scaling in Finance: Discontinuity, Concentration, Risk* (Springer-Verlag, 1997).

10. Andrei Shleifer, *Inefficient Markets: An Introduction to Behavioral Finance* (Oxford University Press, 2000), 121–22.

11. John Y. Campbell and Robert J. Shiller, "The Dividend-Price Ratio and Expectations of Future Dividends and Discount Factors," *Review of Financial Studies*, vol. 1 (1998); John Y. Campbell and John Ammer, "What Moves Stock and Bond Markets: A Variance Decomposition for Long-Term Asset Returns," *Journal of Finance*, vol. 48 (1993).

12. Warren E. Buffett and Lawrence A. Cunningham, *The Essays of Warren Buffett: Lessons for Corporate America* (The Cunningham Group, 1997), 72.

13. Warren E. Buffett, "The Superinvestors of Graham and Doddsville," *Hermes* (Columbia Business School), Fall 1984.

14. Benjamin Graham, *The Intelligent Investor* (1st. ed. 1949; rev. ed Harper & Row, 1973), 36–37.

15. Ibid.

CHAPTER 4

1. Alex Berenson, "On Hair-Trigger Wall Street, A Stock Plunges on Fake News," *The New York Times*, August 26, 2000.

2. Susan E. Hurd and Jonathan M. Winer, "On-Line Securities Fraud Under Scrutiny," *The New York Law Journal*, February 22, 2000.

3. Professor Howard M. Friedman of the University of Toledo Law School furnished testimony providing some of these examples before the Permanent Investigations Subcommittee of the Senate Governmental Affairs Committee on March 22, 1999.

4. *SEC v. Francis Tribble & Sloane Fitzgerald*, SEC Litigation Release No. 15959, October 27, 1998.

5. *SEC v. Remington-Hall Capital Corp. & Douglas T. Fonteno*, SEC Litigation Release No. 15943, October 22, 1998.

6. Alex Berenson, "Two Accused of Using E-Mail to Commit Stock Fraud," *The New York Times*, February 25, 2000.

7. Jeffrey Keegan, "Regulators Step Up Fight against Internet Fraud," *Investment Dealers Digest*, August 7, 1998.

8. Philip L. Carret, *The Art of Speculation* (1st ed. 1930; rev. ed. Fraser, 1984).

9. Edwin LeFèvre, *Reminiscences of a Stock Operator* (1st ed. 1923; rev. ed. John Wiley & Sons, 1994).

10. Benjamin Graham, *The Intelligent Investor* (1st ed. 1949; 4th rev. ed. Harper & Row, 1973), 142.

11. Leslie Eaton, "Internet Investing: Spotlight on Risk," *International Herald Tribune*, December 6, 1996.

12. *SEC v. Aziz-Golshani*, No. 99–13139 (CBM) (Federal Central District of California, December 15, 1999); Rebecca Buckman and Michael Schroeder, "Web Postings Draw Charges of Stock Fraud," *The Wall Street Journal*, December 16, 1999; Gretchen Morgenson, "Internet's Role Is Implicated in Stock Fraud," *The New York Times*, December 16, 1999.

13. SEC Litigation Release No. 16399 (January 5, 2000) (reporting on *SEC v. Yun Soo Oh Park*, Federal Northern District of Illinois, Case No. 00C 0049); Jennifer Friedlin, "The SEC Files Civil Fraud Charges against Tokyo Joe," *TheStreet.com* & *NYTimes.com*, January 2000; John C. Coffee, Jr., "Tokyo Joe and the First Amendment," *The New York Law Journal*, January 20, 2000.

14. "Net Damage: PairGain Hoax Revealed," *Investor Relations Business*, April 26, 1999; Associated Press, "PairGain Worker Sentenced in Fraud Case," *The New York Times*, August 31, 1999.

15. Alex Berenson, "S.E.C. Reaches Settlement in Web-Based 'Pump and Dump' Case," *The New York Times*, March 3, 2000; Michael Schroeder, "Georgetown Students Draw Web Investors—and an SEC Bust," *The Wall Street Journal*, March 3, 2000.

16. William M. Bulkeley, "Presstek Suit Alleges Short Sellers Posted False Statements On-Line," *The Wall Street Journal*, September 18, 1997.

17. Gretchen Morgenson, "S.E.C. Says Teenager Had After-School Hobby: Online Stock Fraud," *The New York Times*, September 21, 2000.

18. Lawrence Harris, "Volatility, Portfolio Insurance, and the Role of Specialists and Market Makers," *Cornell Law Review*, vol. 74 (1989), provided part of the foundation for the following discussion.

19. Michael Schroeder and Randall Smith, "Sweeping Changes in Market Structure Sought: Major Firms Propose Central Order System and Single Regulator," *The Wall Street Journal*, February 29, 2000; Alex Berenson, "Top Wall St. Executives Urge Trading Overhaul," *The New York Times*, March 1, 2000.

20. Michael Schroeder, "NASD, NYSE Discussed Merging to Keep Up With Market Changes," *The Wall Street Journal*, March 3, 2000; Greg Ip and Randall

Smith, "Instinet, Datek Recently Held Merger Talks," *The Wall Street Journal*, March 3, 2000.

21. Thomas Kalinke, "Sleepless in New York: Evening Hours at the Exchange," *Financial History*, vol. 69 (Spring 2000).

22. Rebecca Buckman, "Heavy Losses: The Rise and Collapse of a Day Trader," *The Wall Street Journal*, February 28, 2000.

23. Senate Governmental Affairs Committee, Permanent Subcommittee on Investigations, February 25, 2000; Bloomberg News, "Day Trading's Risks and Pressures Are Described to a Senate Panel," *The New York Times*, February 25, 2000.

24. Gerald M. Loeb, *The Battle for Investment Survival* (1st ed. 1935; rev. ed. John Wiley & Sons, 1996).

25. Warren E. Buffett and Lawrence A. Cunningham, *The Essays of Warren Buffet: Lessons for Corporate America* (The Cunningham Group, 1997), 90.

26. Edward Wyatt, "Day Traders Are Formidable Market Force," *The New York Times*, April 14, 1999.

27. The Charles Schwab Corporation, 1999 Annual Report, 41–42; Patrick McGeehan, "Profit Up at Citigroup, Merrill and Schwab," *The New York Times*, April 18, 2000.

28. Patrick McGeehan, "The Unmutual Fund," *The New York Times*, May 18, 2000.

CHAPTER 5

1. Benjamin Graham, *The Intelligent Investor* (1st ed. 1949; 4th rev. ed. Harper & Row, 1973), 110.

2. Warren E. Buffett and Lawrence A. Cunningham, *The Essays of Warren Buffett: Lessons for Corporate America* (The Cunningham Group, 1997), 120, 122, 134.

3. Ibid., 110.

4. John C. Bogle, *Common Sense on Mutual Funds* (John Wiley & Sons, 1999).

5. Gerald M. Loeb, *The Battle for Investment Survival* (1st ed. 1935; rev. ed. John Wiley & Sons, 1996).

6. Buffett and Cunningham, *Essays*, 79; Graham, *Intelligent Investor*, 54, 282–283.

7. Gretchen Morgenson, "Buying on Margin Becomes a Habit," *The New York Times*, March 24, 2000.

8. Gretchen Morgenson, "Stock-Trading Cheerleader Now Faces $45 Million Debt," *The New York Times*, April 19, 2000.

9. Nick Leeson, *Rogue Trader* (Warner, 1997).

10. Graham, *Intelligent Investor*, 228–231.

11. Buffett and Cunningham, *Essays*, 57.

12. Charles T. Munger, "A Lesson on Elementary, Worldly Wisdom As It Relates to Investment Management and Business," *Outstanding Investor Digest*, vol. X (May 5, 1995).

13. Edwin LeFèvre, *Reminiscences of a Stock Operator* (1st ed. 1923; rev. ed. John Wiley & Sons, 1994).

14. Graham, *Intelligent Investor,* 245.

15. Ibid., 124–125

16. Bill Spindle, "Been There? Euphoric '80s in Japan Ended in Long Slide," *The Wall Street Journal,* January 18, 2000.

17. Steve Liesman and Jacob M. Schlesinger, "Blunted Spike: The Price of Oil Has Doubled This Year; So, Where's the Recession?" *The Wall Street Journal,* December 15, 1999; Joseph Kahn, "Surge in Oil Prices Is Raising Specter of Inflation Spike," *The New York Times,* February 21, 2000.

18. Graham, *Intelligent Investor,* 162.

19. Gretchen Morgenson, "Investing's Longtime Best Bet Is Being Trampled by the Bulls," *The New York Times,* January 15, 2000.

CHAPTER 6

1. Donald Schwartz, late professor at the Georgetown University Law Center, prepared the original version of this parable, rewritten for publication here and previously appearing in other forms in Lawrence A. Cunningham, *Introductory Accounting and Finance for Lawyers* (West Group, 2d ed., 1999) and Lewis D. Solomon, et al., *Corporations Law and Policy* (West Group 4th ed., 1998).

2. Carol Loomis, "Mr. Buffett on the Stock Market," *Fortune,* November 22, 1999.

3. Charles T. Munger, author of "A Lesson on Elementary, Worldly Wisdom As It Relates to Investment Management and Business," *Outstanding Investor Digest,* vol. X (May 5, 1995), furnished this example.

4. Warren E. Buffett and Lawrence A. Cunningham, *The Essays of Warren Buffett: Lessons for Corporate America* (The Cunningham Group, 1997), 71.

CHAPTER 7

1. Benjamin Graham, *The Intelligent Investor* (1st ed. 1949; 4th rev. ed. Harper & Row, 1973), 63.

2. Warren E. Buffett and Lawrence A. Cunningham, *The Essays of Warren Buffett: Lessons for Corporate America* (The Cunningham Group, 1997), 92–93.

3. Benjamin Graham, *The Interpretation of Financial Statements* (1st ed. 1937; rev. ed. Harper Business, 1998), 77.

4. Buffett and Cunningham, *Essays,* 208.

5. Ibid., 91–92.

6. Adrian J. Slywotzky and David J. Morrison, authors of *Profit Patterns* (Times Business, 1999), identify and discuss the patterns described in the accompanying text.

7. Bill Miller, "Amazon.com's Allure," *Barron's,* November 15, 1999.

8. Buffett and Cunningham, *Essays,* 96–97.

9. Graham, *Intelligent Investor,* 286.

10. Buffett and Cunningham, *Essays,* 99.

11. The psychology literature calls the resistance bias a "principle of conservatism" and the pattern-seeking bias a "representativeness heuristic." Both labels seem not only unwieldy but imprecise when adapted for thinking about investor behavior. Nevertheless, investment theorists cling to these terms in arguing that these cognitive biases play a role in explaining market inefficiencies. For an example, consider Andrei Shleifer, *Inefficient Markets: An Introduction to Behavioral Finance* (Oxford University Press, 2000).

12. Buffett and Cunningham, *Essays,* 87.

13. Ibid., 53.

CHAPTER 8

1. Leopold A. Bernstein and John J. Wild, *Analysis of Financial Statements* (5th ed. McGraw-Hill, 2000), 102–03.

2. Benjamin Graham, *The Interpretation of Financial Statements* (1st ed. 1937; rev. ed. Harper Business, 1998), 32.

3. For more, consult ibid. or Lawrence A. Cunningham, *Introductory Accounting and Finance for Lawyers* (West Group, 2nd ed., 1999), on which this and the next chapter draw (the title is intended to show that it is for the nonaccountant; it is not exclusively for lawyers).

CHAPTER 9

1. Benjamin Graham, *The Intelligent Investor* (1st ed. 1949; 4th rev. ed. Harper & Row, 1973), 277.

2. Warren E. Buffett and Lawrence A. Cunningham, *The Essays of Warren Buffett: Lessons for Corporate America* (The Cunningham Group, 1997), 101. Note also Subrata N. Chakravarty, "Three Little Words," *Forbes,* April 6, 1998.

3. Buffett and Cunningham, *Essays,* 187.

4. The per share figures throughout this chapter do not take into account any stock splits occurring in 2000 or beyond.

5. Graham, *Intelligent Investor,* 14–15.

6. Michael Metz and David Kerdell, "Graham and Dodd Revisited," *Portfolio Strategy* (CIBC Oppenheimer, December 11, 1998).

7. Benjamin Graham, *The Interpretation of Financial Statements* (1st ed. 1937; rev. ed. Harper Business, 1998), 15, 23.

8. Ibid., 49.

9. Ibid., 48–49.

10. Philip L. Carret, *The Art of Speculation* (1st ed. 1930; rev. ed. Fraser, 1984).

11. Graham, *Intelligent Investor,* 277–282.

12. John Burr Williams, *The Theory of Investment Value* (1st ed. 1938; rev. ed. Fraser, 1997).

13. Robert Shiller, *Irrational Exuberance* (Princeton University Press, 2000) (noting the studies referred to and reporting on others done directly that show slightly lower expected returns), 52–55; Graham, *Intelligent Investor*, 122.

14. Buffett and Cunningham, *Essays*, 85.

15. Stern Stewart, the firm that trademarked the term "economic value added," publishes volumes of material on the concept, including G. Bennett Stewart III, "EVA™: Fact and Fantasy," *Journal of Applied Corporate Finance*, vol. 7 (1994).

16. The Coca-Cola Company defines "economic value added" in a glossary in its annual report as year-to-year growth in after-tax operating income in excess of a varying estimated charge for average operating capital employed.

17. Graham, *Interpretation*, 75–76.

CHAPTER 10

1. David Burgstahler and Ilia Dichev, "Earnings Management to Avoid Earnings Decreases and Losses," *Journal of Accounting and Economics*, vol. 24 (1997).

2. Michael Schroeder, "SEC to Adopt Disclosure Rules for Companies," *The Wall Street Journal*, December 16, 1999.

3. *New York Stock Exchange Listed Company Manual*, Section 303.01, Audit Committees (available from http://www.nyse.com/listed). Big accounting firms used these rules and recommendations to formulate statements of audit committee standards. For example, see PriceWaterhouseCoopers, *Audit Committees: Best Practices for Protecting Shareholder Interests* (1999); KMPG, *Shaping the Audit Committee Agenda* (1999).

4. Graham's lampooning appears in Warren E. Buffett and Lawrence A. Cunningham, *The Essays of Warren Buffett: Lessons For Corporate America* (The Cunningham Group, 1997), 159–65. Briloff's work includes *More Debits Than Credits* (Harper & Row, 1976) and *Unaccountable Accounting* (Harper & Row, 1972).

5. Some of these charade discussions are adapted from Lawrence A. Cunningham, *Introductory Accounting and Finance for Lawyers* (West Group, 2nd ed., 1999).

6. Buffett and Cunningham, *Essays*, 193.

7. Benjamin Graham, *The Intelligent Investor* (1st ed. 1949; 4th rev. ed. Harper & Row, 1973), 167.

CHAPTER 11

1. Benjamin Graham, *The Intelligent Investor* (1st ed. 1949; 4th rev. ed. Harper & Row, 1973), 155.

2. Ibid., 286.

3. Warren E. Buffett and Lawrence A. Cunningham, *The Essays of Warren Buffett:*

Lessons for Corporate America (The Cunningham Group, 1997), 147.

4. For additional analysis and sources, consult Lawrence A. Cunningham, "Commonalities and Prescriptions in the Vertical Dimension of Global Corporate Governance," *Cornell Law Review*, vol. 84 (1999), on which this and the following chapters draw.

5. Graham, *Intelligent Investor*, 270.

6. *AMP, Inc. v. Allied-Signal, Inc.*, 1998 US District LEXIS 15617 (Federal Eastern District of Pennsylvania, October 8, 1998), reversed on other grounds by the Federal Third Circuit Court of Appeals, 168 Federal Reporter 3d 649 (January 20, 1999).

7. Buffett and Cunningham, *Essays*, 47.

CHAPTER 12

1. Warren E. Buffett and Lawrence A. Cunningham, *The Essays of Warren Buffett: Lessons for Corporate America* (The Cunningham Group, 1997), 138.

2. Ibid., 86–87, 96.

3. Roberta Romano, "Corporate Law and Corporate Governance," *Industrial and Corporate Change*, vol. 5 (1996); Sanjai Bhagat and Bernard Black, "The Uncertain Relationship between Board Composition and Firm Performance," *Business Lawyer*, vol. 54 (1999).

4. Buffett and Cunningham, *Essays*, 40.

5. James A. Brickley, Jeffrey L. Coles, and Gregg Jarrell, "Leadership Structure: Separating the CEO and Chairman of the Board," *Journal of Corporate Finance*, vol. 3 (1997).

6. Ira M. Millstein and Paul W. MacAvoy, "The Active Board of Directors and Performance of the Large Publicly Traded Corporation," *Columbia University Law Review*, vol. 98 (1998).

7. Buffett and Cunningham, *Essays*, 47–54.

8. Investor Responsibility Research Center (press release), "Investors, CEOs, Split on Best Governance Practices for Dot-Com Companies," January 26, 2000.

9. SEC Rule 14a-8 under the Federal Securities Exchange Act of 1934.

10. Benjamin Graham, *The Memoirs of the Dean of Wall Street* (McGraw-Hill, 1996; posthumous publication, Seymour Chatman, ed.), 201–212. The company was Northern Pipeline, and the year was 1928 (Graham was 34 years old). Ibid., 320.

11. Benjamin Graham, *The Intelligent Investor* (1st ed. 1949; 4th rev. ed. Harper and Row, 1973), 270.

CHAPTER 13

1. Joseph Kahn, "AMP Rejects Allied Signal's Takeover Bid of $10 Billion," *The New York Times*, August 22, 1998.

2. John A. Byrnes, "The Blame When the Boss Fails," *Business Week*, December 27, 1999.

3. Consult Kevin Murphy, "Corporate Performance and Managerial Remuneration: An Empirical Analysis," *Journal of Accounting and Economics*, vol. 7 (1985), and Hamid Mehran, "Executive Compensation Structure, Ownership, and Firm Performance," *Journal of Financial Economics*, vol. 38 (1995).

4. Ben & Jerry's Homemade, Inc., 1992 Annual Report (5:1 ratio raised in 1990 to 7:1); Ben & Jerry's Homemade, Inc., 1998 Annual Report (16:1 ratio at its "historical high" and would be higher if "the present value of unexercised stock options were included").

5. Lee Gomes, "McAfee.com to Make Long-Awaited IPO," *The Wall Street Journal*, December 2, 1999.

6. Haig Simonian and Nikki Tait, "U.S. Executives Earn Much More," *The Financial Times* (London), August 3, 1998.

7. Warren E. Buffett and Lawrence A. Cunningham, *The Essays of Warren Buffett: Lessons for Corporate America* (The Cunningham Group, 1997), 54–55.

8. "Accounting for Stock-Based Compensation," *Statement of Financial Accounting Standards No. 123* (Financial Accounting Standards Board, 1995).

9. Gretchen Morgenson, "Investors May Now Eye Costs of Stock Options," *The New York Times*, August 29, 2000 (reporting studies performed by Pat McConnell of Bear Stearns); Manitou Investment Management Ltd., *The Long View: The Amazing Stock Option Bubble* (October 1999) (reporting studies performed by the British research firm Smithers and the U.S. investment banking firm Sanford Bernstein).

10. David Leonhardt, "In the Options Age, Rising Pay (and Risk): Will Today's Huge Rewards Devour Tomorrow's Earnings?" *The New York Times*, April 2, 2000.

11. Buffett and Cunningham, *Essays*, 58.

12. Reuters, "Study Says Mergers Often Don't Aid Investors," *The New York Times*, December 1, 1999.

13. Buffett and Cunningham, *Essays*, 143.

14. Mattell, Inc., SEC Form 8-K (filed July 22, 1999).

15. Mattell, Inc., SEC Form 8-K (filed October 22, 1999).

16. Buffett and Cunningham, *Essays*, 123–127.

17. Beginning in 1999, the author helped direct a project on firm structures for the Independence Standards Board, and his views expressed here do not necessarily represent those of that project or of the board.

18. Buffett and Cunningham, *Essays*, 168.

CHAPTER 14

1. David Gladstone, *Venture Capital Handbook* (Prentice-Hall, 1988), 101–104.

2. Warren E. Buffett and Lawrence A. Cunningham, *The Essays of Warren Buffett: Lessons for Corporate America* (The Cunningham Group, 1997), 36

(this is one of Berkshire Hathaway's famous "Owner Related Business Principles").

3. This discussion draws on the annual letters of John F. (Jack) Welch to General Electric Co. shareholders from 1985 through 2000. Some of them were coauthored with other GE executives.

4. This discussion draws on the annual letters of Michael D. (Mike) Eisner to Walt Disney Co. shareholders from 1988 through 2000.

5. This discussion draws on the annual letters of Roberto C. Goizueta to Coca-Cola Co. shareholders from 1985 through 1996, plus an article enclosed with one of them by Mr. Goizueta called "The Emerging Post-Conglomerate Era: Changing the Shape of Corporate America," *Leaders*, April–June 1989.

COMPANY INDEX

NAME INDEX

SUBJECT INDEX

ABOUT THE AUTHOR

Lawrence A. Cunningham is professor of law at the Benjamin N. Cardozo Law School of Yeshiva University in New York City and director of The Samuel and Ronnie Heyman Center on Corporate Governance at Cardozo, where he has taught since 1992. From 1988 to 1992, he was an associate with Cravath, Swaine & Moore, where he practiced corporate and securities law. Professor Cunningham has written numerous books and dozens of articles on accounting, business, finance, investing, and related policy matters, including an internationally acclaimed collection of Warren Buffett's letters to Berkshire Hathaway shareholders, *The Essays of Warren Buffett: Lessons for Corporate America*, and the widely used textbook *Introductory Accounting and Finance for Lawyers*. Professor Cunningham has taught and lectured widely, in the United States and abroad, at schools and business organizations of all kinds. He has served as a consultant to corporate boards of directors, law and accounting firms, and regulatory and standard-setting bodies. He has been featured in *Forbes* and *Money*, and on *CNN* and *The Motley Fool Radio Show*, and has appeared on or been quoted in scores of other broadcast and print media. Professor Cunningham is a magna cum laude graduate of Cardozo and earned his B.A. in economics from the University of Delaware. He was born and raised in Wilmington, Delaware, and now resides in New York City with his wife, JoAnna Cunningham. Professor Cunningham is an investor and may hold securities of some of the companies discussed in this book.